HISTORIC CHARLOTTE

*An Illustrated History of
Charlotte & Mecklenburg County
by Dr. Dan L. Morrill*

A publication of Historic Charlotte, Inc.

Historical Publishing Network
A division of Lammert Publications, Inc.
San Antonio, Texas

PREFACE

This is not an encyclopedic history of Charlotte and Mecklenburg County. The story is too complex and too big for the scope of a project such as this. This writer asserts that two major themes have been present in the history of Charlotte and Mecklenburg County from the earliest days of Scots-Irish and German settlement in the 1740s until today. One is an intense desire for economic development and expansion. The other is the on-going saga of race. Whenever the pressures of the two have come into direct conflict, especially in the 1890s and in the 1960s and 1970s, economic considerations have won out. This history ends in the 1980s, because happenings thereafter belong to the realm of current events. Also, in this writer's opinion, they produced changes in degree, not in kind.

This writer is deeply indebted to his wife, Mary Lynn Caldwell Morrill, who in this as in all other aspects of his personal life has shown untiring support, patience, and understanding. A direct descendant of Alexander Craighead, she possesses all of the best qualities of her Scots-Irish heritage. This book is dedicated to her.

First Edition

Copyright © 2001 Historical Publishing Network

All rights reserved. No part of this book may be reproduced in any form or by any means, electronic or mechanical, including photocopying, without permission in writing from the publisher. All inquiries should be addressed to Historical Publishing Network, 8491 Leslie Road, San Antonio, Texas, 78254. Phone (210) 688-9006.

ISBN: 1-893619-20-6
Library of Congress Card Catalog Number: 2001097082

Historic Charlotte: An Illustrated History of Charlotte and Mecklenburg County

author:	Dan L. Morrill
photo research:	Bruce Schulman
contributing writers for "sharing the heritage":	Joe Goodpasture
	Marie Beth Jones

Historical Publishing Network

president:	Ron Lammert
vice president:	Barry Black
project representatives:	Tom Carter
	Jeff Clark
	Rob Steidle
director of operations:	Charles A. Newton, III
administration:	Angela Lake
	Donna Mata
	Dee Steidle
graphic production:	Colin Hart
	John Barr

CONTENTS

Native Americans and the Arrival of The White Man

Off Elm Lane there is a massive boulder that sits beside a creek bed. Children from a nearby suburban neighborhood often scamper to the top of the "Big Rock," perhaps unaware of the hate-filled graffiti that mars its ancient face. The Big Rock was a campsite, rendezvous point, and observation post for the first human beings who inhabited what is now Mecklenburg County. They were Paleo or Ancient Native Americans whose forebears had migrated from Asia across the Bering Strait some 40,000 years ago. These initial nomads reached the Carolina Piedmont about 12,000 years ago. They had wandered over the Blue Ridge and Smoky Mountains in pursuit of big game. Living in highly mobile and lightly equipped groups, the Paleo Indians ambushed their prey by thrusting spears into their flanks at close range.

The first Native Americans who resided here lived in tiny bands of one or a few families, rarely came into contact with other human beings, and inbred for centuries. They have left no evidence of permanent settlements, burial sites, pottery or agriculture; and, like the great majority of Native Americans, they never developed a written language. There is a small crevice or indentation on the backside of the eastern wall of the Big Rock. It would have provided protection from the strong, cold winds that blew across the almost treeless grasslands that covered the surrounding country-side in ancient times.

About 10,000 years ago the glaciers started to retreat, and deciduous forests began to predominate in this part of North America. Their habitat destroyed or massively altered, some large mammals, like the mammoth, disappeared, while others, like the camel and the horse, moved elsewhere. Paleo Indian traditions began to die out as the Native Americans adapted to their new environment. Archeologists have named their successors the "Archaic" culture.

Archaic people foraged for plants and hunted smaller game, such as rabbit, squirrel, beaver and deer. Still nomads, they roamed within smaller territories than their predecessors. Indians of this era were more technologically proficient than their forbears. One of their most ingenious inventions was the *atlatl*, a spear-throwing device that enabled them to kill deer and other large game more easily.

They also used grinding stones and mortars to crush nuts and seeds, carved bowls from soapstone, and polished their spear points into smooth and shiny projectiles.

A momentous event in the history of the Native Americans of this region occurred about 2000 years ago. Indians of the so-called "Woodland" tradition began practicing agriculture and establishing permanent settlements. The great majority of the Native Americans who inhabited what is now the Carolina Piedmont, including the Catawbas of this immediate area, were still following these Woodland customs when the first white men arrived in the 16th century. People of this tradition developed a sophisticated culture, replete with religious ceremonies and complex

ethical systems. Their religion was polytheistic, meaning that Woodland Indians believed in many gods. They also had no concept of private property. Such notions would come into direct conflict with the cultural values that white settlers would bring to the Carolina Piedmont.

The first English-speaking people to move through this region were merchants who brought finished goods on the backs of horses or on their own backs to trade for animal hides prepared by the Catawbas and other Native American tribes. The Catawbas and other inland tribes also traveled widely. Long before the arrival of the white man, Native Americans had established trade routes along footpaths that stretched from the mountains to the sea. White explorers and traders became familiar with this system of reliable, well-established Indian trails and adopted it for their own use.

A fundamental transformation of the Yadkin-Catawba territory occurred in the 18th century, when the era of Native American

domination of the region came to a precipitous end. European civilization became predominant within a very few years. The initial white settlers drove their wagons into the Carolina Piedmont in the 1740s. First in a trickle then a virtual flood, these immigrants, who were mostly from Pennsylvania, Maryland, and Delaware, came swarming down the Great Philadelphia Wagon Road to establish farms. Unlike the white traders who had preceded them, these families planned to stay.

The white pioneers changed what they found. To them the ancient home of the Native Americans was a wilderness to be tamed. The new settlers built houses, taverns, and mills, established ferries, and cleared fields. The Catawbas were powerless to resist. By the 1760s, after only a decade of persistent white occupation, much of the Catawba's lands had been sold, bartered, or lost. The Catawba nation had dwindled to a population of about 1000, for in addition to tribal warfare they suffered from contact with European diseases and vices: chiefly smallpox and whiskey. In 1764, two years after the death of the last famous Catawba chief, King Haiglar, the colonial governor of South Carolina granted the Catawba fifteen square miles on the border of North Carolina and South Carolina. By 1840 the area had dwindled to 652 acres, and there were only seventy-five Catawba left.

Most of the pioneers who moved into the Piedmont in the mid-1700s were Scots-Irish Presbyterians or German Lutherans. Their primary reason for coming was to escape oppression and to be "left alone." Certainly that sentiment was paramount among the Scots-Irish. Scotsmen and Scotswomen who had moved from Scotland to the Ulster region of Ireland in the early 1600s, the Scots-Irish were only too aware of the discriminatory actions the English could enact. The response of growing numbers of these beleaguered Presbyterians was to move again, this time to North America.

About 250,000 Scots-Irish immigrated to the New World in the first quarter of the 18th century, most entering through Philadelphia, Baltimore, or Lewes, Delaware. Learning that the land near the coast was already taken, the former residents of Ulster trekked inland and

created farms until they reached the Alleghany Mountains. They then turned south and began filtering into Virginia and the Carolinas.

Tradition holds that the first Scots-Irish pioneer to bring his family to Mecklenburg County was Thomas Spratt. A marker in the 1900 block of Randolph Road marks the spot where Spratt constructed his home. Erected by the Colonial Dames in 1926, the marker reads:

SITE OF THE FIRST COURT HELD IN MECKLENBURG COUNTY. FEBRUARY 26, 1763. HOME OF THOMAS SPRATT, FIRST PERSON TO CROSS THE YADKIN RIVER WITH WHEELS HERE WAS BORN ANNE SPRATT, FIRST WHITE CHILD BORN BETWEEN CATAWBA & YADKIN RIVERS.

The chief spokesperson for the Scots-Irish settlers of what is now Mecklenburg County was Alexander Craighead. He was summoned to be minister at Sugaw Creek Presbyterian Church and Rocky River Presbyterian Church in 1758. Craighead, whose grave is located in the oldest burial ground of Sugaw Creek Presbyterian Church on Craighead Road off North Tryon Street, was born in Donegal, Ireland and died in Mecklenburg County in March 1766. He traveled as a child with his parents to Pennsylvania in the early 1700s. Ordained in 1735, Craighead

✧
Above: The marker on Randolph Road
where Thomas Spratt constructed his home.
PHOTO TAKEN BY BRUCE R. SCHULMAN.

became an outspoken critic of the Church of England and even succeeded in alienating the majority of his fellow Presbyterians. To Craighead's way of "New Side" thinking, even the Presbyterian Church was tainted because of its commitment to maintaining traditional dogma rather than emphasizing the importance of faith and spontaneous emotion in religious matters and because of its willingness to make peace with British officials.

Alexander Craighead faced a monumental challenge in Mecklenburg County. The great majority of people were illiterate. Squabbling and fighting were routine. Arthur Dobbs, the Royal Governor of North Carolina, visited what is now Mecklenburg County in 1755. He observed that the great majority of the inhabitants were impoverished. Most families had six to ten children, all "going barefooted," and the mothers were barely clothed. Charles Woodmason, an Anglican minister, described the Scots-Irish residents of Mecklenburg County as "vile, leveling commonwealth Presbyterians. They are," he continued, "profligate, audacious Vagabonds...Hunters going Naked as Indians." Admittedly, officials of the Church of England were predisposed to castigate the Scots-Irish Presbyterians of the Carolina hinterland. Still, their observations were not created entirely out of whole cloth.

❖

Above: Sanctuary of Providence Presbyterian Church. Dating to 1858, the sanctuary serves one of the original congregations of the county.

PHOTO TAKEN BY BRUCE R. SCHULMAN.

Below, left: Princess Charlotte of Mecklenburg, for whom both the City of Charlotte and Mecklenburg County were named. Charlotte married King George III of England and became the Queen.

SPECIAL COLLECTIONS, ATKINS LIBRARY,
UNIVERSITY OF NORTH CAROLINA AT CHARLOTTE.

Below, right: The Providence Presbyterian Church graveyard. Pictured at right is the grave of John McKee dating from 1764.

PHOTO TAKEN BY BRUCE R. SCHULMAN.

INDEPENDENCE AND REVOLUTION

Alexander Craighead's principal legacy was to instill among the people of his congregations a fierce determination to resist the imposition of unwanted authority. "Social historians studying the more than two-century story of Mecklenburg might well agree that this community's character has its roots in the independent-mindedness of her early citizenship," writes LeGette Blythe in his popular 1961 history of Mecklenburg County. Dramatic proof of this commitment to noninterference occurred during the so-called "Sugar Creek War" in 1765, the year preceding Craighead's death and three years following the creation of Mecklenburg County from a portion of Anson County in 1762.

Conflict arose when Henry McCulloh, one of Governor Dobbs's partners in land speculation and an agent for another absentee property owner, Lord George Augustus Selwyn, assembled a team of surveyors in the area to determine the boundaries of Lord Selwyn's land. A group of local ruffians, led by Thomas Polk, warned McCulloh to desist or he would be "tied Neck and heels and be carried over

◆

The log cabin at the McIntyre Farm.
The skirmish fought here helped give rise
to Charlotte's reputation as a "Hornets'
Nest" of rebellion.

COURTESY OF CAROLINA ROOM, PUBLIC LIBRARY OF
CHARLOTTE AND MECKLENBURG COUNTY.

✧

Above: A drawing of the first courthouse, a log structure erected in the intersection of Trade and Tryon Streets.

COURTESY CHARLOTTE-MECKLENBURG HISTORIC LANDMARKS COMMISSION.

Below: An interior view of the first Mecklenburg County courthouse. This replica was built in 1968 for Charlotte's bicentennial.

COURTESY OF CAROLINA ROOM, PUBLIC LIBRARY OF CHARLOTTE AND MECKLENBURG COUNTY.

the Yadkin, and that he might think himself happy if he got off so." Undeterred, McCulloh attempted to perform his duties and ordered the "parcel of blockheads" to stand aside, whereupon the squatters, their faces blackened, attacked McCulloh's men. McCulloh retreated and departed for New Bern.

An even more dramatic manifestation of defiance of Royal authority by the Scots-Irish of Mecklenburg County happened in May 1775. Allegedly, a group of leading citizens of Mecklenburg County drafted and signed the so-called Mecklenburg Declaration of Independence on May 20, 1775 and were therefore the first colonists to break their legal ties to Great Britain. It was not until 1819, forty-four years later, when Virginia and Massachusetts were arguing over which of the two states had been first to break with Great Britain, that U.S. Senator Nathanial Macon and William Davidson, the latter representing the Mecklenburg County district in the U.S. House of Representatives, claimed that the Scots-Irish of North Carolina were the first to declare their independence.

Even its staunchest defenders admitted that no copy of the actual document existed. "Nearly all of my father's papers," declared a son of John McKnitt Alexander, "were burned in the spring of 1800." To bolster their case, supporters of the so-called "Meck Dec" interviewed several alleged signers. These elderly gentlemen agreed that they had attended a meeting in May 1775 but could not recall the exact date. William Polk, son of Thomas Polk, published a pamphlet containing these testimonials and declared the matter settled.

Trouble for the backers of the "Meck Dec" surfaced in 1838. An archivist uncovered an article in the July 12, 1775, issue of a Massachusetts newspaper that reproduced a series of resolutions that had reportedly been drawn up in Charlotte on May 31, 1775. Unlike the Mecklenburg Declaration of Independence, the Mecklenburg Resolves expressed the hope that the exercise of independent authority by officials of Mecklenburg County would end if Great Britain would "resign its unjust and arbitrary pretensions with respect to America." Any doubt about the authenticity of the Mecklenburg Resolves disappeared in 1847, when scholars found the entire text published in the *South Carolina Gazette* of June 13, 1775.

The fact that the leaders of Mecklenburg County backed a conditional separation from British rule just eleven days after they allegedly declared their independence seems oxymoronic. Also, none of the participants who was interviewed years after the dramatic events of May 1775 made any mention of the Mecklenburg Resolves. One cannot help but wonder whether these aged men remembered the meeting where the Mecklenburg Resolves was signed, not the Mecklenburg Declaration of Independence.

Defenders of the authenticity of the "Meck Dec" have labored tirelessly to prove their case. They note that a diarist in the Moravian settlement at Salem, now part of Winston Salem, recorded in June 1775 that the citizens of Mecklenburg County had "unseated all Magistrates and put Select Men in their places." The bearer of this news to the Moravians was Captain James Jack, who delivered a document or documents to North Carolina representatives to the Continental Congress then meeting in Philadelphia. The question is what did Captain Jack have in his satchel, the Mecklenburg Declaration of Independence, the Mecklenburg Resolves, or both? The evidence suggests that it was the Mecklenburg Resolves. Captain Jack, for example, traveled through Salisbury when the court was in session in early June 1775. The timing of his arrival in Rowan County is congruous with May 31st, not May 20th, when the Mecklenburg Declaration of Independence was purportedly signed.

According to Chalmers Davidson, Professor of History and later archivist at Davidson College, Archibald Henderson pro-

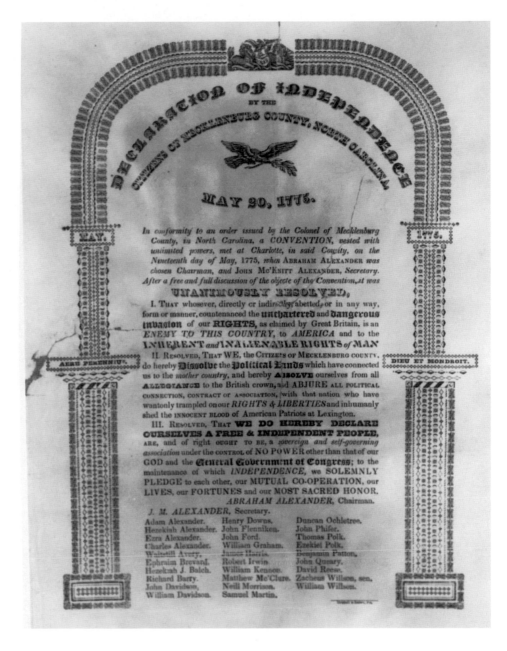

vided the strongest evidence for the authenticity of the "Meck Dec." A member of the faculty at the University of North Carolina at Chapel Hill, Henderson calculated that the news of the Battle of Lexington outside Boston had arrived in Charlotte on May 19th, the date when the heads of Mecklenburg militia units and other leaders had supposedly gathered to consider an appropriate course of action in light of this auspicious news and the day preceding the signing of the Mecklenburg Declaration of Independence.

The controversy over the "Meck Dec" is unending. Despite solid evidence produced against it by a distinguished list of scholars, supporters of the document are unyielding. Edward S. Perzel of the University of North

❖

The Mecklenburg Declaration of Independence. This, the oldest known extant copy, was printed in 1826 in Knoxville, Tennessee. Lack of an original copy or contemporary references to the "Meck Dec" call its authenticity into question.

SPECIAL COLLECTIONS, ATKINS LIBRARY, UNIVERSITY OF NORTH CAROLINA AT CHARLOTTE.

Carolina at Charlotte, a disbeliever, knows what it is like to be a skeptic. "This is very, very serious to a lot of people here," he declared. "When they figure out who I am, they're just not nice."

There is no controversy concerning Mecklenburg County's role in the American Revolutionary War. In 1780-1781 British and Tory troops invaded the Carolina hinterland and brought the war literally to Charlotte's doorstep. Tories were settlers who supported the king. After Charleston, South Carolina had fallen to the British on May 12, 1780, Charles Cornwallis, the newly-appointed commander of the British army in the South, was instructed to take his troops inland and provide protection for the backers of the King. Among his subordinate officers was Banastre Tarleton, a highly aggressive commander of cavalry.

Any realistic expectations that the Patriots or Whigs could stop Cornwallis appeared to end on August 16th in the pine forests outside Camden, South Carolina, where Cornwallis and Tarleton overwhelmed General Horatio Gates's force in a bloody frontal assault. The people of Charlotte and Mecklenburg County faced an ominous threat in the late summer and early fall of 1780. Local folks recognized that a powerful occupying force was about to come into their midst.

Cornwallis and his 2,300 men marched out of Camden on September 8, 1780. The initial British objective in North Carolina was Charlotte and Mecklenburg County, where numerous gristmills along its fast-flowing

creeks would allow Cornwallis to replenish his supplies before proceeding on to Salisbury and eventually to Hillsborough. Opposing him was General William Lee Davidson, commander of the patriot militia in western North Carolina. A 35-year-old former Indian fighter, Davidson was determined to slow down the British advance. He dispatched William R. Davie and a small force of mounted militiamen into the Waxhaws to torment the redcoats. Davie, a South Carolinian, did just that. At daylight on September 20th, he led his men on a daring strike at Wahab's Plantation in what is now Union County. The British army, however, moved inexorably toward Charlotte.

Cornwallis reached Charlotte on September 26, 1780. Davidson had ordered Davie's militia, assisted by local irregular troops commanded by Joseph Graham, to fight a delaying action. Outnumbered about ten to one, Davie's small force of about 300 men looked southward down Tryon Street from the courthouse, then located in the middle of Charlotte, and waited for Cornwallis's redoubtable army to appear. According to Davie, Charlotte was a town containing "about twenty Houses built on two streets which cross each other at right angles in the intersection of which stands the Court-House." Graham described the structure as "a frame building raised on eight brick pillars ten feet from the ground, which was the most elevated in the place." A rock wall some three and a half feet high extended between the pillars so that the local residents could use the ground beneath the courthouse as a marketplace.

Davie placed some of his soldiers behind the rock wall beneath the courthouse and sent others down Tryon Street to hide among the fences, houses, and outbuildings to protect his flanks. The first of the enemy to arrive were the green-coated cavalrymen of Tarleton's Legion. Tarleton was ill, so command of the unit fell to the Major George Hanger. Convinced that the patriot militia could be easily dislodged, Hanger ordered his men to gallop pell-mell toward the courthouse, swords swinging menacingly overhead. Davie instructed the militia to hold their fire until the last moment.

A sheet of flame announced the presence of the patriots behind the rock wall beneath the courthouse. Stunned by a well-executed volley, Hanger and his men turned back. A second attempt also failed. Unable to protect his flanks against the sheer number of troops that Cornwallis could throw against him, Davie eventually had to order his militia to mount their horses and retreat northward on Tryon Street toward Salisbury. In keeping with the military tactics of the day, the Tory cavalry vigorously pursued the departing patriots in order to prevent them from forming another battle line and delivering an effective volley. The Tories caught up with George Locke, a young lad from Rowan County, swooped down upon him, and cut his body to pieces. A marker in the median of Tryon Street just south of its intersection with the connector road from I-85 commemorates Locke's death.

Charles Cornwallis and his army encamped in Charlotte from September 26th until October 12th. Davie and his militiamen continuously harassed the foraging parties that Cornwallis dispatched into the dense forests that surrounded Charlotte. The British attempted to win the support of the people of Mecklenburg County. Davie reported that a large contingent of redcoats and Tories marched "in the direction of the Catawba, near Tuckasegie Ford." According to the patriot commander, the enemy was "cajoling and flattering the people to take Paroles."

Cornwallis's efforts to pacify the local population were unsuccessful, causing the British to label Mecklenburg County a "Hornets' Nest." One particularly unpleasant episode for the

redcoats and Tories occurred in the first week of October at McIntyre's Farm on Beatties Ford Road. Some 300 troops, marching toward a gristmill on Long Creek near Hopewell Presbyterian Church, were engaged in gathering livestock and farm produce along the way.

Local farmers had been warned of the approach of the enemy and were laying in ambush in the woods bordering the farm with rifles in hand. Incensed when the redcoats and Tories "shouted joyously amidst their plunder," the farmers opened fire on their unsuspecting victims and sent them scurrying back to Charlotte. "A large number of the dragoons were shot down," reported one observer.

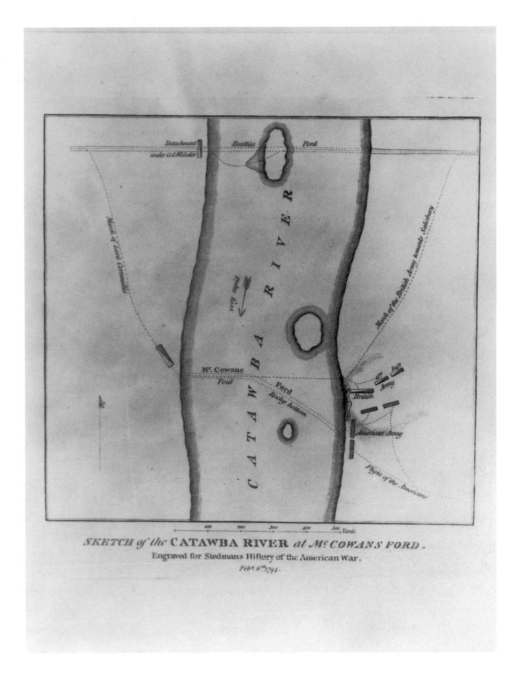

SKETCH of the CATAWBA RIVER at McCOWANS FORD.
Engraved for Stedmans History of the American War.
Feby 6th 1794.

❖

A map of the battle site at McCowan's Ford. Here, American General Davidson was killed trying to delay the advance of British Lord Cornwallis.

SPECIAL COLLECTIONS, ATKINS LIBRARY, UNIVERSITY OF NORTH CAROLINA AT CHARLOTTE.

Above: Revolution by Werner Willis.

Below: The James K. Polk birthplace. The structures are careful reproductions on the site in Pineville where our 11th president was born.

FROM THE COLLECTION OF DAVID T. RITCH.

A far greater calamity for the British happened on the afternoon of October 7, 1780, at the Battle of Kings Mountain about thirty miles southwest of Charlotte. Patrick Ferguson and his entire force of some 900 men were shot dead or captured by a roughly equal contingent of Patriot militiamen. An important consequence of the major setback at Kings Mountain was that Cornwallis decided to retreat into South Carolina and await reinforcements from Charleston. He took his army to Winnsboro. The respite for the people of Mecklenburg County from the Revolutionary War did not last long, however.

Nathanael Greene rode into Charlotte on December 2, 1780 and assumed command of the Continental Army of the South, which General Gates had recently brought to town. The most famous of Greene's subordinate officers at Charlotte was the volatile but unsurpassed tactician Brigadier General Daniel Morgan. A resident of the Virginia frontier, Morgan was a boisterous, coarse, irreverent, and rowdy backwoodsman. "Outsiders in particular found Morgan a dangerous man to cross," writes historian Don Higginbotham.

Greene sat at a table in the Mecklenburg County Courthouse in the heart of Charlotte and finalized his plan of military operations. He realized that his army could not remain in Mecklenburg County because troops from both sides had picked the countryside clean. Greene left Charlotte with the larger part of his army on December 16th and marched to a new camp just across the Pee Dee River from Cheraw, South Carolina. He placed the rest of his troops under Morgan's command. The Old Waggoner led his soldiers out of Charlotte on December 20th and headed westward across the Catawba and Broad Rivers.

Morgan's troops won a decisive victory over a British and Tory army headed by Banastre Tarleton at Cowpens in upper South Carolina on January 17, 1781. Cornwallis then set out from Winnsboro in an effort to catch Morgan's troops before they could cross

the Catawba and join up with Greene's soldiers who were retreating northward through Salisbury. The British marched through Lincoln County and reached McCowan's Ford at the opposite shore from Mecklenburg County shortly after Morgan and his men had reached the other side.

Nathanael Greene arrived in Morgan's camp on January 30, 1781. On the same day, the waters of the Catawba receded enough to allow Cornwallis to begin making plans to cross the river. Greene ordered William Lee Davidson to delay the British advance while Morgan and his troops dashed for Salisbury and the Trading Ford on the Yadkin River.

Joel Jetton, a patriot militiaman, awoke suddenly on the morning of February 1st at McCowan's Ford when he heard the whinnying of horses and the sloshing of water. Coming straight at him were three mounted British officers and hundreds of redcoats. "The British! The British!" Jetton yelled as he scurried up the bank and awoke his startled compatriots. The militia opened fire, making the muddy waters of the Catawba turn red with British blood.

The gunfire caused General Davidson to rush to McCowan's Ford, where he began rallying the militia and organizing reinforcements. The British, who had now gained the shore in sufficient strength to deliver volleys, fired their muskets at the patriots. A musket ball penetrated Davidson's chest, killing him instantly. Thereafter, any semblance of resistance on the part of the militia evaporated, as young and old alike fled for their lives.

Davidson's ultimate sacrifice paid great dividends for Greene and Morgan. It gave the patriot army the critical head start it needed to reach the Yadkin at the Trading Ford, seven miles beyond Salisbury, and to cross the river in boats before the first elements of Cornwallis's army arrived on the night of February 3rd.

Mecklenburg County was no longer affected directly by the American Revolutionary War. As the tide of battle surged back into South Carolina and eventually into Virginia, where Cornwallis was entrapped at Yorktown and forced to surrender his army to General George Washington on October 19, 1781, the farmers of the Carolina Piedmont returned to the performance of their daily chores. The great majority of the early settlers of Mecklenburg County scratched out a meager living in the fields they labored to keep free from unwanted trees. These subsistence farmers grew what they ate and made what they wore. The staple crop was corn They were poor and malnourished. Infectious diseases like measles, influenza, whooping cough, and

✧

A re-enactor portrays Hezekiah Alexander at the circa 1740 Hezekiah Alexander House on the grounds of the Charlotte Museum of History.

✧

The Robinson Rock House, located near Reedy Creek, is another pioneer house built of stone. This house has not fared as well as the Hezekiah Alexander House, several miles to its southwest.

COURTESY OF CHARLOTTE-MECKLENBURG HISTORIC LANDMARKS HISTORIC LANDMARKS OMMISSION.

dysentery could easily take anyone away. Go to the cemeteries of the oldest Presbyterian Churches in Mecklenburg County, such as Providence, Steele Creek, Hopewell, Sugaw Creek, and Philadelphia, and you will encounter the numerous graves of infants and of women who died in childbirth.

There were a few people of considerable wealth living in Mecklenburg County in the Colonial era. One was Hezekiah Alexander, whose imposing rock house erected in 1774 off what is now Shamrock Drive is the most impressive remnant of the local built or man-made environment of the Colonial era. In 1767, Alexander, a blacksmith by trade, sold his property in Pennsylvania and moved to Mecklenburg County, where he already owned land and where he had influential relatives. Recognizing that more and more settlers were moving into the Yadkin-Catawba territory, Alexander employed his sons and nephews as teamsters and had them haul Mecklenburg's cash crops, mainly flour, cattle, furs, and pink-root (a drug used to treat hookworm), to Philadelphia, where they were traded for manufactured goods and slaves. The return of the wagons would assure Alexander a hefty profit.

The largest landholder in Colonial Mecklenburg was Thomas Polk, whose house stood on the northeastern corner of the Courthouse Square in Charlotte. "Polk's name appears throughout the deed records for the county, buying and selling tracts that would eventually amount to a personal holding of over 15,000 acres," writes historian H. Beau Bowers. Like most of Mecklenburg's upper class, Polk also owned slaves. "In a backcountry not noted for large-scale agriculture or the presence of bonded labor," Bowers asserts, "the possession of slaves stood out, almost as noticeably as stone houses, as one indicator of an individual's wealth." Thomas Polk and his relatives owned 81 slaves. The Alexander clan possessed more than 160.

The members of Mecklenburg County's upper class also dominated the political and cultural life of the community before and after the American Revolution. As immigrants continued to flood into the Yadkin-Catawba territory, pushing the population of Mecklenburg County upward to 11,395 in 1790, the wealthier residents made sure that the social system they dominated remained intact.

Mecklenburg County did receive a famous visitor in 1791—General and former President George Washington. Arriving on May 28, Washington was on an extended tour of the South. Lots of folks gathered in Charlotte to greet their illustrious guest. So many came that not a few had to sleep in their covered wagons. Thomas Polk, the wealthiest man in town, hosted a big party in the yard of his Federal style house on the Square. Washington spent the night in an Inn on West Trade Street operated by a Captain Cook.

Washington departed from Charlotte the next morning and began his journey to Salisbury. The President was not impressed with Charlotte. Writing in his diary, he called it "a trifling place." Maybe it was, but two events of the 1790s, one national in scope and the other regional, were to inaugurate a period of unprecedented economic growth in Mecklenburg County. One was the invention of the cotton gin by Eli Whitney in 1793. The other was the discovery of gold by a boy named Conrad Reed in 1799.

SLAVES AND THEIR CABIN, 1850.

COTTON AND SLAVES

Slavery was a fundamental component of the social hierarchy of pre-Civil War Mecklenburg County. In 1860, slaves composed approximately 40 percent of the local population (6800 of 17,000), making Mecklenburg County one of the highest in terms of the number of bondspeople in the North Carolina Piedmont. Anyone who doubts the impact of the institution of human bondage upon Charlotte-Mecklenburg in the years before and during the Civil War need only examine the historical record. In Charlotte, for example, where 44 percent of the people were slaves in 1850, town officials passed ordinances that closely circumscribed the behavior of blacks. Bondspeople were not allowed to be out on the streets after 9:30 P.M without written permission of their owners. They could not buy or sell alcohol or even smoke a pipe or a cigar in public. Slaves could not leave their plantations without a pass or assemble without the permission of their owners. Slaves could not hold worship services and were forced to go to the white man's churches. Any African American who defied these ordinances was harshly punished. "A severe lashing awaited blacks found guilty of breaking any of these ordinances," writes historian Janette Greenwood.

Bondspeople represented a major financial investment on the part of their owners, so it is not surprising that their masters exerted great effort to capture runaways. In 1860 the average sales price for a healthy, young bondsmen was equivalent to the price of an average house. Admittedly with inflated Confederate dollars, slaves sold in Charlotte in August 1864 brought the following prices. "Boy 18 years old $5,150, boy 11 years $4,100, girl 16 years $4,300, woman 35 years $3,035, girl 16 years (very likely) $5,000, boy 21 years $5,200, man and wife and 2 children aged 2 and 4 years (the man with one eye) $6,500."

This writer does not know of any intact slave houses that survive in Mecklenburg County. The physical record of human bondage is present in several slave cemeteries, however. Perhaps the most evocative is the McCoy Slave Burial Ground off McCoy Road just east of Beatties Ford Road. A rock monument, most likely erected in the 1920s, contains the following inscription.

A slave cabin, 1850

◇

Above: The monument from the McCoy Slave Burial Ground.

COURTESY BRUCE R. SCHULMAN.

Bottom, left: An estate sale, which featured twelve slaves among the household goods.
SPECIAL COLLECTIONS, ATKINS LIBRARY,
UNIVERSITY OF NORTH CAROLINA AT CHARLOTTE.

Bottom, right: A Bill of Sale for a family of three. The mother and two children were sold for $2,035 in 1854.
SPECIAL COLLECTIONS, ATKINS LIBRARY,
UNIVERSITY OF NORTH CAROLINA AT CHARLOTTE.

ERECTED BY
ALBERT McCOY'S
CHILDREN TO HIS SLAVES
UNCLE JIM AND HIS WIFE LIZZIE
UNCLE CHARLES & FAMILY

Some visitors to this site are offended by the marker's language. They consider it to be paternalistic and demeaning. Others are touched by what they regard as a gesture of gratitude on the part of the descendants of the slave owner. Regardless, there is certainly no

question about the sincerity of the McCoy family's motives. They remember Jim and Lizzie with great affection.

The Neely Slave Cemetery is another poignant reminder of the days when human bondage held sway in Mecklenburg County. It is situated in a small grove of trees in an office park near Carowinds Amusement Park. Thomas Neely, who had arrived in southwestern Mecklenburg in 1754 and who owned fewer than ten slaves at the time of his death in 1795, was a generous, kind-hearted, and compassionate master. He made special provisions in his will for the welfare of his chattel labor. He stipulated that "our negro Joe . . . to be taught to read" and wanted his son to give "our negro wench Susy two days every week for the purpose of providing herself in clothing."

Sarah Frew Davidson, the mistress at Rosedale Plantation near Charlotte, encouraged some of her slaves to become literate. Her motive was religious. "After tea attended to the instruction of our young servants," Sarah recorded in her journal on February 7, 1837. "Being much troubled and perplexed relative to my duty on this subject and believing that religious instruction can not be well

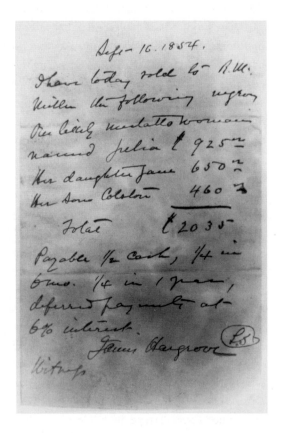

communicated without some knowledge of letters, about six weeks ago I commenced learning them to read."

Slaves in the South placed great emphasis upon performing "a good burial," because death was an act of liberation, a breaking of the chains of bondage. "The slave funeral was at once a 'religious ritual, a major social event, and a community pageant,' drawing upon a mixture of cherished traditions," explains historian Emily Ramsey.

Typically, the funeral began after sunset. A procession of mourners, carrying torches to light the pathway, would leave the slave houses and proceed across the fields and meadows toward the burial ground, which was usually located in a far corner of the plantation. The coffin and the pallbearers would go first, followed by the dead person's family, then the master and his family, and finally the members of the slave community. Mournful spirituals accompanied the entire proceedings, and sobbing and lamentations were acceptable behavior throughout the ceremony. Simple fieldstones mark the burial sites in the Neely Slave Cemetery. The ground is now covered with periwinkle. Archeologists have identified 42 graves.

One of the most confounding aspects of the institution of human bondage was its capriciousness. Masters were in total control and could distribute rewards or punishments as they saw fit. Indeed, their influence extended even beyond death. George Elliot, a Mecklenburg County planter who died in 1804, stipulated in his will that two of his slaves would be set free. "For the many faithful, honest, and meritorious labors and services which I have received for near forty years from my honest slaves . . . Tom and Bet, I hereby liberate them and each of them from slavery." He gave Tom and Bet money and even the use of part of his plantation for their lifetimes. The same master, however, withheld freedom from his other slaves and gave them instead to members of his family. "I will give and bequeath to my son Richard Elliot one Negro boy named Zena, to him, his heirs and assigns forever," George's will proclaimed. "I will give and bequeath to my daughter Jane Dun, to her, her heirs and assigns one Negro girl named Patsey forever."

The system of human bondage that held sway in the Old South is obviously repugnant from the perspective of the prevailing values of today. However, one should consider slavery within the context of the time in which it existed. While it is undeniable that some bondspeople were whipped and otherwise

❖

Above: A grave marker in Pinewood Cemetery. Set aside by design from white Elmwood Cemetery, the fence separating the two was removed in the late 1960s. The marker dates from 1925, illustrating the six-decade long period George Miller lived as a free man after years of bondage.

COURTESY BRUCE R. SCHULMAN.

Left: A headstone from the W.T. Alexander Slave Cemetery.

COURTESY OF CHARLOTTE-MECKLENBURG HISTORIC LANDMARKS COMMISSION.

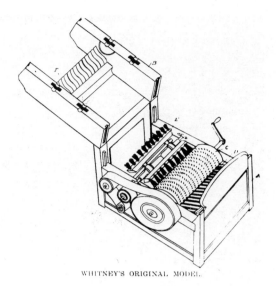

WHITNEY'S ORIGINAL MODEL.

Above: Eli Whitney's cotton gin. With this tool, cotton production—and the demand for slave labor—grew dramatically during the first half of the 19th century.
SPECIAL COLLECTIONS, ATKINS LIBRARY, UNIVERSITY OF NORTH CAROLINA AT CHARLOTTE.

Below: Cedar Grove, built in 1831.
COURTESY OF CHARLOTTE-MECKLENBURG HISTORIC LANDMARKS COMMISSION.

Cedar Grove Plantation, built in 1831 by James G. Torrance

mistreated, others were treated quite well, such as those who belonged to John Starr Neely. Do not forget that Sarah Frew Davidson taught the slave children on her plantation to read and write.

It is also worth noting that slaves were not alone in being beaten in antebellum Mecklenburg County. Early nineteenth century disciplinary customs dictated that unruly white youngsters be whipped. White parents had no compunctions about beating their children. Indeed, their children expected to be whipped—often and severely. "Spare the rod and spoil the child" was a popular dictum of the day. There is a small brick building near the intersection of Sugar Creek Road and North Tryon Street. It was once a school. The sons of slave owners started coming here in 1837 to prepare for higher education. The first full-time teacher was Robert I. McDowell, an honor graduate of Hampton-Sydney College. He would have readily whipped any student who deviated from accepted norms of behavior in the classroom.

The cotton gin, invented by Eli Whitney in 1793, enabled farmers to ship about twelve times as much cotton to market than they could before, and the world price decreased by approximately one half. This meant that industrious individuals who owned substantial amounts of land and the requisite labor supply could increase their annual income by 600 percent. Before the cotton gin, virtually no cotton was grown in the Piedmont. "The machine allowed cotton to be cheaply cleaned so that it could be spun into thread. All over the South a plantation economy quickly developed to produce short-staple cotton to fill the new demand," historian Tom Hanchett explains. In 1790 the United States produced about 3,000 bales of cotton. The figure increased to 178,000 in 1810 and ballooned to more than 4 million bales on the eve of the Civil War.

The most successful of Mecklenburg's cotton farmers made their enhanced economic status known by building fancy, new houses. These antebellum plantation mansions still adorn the Mecklenburg landscape. "The model for much of the architecture of the early nineteenth century was directly or indirectly that of ancient Greece and Rome," one scholar notes. The Federal style was the most popular. Devised by the Adam brothers in Great Britain and sometimes called the Adam style, buildings of this genre most commonly have small entry porches, windows aligned horizontally and vertically in symmetrical rows, cornices decorated with tooth-like dentils, side-gabled roofs, and semi-circular or elliptical fanlights.

An excellent example of the Federal style is Rosedale, Sarah Frew Davidson's home at 3427 North Tryon Street in Charlotte. Built shortly after 1800 and for many years the centerpiece of the William Davidson Plantation, Rosedale has exquisite interior appointments. Other imposing Federal style houses in Mecklenburg County include Latta Place, Oak Lawn, White Oaks, the W. T. Alexander House, Holly Bend, and Cedar Grove.

Many of Mecklenburg's planters were members of Hopewell Presbyterian Church, still an active congregation on Beatties Ford Road. Nowhere in Mecklenburg County does the aura of the Old South linger with greater impact than in the sanctuary of this venerable house of worship, intentionally built without a steeple. Imagine what attending a service in Hopewell Presbyterian Church in the 1850s would have been like. The hierarchical social order of antebellum Mecklenburg would have been apparent to even the most casual observer. Seats were rented to raise money to pay the minister's salary and to meet other church expenses. Downstairs the slave owners and their families would have sat in their subscribed pews. The wealthiest planters would have sat near the front, and their less fortunate compatriots would have occupied pews toward the rear. The poorest whites would have had to sit in the balcony, their seats separated from those occupied by the slaves only by a wooden divider.

Juliana Margaret Conner, a Charleston belle who visited Hopewell Presbyterian Church in 1827, was not overly impressed by even the wealthiest and most politically powerful people she met. She called Charlotte a "place not offering anything worthy of note or interest" and remarked that none of the women at Hopewell was properly attired for church. "There were not two bonnets which differed in shape and color in the whole congregation," she exclaimed. Conner described the backcountry gentry as an essentially a boring lot who lived a humdrum, "almost primitive" existence of "no excitement." The Piedmont planters knew nothing of culinary delicacies, feasting instead upon foods like "ham and chickens, vegetables, tarts, custards and sweetmeats...corn or wheat cakes and coffee."

✧

A docent demonstrates cooking techniques of the early 1800s at Latta Place. As with most large homes, the kitchen was built away from the main house because of the risk of fire.
COURTESY BRUCE R. SCHULMAN.

HISTORIC CHARLOTTE

Left: Hopewell Presbyterian Church,
one of the oldest congregations in
Mecklenburg County.
COURTESY OF CHARLOTTE-MECKLENBURG
HISTORIC LANDMARKS COMMISSION.

Below: The Hugh Torance House and Store.
Adjacent to the Cedar Grove plantation house.
The store brought in manufactured goods from
the North for sale to families across North
Mecklenburg. The oldest part of the structure
dates to the end of the 18th century.
COURTESY BRUCE R. SCHULMAN.

The minister at Hopewell would have preached with great emotional fervor, his sermon emphasizing the depraved nature of mankind and the absolute necessity of God's grace for salvation. Each fall and spring Hopewell Presbyterian Church would have celebrated "Communion Season." All members, including the slaves, would have come forward to sit at a table where the minister or an elder would have served each individual bread and wine out of a common cup. To the leaders of the Hopewell community there was no conflict between slavery and the lessons of the Bible. To their way of thinking, most slaves lacked discipline and culture and had to be treated like children but always within a system of strictures based upon God's law. "For centuries, a wide range of social thinkers had seen the institution as fully compatible with human progress and felicity," writes Peter Kolchin in his book, *American Slavery 1619-1877.* Jeff Lowrance, the present minister at Hopewell Presbyterian Church, told this writer that he is "embarrassed" that the members of his congregation once followed this misguided line of thinking.

Most slave owners in Mecklenburg County, like their counterparts elsewhere in the South, owned relatively small numbers of bondsmen and bondswomen. "In rough terms," states Peter Kolchin, "about one-quarter of Southern slaves lived on very small holdings of 1 to 9." The percentage in such peripheral cotton growing areas as Mecklenburg County was even higher. The majority of Mecklenburg farmers simply did not have enough money to compete with the likes of James Torance or W. T. Alexander.

GOLD AND RAILROADS

Cotton was not the only source of wealth in antebellum Mecklenburg County. Industrialized gold mining became serious business in the Carolina Piedmont in the first half of the nineteenth century and made Charlotte an important economic center for the first time in its history. Charlotte "was a quiet little village, and seemed to be kept up principally by the mining interest," declared an English geologist who visited here in October 1837. The mid-1800s also witnessed the coming of the railroad to Mecklenburg County and the establishment of Davidson College.

In 1799, Conrad Reed, the twelve-year-old son of John Reed, a Hessian soldier who had fought for the British in the Revolutionary War, was fishing along Little Meadow Creek on the family farm in Carbarrus County. He saw a seventeen-pound rock and decided to take it home, where it was used as a doorstop for three years. A jeweler in Fayetteville identified it as gold in 1802. This was the opening event in the history of the gold mining industry of North Carolina.

News traveled slowly in the North Carolina Piedmont in the early 1800s. There was no immediate gold rush. Until the mid-1820s, farmers took a haphazard approach to mining for the precious ore. "It is laughable," wrote one visitor, "to see these tall, long-tail cotton-coat North Carolinians…poking about like snails, and picking up the quicksilver every now and then, and eagerly squeezing it in their hands, to see how much gold is in it." Few people laughed when a laborer at the Reed Gold Mine gathered fourteen pounds of gold before breakfast and five more pounds before sunset. One geologist reported that workers "dug the gold 'like potatoes.'"

It did not require a lot of capital to become involved in gold mining in the early 1800s. After the fall harvest, when they had little else to do, families, including their slaves, would inspect creek beds

or dig shallow holes, called placer pits, to see what they might find. Mecklenburg County still has hundreds of placer pits. The unsystematic, low cost approach to gold mining began to end in 1825. Matthias Barringer, a farmer living in what is now Stanly County, noticed that gold was especially prevalent in veins of white quartz rock. The implications of this discovery were revolutionary. Miners who heretofore had dug placer pits on the surface of the earth suddenly realized that they would extract a lot more gold by sinking shafts deep into the red hills of the Piedmont. Shaft mining, however, was costly. It took a great deal of money to establish mines of this sort, and North Carolina farmers had little expertise in such enterprises.

The solution was to attract foreign capital and labor. Charlotte, like many other tiny villages in the Piedmont, became a boomtown almost overnight in the early 1830s. After sizeable deposits of gold were discovered at Sam McComb's St. Catherine Mine, hundreds of laborers began arriving from places like Great Britain, Italy, Portugal, and Spain. "The discovery, near Charlotte in 1831, of a nest or bed of gold containing pieces weighing five, seven

and eight pounds…produced a frenzy of excitement," writes historian Fletcher Green.

Nine gold mining companies doing business in Mecklenburg County had received their charters of incorporation by 1834. The largest was the London Mining Company, which leased the St. Catherine Mine and the Rudisill Mine in the vicinity of what is now Ericsson Stadium and Summit Avenue in Charlotte. It brought Italian mining expert Count Chevalier Vincent de Rivafinoli to oversee its local operations. A flamboyant, elegant dresser, Rivafinoli made a strong impression upon the Scots-Irish residents of Charlotte.

Most of the new arrivals in Charlotte possessed none of Rivafinoli's refinements. They were the type of individuals one usually finds in towns on the mining frontier. A correspondent for the *New York Observer* toured the North Carolina gold fields in 1831 and was appalled by what he saw. "I can hardly conceive of a more immoral community than exists around these mines," he exclaimed. "Drunkenness, gambling, fighting, lewdness, and every other vice exists here to an unlawful extent."

Some local citizens fell victim to the shameful influences of gold and the sudden

✧

Left: A statue at The Square recognizes the influence of Charlotte's gold mining past on its present as a financial center. In this statue, a miner pours gold coins from his pan onto a banker's head. The banker was modeled after Alan Greenspan.
COURTESY BRUCE R. SCHULMAN.

Below: A statue at The Square commemorates the importance of railroads in the development of Charlotte.
COURTESY BRUCE R. SCHULMAN.

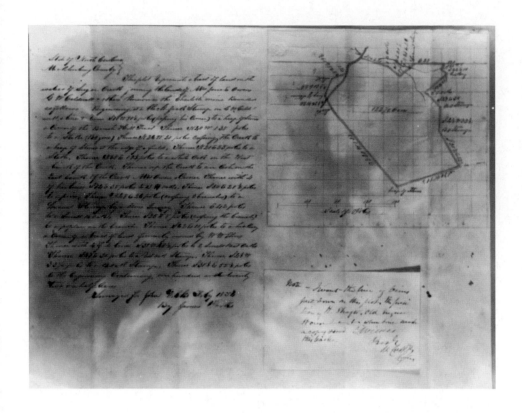

A map and survey of the St. Catherine mine from 1848.

wealth it could provide. One such person was James Capps. A poor farmer residing on a tract of "sterile & apparently valueless land" off Beatties Ford Road about five miles north of Charlotte, Capps discovered gold on his impoverished farm and leased it to foreign investors in 1827. The Capps Mine became the "most productive gold mine in Mecklenburg County, and perhaps in the state," declared the *Western Carolinian*. Suddenly affluent, Capps began carrying portable scales with him wherever he went, so he could weigh the gold dust he needed to purchase whatever he wanted. Unfortunately, Capps used most of his precious ore to buy whiskey. He died from alcoholism in 1828.

Gold mines were not pretty places. The first step in establishing a shaft mine was to erect housing for the workforce that included emigrants, poor farmers, women, children, and slaves whom local slave owners rented out to mining enterprises or whom the companies owned outright. "Taken collectively, southern companies owned directly eighty percent of the total slaves engaged in industry," writes Jeffry Paul Forret in his U.N.C.C. Masters Thesis. The remaining twenty percent were nothing more than rental property. Leasing bondsmen and bondswomen was a widespread practice in the antebellum South.

According to one estimate, 6 percent of rural slaves and 31 percent of urban slaves were on lease from their masters in 1860.

It was not uncommon for slaves to flee from their masters in hopes of finding work in the North Carolina gold mines. The pitiless blacks, aspiring to find enough gold to purchase their freedom, were generally assigned such menial tasks as cutting timber, building fences and dams, and growing hay, corn, and oats for the miners and for the company's mules and horses. One Cabarrus County slave owner complained in 1831 that "his boy Lewis" had left home to "sculk about the gold mines in this county and Mecklenburg."

The majority of the workers in the gold mines of North Carolina were foreigners. "In 1830 alone, Charlotte's population of 717 included sixty-one unnaturalized foreigners," writes historian Jeffrey Forret. The largest number had come from Cornwall in southeastern England, where they had learned the techniques of underground mining by extracting tin and copper for centuries. Illustrative of this truth are the words of a favorite Cornish toast, "fish, tin, and copper."

A newspaper reporter from Charleston, South Carolina toured the St. Catherine Mine in 1831. "I went down a ladder about one hundred feet, perpendicular, and thence along galleries well braced on the sides, and roofed with boards overhead, for some hundred feet further," he declared. "I then followed, in a slanting direction, the vein to the spot where the miners were taking the ore from the earth, and sending it aloft by means of buckets, which are drawn up by mules." The underground workers wore short-sleeved coats and white overalls. "A round-topped, wide-brimmed hat of indurated felt protected the head like a helmet," wrote a reporter for *Harper's Magazine*. "In lieu of crest or plume each wore a lighted candle in front, stuck upon the hat with a wad of clay."

The pace of gold mining in North Carolina began to wane in the late 1830s and early 1840s. The national economic downturn known as the Panic of 1837 hastened the ruin of many unwise speculative investors. Even more significant in prompting miners to abandon their operations in North Carolina was the discovery of huge gold deposits in California in 1848. Southern miners simply packed up their belongings and departed individually and in groups for California, many taking their slaves with them. "One stream in McDowell County which had 3,000 miners at work in 1848," writes historian Fletcher Green, "was practically deserted in 1850." All that remained were abandoned wooden buildings and piles of white quartz rock. Some gold mines did continue to operate in the North Carolina Piedmont, some as late as the Great Depression of the 1930s, but never even close to the level of activity of antebellum days.

The most significant building that survives from the gold mining era in North Carolina is the former United States Branch Mint in Charlotte. It was dismantled and moved from its original location on West Trade Street in 1936 and now serves as the Mint Museum of Art. Designed by Philadelphia architect William Strickland, the facility opened for business on December 4, 1837. The need for a branch mint in the North Carolina gold region arose because of the tendency of many private assayers and minters to produce counterfeit coins. A Congressional committee reported that a lot of "imperfect currency" was circulating in and around Charlotte and the other boomtowns of the Piedmont. The imposing new edifice, which cost $29,700 to build, operated until Confederate authorities took it over in May 1861. The increasing affluence of Mecklenburg County's Scots Irish planter class prompted them to join with their counterparts in surrounding counties to create an institution of higher learning.

Grand buildings were erected on the campus of Davidson College in the 1830s and 1840s. The leaders of the Concord Presbytery of the Presbyterian Church, not wanting their sons to continue having to go to Princeton College in New Jersey to receive a Calvinistic education, voted on March 12, 1835, to establish a college in western North Carolina. William Lee Davidson, II was a member of the committee charged with selecting a site for the "Manual Labour School." He was also the son of General William Lee Davidson, who had died on February 1, 1780 in the Battle of McCowan's Ford. At a meeting held at

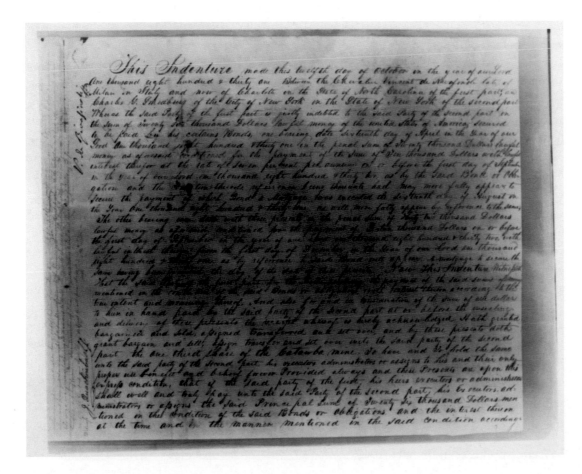

A contract between Charles Smedberg and Count Rivafanoli from October 12, 1831. The mining expert helped improve the efficiency of Charlotte-area gold mines.

Davidson's home, Beaver Dam, on May 13, 1835, "at candlelight after solemn and special prayer to Almighty God for the aid of his grace," the committee decided to recommend purchase of 469 acres of Davidson's land for $1521 for the college's campus. At a later meeting, on August 26, 1835, it was decided to name the institution "Davidson College… as a tribute to the memory of that distinguished and excellent man, General William Davidson, who in the ardor of patriotism, fearlessly contending for the liberty of his country, fell (universally lamented) in the Battle of McCowan's Ford."

Davidson College opened in 1837. The original curriculum included moral and natural philosophy, evidences of Christianity, classical languages, logic, and mathematics. There were three professors, including Robert Hall Morrison, who was also the college's first president, and approximately sixty-four students. The oldest extant structures on the campus are Elm Row and Oak Row. Both were originally dormitories and date from the first year of the institution's operations. The style and placement of the buildings suggest that the Presbyterian elders who founded Davidson College were hoping to duplicate the feel of Thomas Jefferson's famous "Lawn" at the University of Virginia. The exteriors of the buildings retain their original Jeffersonian Classical features. The most elegant of the early college structures are Eumenean Hall and Philanthropic Hall. Both were built in 1848, and each served as the home of a debating society, secret and formal in nature.

The decade of the 1850s was a time of propitious happenings in Charlotte. Indeed, those ten years witnessed to a substantial degree the birth of the community that we inhabit today, at least in terms of civic spirit. Unlike the invention of the cotton gin by Eli Whitney in 1793 or the discovery of gold by Conrad Reed in 1799, both of which had profoundly impacted life in Mecklenburg County, local residents, not outside forces or good fortune, brought this new change about. "With

our citizens, the tide and the spirit of improvements are still as high as ever," declared a Charlotte newspaper in 1853.

There was considerable apprehension about the future economic health of the county after the Panic of 1837 and the discovery of gold in California in 1848. Physician Charles J. Fox and lawyers James W. Osborne and William Johnston led the effort to boost local development by bringing a railroad to Charlotte. By doing so, they elevated resolute and imaginative leadership to the pinnacle of importance it has occupied in Charlotte and Mecklenburg County ever since.

Mecklenburg planters produced bounteous crops of cotton throughout the 1830s and 1840s, but markets were far removed and difficult to reach. Teamsters had to traverse nearly impassable roads to Fayetteville, Cheraw or Camden, where the "White Gold" of the South was loaded onto flat-bottomed scows for shipment to Wilmington, Georgetown or Charleston. "The difficulties faced by farmers in marketing their crop led many to abandon the Carolina Piedmont for greener pastures in the west," writes historian Janette Greenwood.

The population of Mecklenburg County declined from 20,073 in 1830 to 13,914 in 1850. Although a substantial number of those no longer living in Mecklenburg had become

residents of new neighboring counties, such as Union County, Mecklenburg County was unquestionably experiencing economic stagnation. Real estate values fell by about half during the same years. Dramatic action was needed if Charlotte-Mecklenburg was to continue to compete with other communities for economic prominence.

In 1847, Johnston, Fox, and Osborne began sponsoring public meetings in Charlotte and its environs to champion a rail line that would link Charlotte to Charleston

Above: Eumanean Hall, Davidson. Members of the two debating societies would debate issues from across their balconies. President Woodrow Wilson, who attended Davidson College, returned in 1916 and spoke once again from the Eumanean Hall balcony. He noted that he hoped his debating and speaking skills had improved since his college days
COURTESY BRUCE R. SCHULMAN.

Below: Oak Row, Davidson College, was constructed as part of the original Quadrangle on campus. The style and placement of structures on campus was designed to evoke Thomas Jefferson's "Lawn at the University of Virginia."
COURTESY BRUCE R. SCHULMAN.

Southern Station and Stonewall Hotel.

✧

Above: The Southern Railway Station as seen in this early 20th century postcard. Rail remained the dominant mode of intercity travel from the 1850s to the 1950s.

FROM THE COLLECTION OF DAVID T. RITCH.

Below: Efforts to establish rail links to major ports and trading centers began in the 1850s and continues throughout the 1860s. The proceedings described in this book detail Charlotte's efforts to further integrate into the nascent national rail network.

SPECIAL COLLECTIONS, ATKINS LIBRARY,
UNIVERSITY OF NORTH CAROLINA AT CHARLOTTE.

by way of Columbia, South Carolina. The railroad boosters contended that only the laying of track would allow the County's farmers to enjoy "the improvements and advantages of the age in which we live." They named the proposed line the Charlotte and South Carolina Railroad and insisted it would save Mecklenburg County and its neighbors "from poverty and from ruin."

Fundraisers were held in towns throughout the region, including Lincolnton, Salisbury, Concord, Monroe, and as far away as Rutherfordton. The response was overwhelmingly positive. The farmers of the Providence community organized a barbecue and pledged $14,000. A sizeable home could be bought at that time for $3000! By August 1847 the astounding sum of $300,000 had been raised for the road. The dream of connecting Charlotte to Columbia and Charleston by rail was going to become a reality.

On October 28, 1852, a crowd of about 20,000 people gathered to wait for the arrival of the first train. All was anticipation and excitement. Then it happened. The first train lumbered into the Charlotte station, which was situated about where the Charlotte Convention Center now stands.

"More than any other event, the arrival of the railroad in 1852 set Charlotte on its way to being the largest city in the Carolinas," contends historian Thomas W. Hanchett. Heretofore, nothing had distinguished

Charlotte economically from other towns in the southern Piedmont. There had been no greater reason for farmers to congregate for business here than in Lincolnton or Monroe or Concord. The efforts of Fox, Osborne, Johnston, and their supporters made Charlotte the railhead of the region and its transportation and distribution center, a position it has never relinquished.

With Charlotte having the only rail connection from the southern Piedmont into neighboring South Carolina, it was only logical that the largely State-financed North Carolina Railroad, extending from Goldsboro on the Wilmington and Weldon Railroad westward through Raleigh to Greensboro and Salisbury, would terminate in Charlotte. The first train traveled the entire route from Goldsboro to Charlotte on January 31, 1856. "We now have a railroad connection with Raleigh, Petersburg, Richmond, and with all the cities of the North, on to the lines of Canada," the *Western Democrat* proclaimed.

In 1858, the Wilmington, Charlotte and Rutherfordton Railroad Company erected a passenger station on North Tryon Street to serve as the eastern terminus of a thirty-one mile line from Charlotte to Lincolnton, which was completed by April 1861. Dr. Charles Fox headed the campaign to establish Charlotte's fourth railroad of the 1850s, the Atlantic, Tennessee and Ohio Railroad or

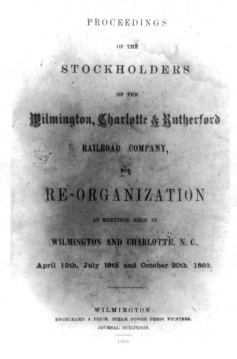

PROCEEDINGS

OF THE

STOCKHOLDERS

OF THE

Wilmington, Charlotte & Rutherford

RAILROAD COMPANY,

FOR

RE-ORGANIZATION

AT MEETINGS HELD IN

WILMINGTON AND CHARLOTTE, N. C.,

April 15th, July 19th and October 20th 1869.

WILMINGTON:
ENGELHARD & PRICE, STEAM POWER PRESS PRINTERS.
JOURNAL BUILDINGS.

1869.

AT&O, which despite its boastful name only ran from Charlotte to Statesville. The Atlantic, Tennessee & Ohio Railroad reached from Charlotte to Davidson in 1861 and to Statesville in March 1863, where it connected with the Western North Carolina Railroad.

Dr. Fox and his associates also wanted to make Charlotte an important cultural place. They provided the impetus for establishing the North Carolina Military Institute. "Those gentlemen who originated and pushed forward the scheme are entitled to much credit for energy and zeal," proclaimed the *Western Democrat*. Fox and his friends raised $15,000 by selling stock to individuals and received $10,000 from the City of Charlotte, also to purchase stock. The voters of Charlotte had approved this financial outlay in a special referendum held on March 27, 1858. Dr. Fox and his fellow boosters bought a tract of land about one-half mile south of Charlotte beside the tracks of the Charlotte and South Carolina Railroad and hired Sydney Reading, a contractor, to oversee the construction of Steward's Hall, a massive, castle like,

three and four-story brick edifice designed to look like the buildings at West Point.

Classes began at the North Carolina Military Institute on October 1, 1859. The institute had two departments. A Primary Department for boys from 12 to 15 and a Scientific Department for young men from 15 to 21. The superintendent of the North Carolina Military Institute was Daniel Harvey Hill, a graduate of West Point and formerly a member of the Davidson College faculty. "As a teacher I have never seen his superior," one of his students exclaimed. D. H. Hill's influence over the educational philosophy of the North Carolina Military Institute was paramount. In keeping with his gloomy appraisal of human nature, Hill insisted that discipline must be rigorously enforced. Just as at Davidson College, he held firmly to the belief that young men, unless closely supervised, would inevitably go astray. "The great sin of the age," he told the Education Committee of the North Carolina Legislature in January 1861, "is resistance to established authority."

✧

The Helper Hotel, Davidson. Constructed in stages from the 1840s to the 1870s, this is the oldest extant building in Mecklenburg County, which originally served as a hotel. Its Jeffersonian Classical style demonstrates its close ties to the college across the street. The father-in-law of two college presidents operated a drug store here.
COURTESY BRUCE R. SCHULMAN.

THE CIVIL WAR

J. W. Ratchford, a student who had left Davidson College to follow D. H. Hill to the North Carolina Military Institute, remembered attending chapel and listening to his mentor speak. Hill spoke about politics. When word arrived that South Carolina had seceded from the United States on December 20, 1860, many of the cadets from South Carolina, including Ratchford, considered withdrawing from school and going home to support their native state. "Gen. Hill made us a talk...one morning, telling us that if we did have a war he expected to go, and advised us to stay at school until it was certain," Ratchford reported.

Rumor and suspicion were rampant in Charlotte-Mecklenburg in the spring of 1861. The *Western Democrat* reported that "several strangers" were prowling about different sections of Mecklenburg County pretending to be peddlers "but acting in such manner as to cause the belief that this was not the real object." The newspaper went on to state that these sneaky fellows were asking all sorts of questions about the status of people's property. One was even discovered "talking with Negroes at a distance from any road or path."

The second half of April 1861 witnessed a flurry of activity at the North Carolina Military Institute. A particularly dramatic scene occurred when the cadets raised a secession flag, made by the ladies of Charlotte, over Steward's Hall so the passengers on the trains moving north out of South Carolina could see it. James H. Lane, a graduate of the Virginia Military Institute and a member of Hill's faculty, described what happened when the next locomotive passed by the campus. "The artillery thundered its greetings to South Carolina as the train passed slowly by; the male passengers yelled themselves hoarse; the ladies waved their handkerchiefs and threw kisses to these brave boys."

North Carolina Governor John W. Ellis summoned D. H. Hill to Raleigh to organize the State's first military instruction camp. The cadets followed soon thereafter. They marched as a body into Charlotte and boarded trains headed for the State capital on April 26th. Crowds lined the platform as the locomotive pulled away from the station. Among the passengers headed for Raleigh was L. Leon, a private in the Charlotte Greys, a local Confederate unit that had been ordered the day before to wrest control of the Charlotte Mint from Federal authorities. "Our trip was full of joy and pleasure, for at every station where our train stopped the ladies showered us with flowers and Godspeed," he recorded in his diary.

The mood of Charlotte and Mecklenburg County was hopeful and resolute at the beginning of the Civil War. Just as they had done for

the cadets at the North Carolina Military Institute, the "young ladies" of Charlotte presented a flag to the "Charlotte Greys." Lizzie Alexander, a Confederate supporter, gave a stirring speech on April 21st when she addressed the Sharon Riflemen on the occasion of their receiving a "handsome flag" from the local ladies. "Permit me in the name of the ladies of Sharon to present you this Flag bearing the Lone Star as an emblem of North Carolina, to whom alone we now owe allegiance," she declared. Eight companies of troops from Mecklenburg County had left for the front by September 1861.

Charlotte's small community of free African Americans also demonstrated their commitment to the Confederate cause. No doubt motivated mostly by desires to appease their white neighbors, black leaders like barber Jerry Pethel, who owned $2300 of real property in 1860, and household laborer Nancy Jenkins led a successful campaign to raise $55 for the Soldiers' Aid Society, an organization headed by prominent white women. "Our country's cause is a common one with master and servant alike," proclaimed an official of the Soldiers' Aid Society, "and it behooves us all to . . . to show the fanatics of the North that we of the South, regardless of colour, stand as a unit to sustain and strengthen the arm of the soldier of our glorious Confederacy."

Above: Mrs. "Stonewall" Jackson.
COURTESY OF CAROLINA ROOM, PUBLIC LIBRARY OF CHARLOTTE AND MECKLENBURG COUNTY.

Left: The home of Mrs. "Stonewall" Jackson, widow of the Confederate General.
FROM THE COLLECTION OF DAVID T. RITCH.

"Let our people plant corn," proclaimed the *Western Democrat*. "Let them wear jeans and homespuns as their ancestors did before them, when they threw off British rule." It became commonplace for supporters of secession to compare the actions of patriots during the War for American Independence with the exploits of Confederates soldiers during the Civil War. President Jefferson Davis drew upon this theme when he addressed a large crowd in Charlotte in September 1864. The Confederate chief executive said he was aware that the "people of this section were the first to defy British authority and declare themselves free." Davis encouraged the citizens of Charlotte-Mecklenburg to continue to back the war effort even in the face of mounting hardships and adversities. By doing so, he contended, local folks would prove that the "spirit of the sires of '75 and '76 still actuated their descendants."

No battles of consequence occurred in Charlotte-Mecklenburg during the Civil War. There was to be no repetition of what had happened in this region during the American Revolutionary War. The absence of fighting did not make Charlotte-Mecklenburg an unimportant place during the Civil War, however. Because it remained in Confederate hands until the very closing days of the conflict and because it was a major railroad junc-tion, this community was of great strategic value to the South.

In the spring of 1862, the Confederates had to abandon the Gosport Naval Yard in Norfolk because of the likelihood of its imminent capture by the North. Charlotte was chosen as one of the principal locations to which to transport the invaluable machinery and irreplaceable workmen. Laborers occupied

the Mecklenburg Iron Works and erected a series of new wooden buildings along the tracks of the North Carolina Railroad in what is now First Ward in the summer of 1862 to house the Charlotte branch of the Confederate Naval Yard. Among the products of the Naval Yard were mines, anchors, gun carriages, and even marine engines.

Charlotte-Mecklenburg had other important industrial plants that served the Confederacy. These included the Confederate State Acid Works, the Mecklenburg Gun Factory, and the New Manufacturing Company. Industrial life was fraught with danger. This was especially true in the case of the North Carolina Powder Manufacturing Company near the Tuckasseegee Ford on the Catawba River. Disaster struck the plant on May 23, 1863, when 700 pounds of powder exploded, killing 5 people, destroying most of the factory, and rattling windows in Charlotte almost ten miles away. Rebuilt, the plant was destroyed again by an accidental explosion in August 1864 that killed "one white man and two mulattoes." The mill never reopened.

The biggest calamity that occurred in Charlotte during the Civil War was the destruction by accidental fire in January 1865 of the

Confederate storage warehouses, depots, and platforms of the North Carolina Railroad and the Charlotte and South Carolina Railroad. "The loss to the Confederate Government is severe," reported the *Western Democrat*. Large quantities of foodstuffs went up in flames, as did "blankets, soldiers clothing, leather, and various other articles." Supplies became critically scarce in Charlotte during the Civil War. Local newspapers complained about the paucity of paper. Factories found it increasingly difficult to obtain lubricating oils. Charlotte fell into "almost complete darkness" in March 1864 when gas supplies ran out.

Charlotte newspapers were full of articles encouraging the people to provide greater support to the men in uniform. "All person wishing to render the Confederacy essential service, can do so by cultivating the common GARDEN POPPY," declared the *Western Democrat* on May 12, 1863. Poppy juice is opium, which was commonly used as a painkiller during the Civil War. Farmers were told to plant "large corn crops, not only corn but everything that will sustain life." On January 12, 1863, Confederate officials in Charlotte issued an urgent plea for soap.

The people of Mecklenburg County had to endure increasingly grim news as the war dragged on. "We have not room to publish a list of the casualties in all of the N. C. Regiments reported, and therefore select the companies from this and the surrounding counties," announced the *Western Democrat* on May 19, 1863. The newspaper proceeded to list the names of those who had fallen in the Battle of Fredericksburg. Imagine the dread and apprehension with which mothers and daughters must have scanned the pages.

Unlike some sections of North Carolina, Charlotte-Mecklenburg remained steadfast in its commitment to the Confederate cause. "If the whole South was imbued with the same spirit of resistance to Yankee tyranny and oppression as that which characterizes the people of good old Mecklenburg," commented one soldier who visited Charlotte in 1863, "no one need fear the result of the mighty struggle which is now going on." The Charlotte press lashed out with special vengeance against so-called "croakers"—those who unduly criticized the Confederate government and who sought to make peace with the North. One anti-war group, headed by Thomas Gluyas, did meet at Whitley's Mill in the Long Creek community of Mecklenburg County in 1863 but was never able to gain broad support locally.

Even the optimism of the *Western Democrat* began to wane during the last year of the Civil War. The newspaper announced that increasing numbers of unruly deserters from Confederate ranks were finding their way into Mecklenburg County. Famished and half-naked, these desperate men were further diminishing public morale by engaging in criminal activities. "On Wednesday night last, two armed men (supposed to be deserters) went to the house of Mr. Sam Davis, who lives on Potter Road about 12 miles from this place, and demanded his money," the *Western Democrat* declared on December 22, 1863.

Its relatively secure location made Charlotte an ideal place to treat the Confederate sick and wounded. In July 1863 officials erected "extensive hospital buildings on the Fair Gounds, about 1 mile from the Public Square." Steward's Hall housed a medical laboratory, where surgeons and doctors devised compounds to help make the infirm soldiers well. The women of Charlotte were

indefatigable in gathering provisions for the military hospitals of Charlotte. Mayor S. A. Harris implored the "people of Mecklenburg County to send to Charlotte meat, flour, meal and all kinds to vegetables, to be prepared here for the large number of our wounded soldiers who are arriving daily."

By 1865 hordes of wounded were being transported by rail to Charlotte from such cities as Raleigh and Columbia. Refugees came too. So desperate did the situation become that local officials urged refugees to stay at home or seek shelter elsewhere. "The citizens of town are doing what they can towards supplying the wants of the sick soldier, but they have not the means to do much," lamented the *Western Democrat* on March 28, 1865.

On February 21, 1865, the *Western Democrat* warned its readers that it did not know how long it could continue to appear. Expecting William Tecumseh Sherman's army to arrive any day, the editors declared that they would keep the presses rolling "until the enemy prevents us from publishing." Union

troops did destroy the bridge that carried the Charlotte and South Carolina Railroad over the Catawba River but Sherman's army turned eastward toward Goldsboro.

Everywhere there was hunger. Everywhere fear. Everywhere suffering. "In addition to the demands of the hospitals, thousands of soldiers are passing though our town, requiring something to eat," reported the *Western Democrat*. President Jefferson Davis delivered a somber speech when he arrived by horseback in April 1865 on his flight southward from Richmond. "I am conscious of having committed errors," he declared, "...but in all that I have done, in all that I have tried to do, I can lay my hand upon my heart and appeal to God that I have had but one purpose to serve, but one mission to fulfill, the preservation of the true principles of Constitutional freedom, which are as dear to me today as they were four years ago."

As civil authority collapsed, looters began moving unmolested through the streets of Charlotte, smashing storefronts and stealing whatever they could find. Town leaders wel-

✧

Grace AME Zion Church, founded in 1886 after a dispute over alcohol. The new congregation favored banning alcohol and sought to establish a congregation "to rid our youth of fogey ideas, sentiments, etc. and to bring them up to proper moral sentiments and religious beliefs."
COURTESY OF CHARLOTTE-MECKLENBURG HISTORIC LANDMARKS COMMISSION.

comed Union troops who took control of Charlotte without a struggle in May 1865. The first order of business was the restoration of order and the imposition of a loyalty oath. ". . . all persons who wish to engage or are engaged in any business, are required to take the oath of allegiance to the United States," announced Colonel Willard Warner.

"When our soldiers returned to their former homes," wrote J. B. Alexander, a prominent Charlotte physician, "they felt the bitterness of defeat, and were stared in the face by poverty." Paul B. Barringer, then a young boy living in nearby Concord, remembered what his uncle said to the family slaves. "My uncle called all of them in and told them that they were now free and from henceforth could go where they willed, Mr. Lincoln's proclamation having been made good on the field of battle."

"A friend calls our attention to the fact that numbers of Confederate soldiers, who have recently been released, are daily arriving at Charlotte, many of them sick," reported the *Western Democrat* on July 3, 1865. Others, like John Starr Neely, had to walk home. Imprisoned by the Yankees after serving as a guard in the Confederate prison in Salisbury, Neely did not get back to Mecklenburg County until 1866. Writing in the first issue of *The Land We Love*, a monthly magazine he founded in 1866, D. H. Hill gave full vent to the agony he felt over the South's defeat. "All the rivers of plenty have been dried up! The grass sprouts and grows from blood only; the rains of peace can not wash it away! Want, want, want, cries! Suffering groans!" The *Western Democrat* shared Hill's dreary assessment of the local economy. "Everybody is complaining of the scarcity of money, and nobody seems to have any," the newspaper complained on June 13th.

Blacks swarmed into Charlotte from the surrounding countryside. Bondspeople left the plantations to give expression to their new status as free people. The same impulse caused

African Americans to establish their own churches. "The unifying theme underlying the diverse efforts of the freed people remained the drive for autonomy and independence," explains historian Peter Kolchin. Kathleen Hayes of Charlotte summoned the black members of First Presbyterian Church to "come down out of the gallery and worship God on the main floor." Rev. Samuel C. Alexander, a white Presbyterian missionary from Pittsburgh, Pennsylvania, came to Charlotte soon after the war and purchased property at Davidson and Third Streets, where Hayes and her small band commenced to worship.

Missionaries for the A. M. E. Zion Church arrived in Charlotte in May 1865 and established new houses of worship. Edward H. Hill arrived and founded Clinton Chapel. It stood on South Mint Street between First and Second Streets. Reverend Hill licensed Bird Hampton Taylor, put him in charge of Clinton Chapel, and continued his organizing activities. Before he died later that year, Hill had laid the groundwork for nearly twenty new churches within a fifty-mile radius of Charlotte. Thomas Henry Lomax, a native of Cumberland County, came to Charlotte about 1873 and founded Little Rock A.M.E. Zion Church. Grace A.M.E. Zion Church was established in 1887 by dissident members of Clinton Chapel.

African Americans residing in Mecklenburg County also witnessed the founding of Biddle Memorial Institute, now Johnson C. Smith University. Three white Presbyterian ministers, Samuel C. Alexander, Sidney S. Murkland, and Willis L. Miller, were eager to impart Christianity and such middle class values as punctuality and frugality to the newly freed black men of the region. Excluded from the Concord Presbytery and vilified by many of their white neighbors, the three courageous preachers became agents of the Freedmen's Committee of the Presbyterian Church of the North.

Willis Miller traveled to Missouri in May 1867 to meet with denominational leaders. He "urged the favorable consideration of the grave need for an educational center in the midst of the suffering field," explains historian Inez Moore Parker. Miller was successful in win-

ning the support of the General Assembly of the Presbyterian Church, U.S.A. He and his associates came to Charlotte, purchased a lot, and moved a building formerly used as a hospital for Confederate troops to the Charlotte site and opened the school soon thereafter. Mrs. Henry J. Biddle of Philadelphia, Pennsylvania made a generous donation to the college and requested that it be named "Henry J. Biddle Memorial Institute" in honor of her husband who had been killed in the Civil War.

❖

Confederate Monument in Elmwood Cemetery, Mecklenburg County's most prominent memorial to the soldiers of the Civil War.
COURTESY BRUCE R. SCHULMAN.

RECONSTRUCTION

Whites were appalled over what was happening in Charlotte and its environs in terms of the advancement of African Americans. The traditional white upper class of Charlotte and Mecklenburg County joined their compatriots throughout North Carolina and the South in opposing the creation of greater social and economic equality for the rank-and-file citizenry, black and white. "The Negro is a good thing for fanatics, demagogues and hypocritical philanthropists to prate about," proclaimed the *Western Democrat*. D. H. Hill minced no words about how he felt. "As children need parents, so do Negroes need masters," declared a newspaper editorial that Hill reprinted in *The Land We Love*.

Historian Paul D. Escott contends that "continuity in power relationships and in the elite's undemocratic attitudes" spanned the Civil War. "The men who benefited from the aristocratic customs and laws of 1850," he asserts, "fought tenaciously to protect their power and privilege during the Civil War and Reconstruction." Such influential whites as railroad promoter William Johnston and physician J. B. Alexander believed that blacks and lower class whites were incapable of exercising prudent political judgments. Consequently, Johnston, Alexander and other men of their upper-class persuasion worked tirelessly to maintain the social hierarchy of antebellum Charlotte and Mecklenburg County after the Civil War.

Most wealthy and middle class whites in the South reacted angrily when the United States Congress wrested control of Reconstruction policies from President Andrew Johnson and passed a series of laws in 1867 that established what many Southerners regarded as onerous requirements for being accepted back into the Union. The Radical Republicans, upset by the refusal of Southern white politicians to let blacks vote and exercise full civil rights, divided the South into five military districts and stipulated that all states in the former Confederacy had to enact universal manhood suffrage and approve new constitutions consistent with the Constitution of the United States. This meant that free blacks would be able to vote in North Carolina for the first time since 1835 and that their ranks would now include hordes of former bondspeople.

Elections for a constitutional convention were held under duress in North Carolina in November 1867. Controlled by African Americans and pro-Unionist whites, despairingly known as "Carpetbaggers" and "Scalawags," the convention completed its work in March 1868; and soon thereafter North Carolina was readmitted to the Union. The new constitution eliminated all property qualifications for voting or holding office and provided for a "general and uniform system of Public Schools." Even more ominously for elitist and middle class whites, it eliminated the system of county Justices of the Peace and created elected county commissions as the governing body of local government.

Newspaperman William W. Holden, who had served briefly as Provisional Governor in 1865 and who had brought about the establishment of the Republican Party in North Carolina two years later, was elected Governor in April 1868. Republicans carried 58 of North Carolina's 89 counties. "Prominent men of the old elite saw their worst nightmare—an alliance among the lower classes of both races—materializing under the protection of the federal government," says Escott.

Thomas McAlpine, Charlotte agent for the Freedmen's Bureau, was concerned about the retribution that embittered whites were meting out against African Americans who had voted with the Republicans. Deliveryman Allen Cruse fired five black employees who

supported Holden. One black voter in Mecklenburg County had his mule killed on the night of the election.

The most ominous form of white payback against "unruly" blacks was political terror and physical intimidation. In 1866, six Confederate veterans met in Pulaski, Tennessee and founded the Ku Klux Klan. Its membership quickly spread into other states, including North Carolina. Although there is no definitive evidence that it operated in

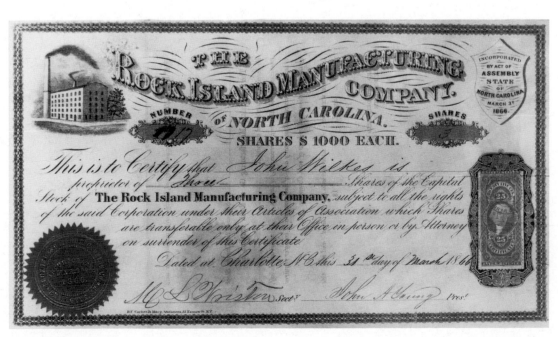

CHARLOTTE FEMALE INSTITUTE.

A Boarding and Day School for Young Ladies, delightfully situated in a retired and pleasant portion of the City of Charlotte, N. C.

Officers and Instructors.

Rev. R. BURWELL, Principal and Instructor in Mental and Moral Philoso-

sought to use the doctrines of White Supremacy to solidify their electoral base.

The scheme was simple and ultimately successful. Poor whites would be weaned from forming alliances with African Americans on the basis of their shared economic interests and would be made to understand they should stand shoulder to shoulder with members of their own race. In return, affluent and middle class whites promised to create jobs for impoverished whites and for cooperative blacks by advancing the economic recovery of the South. In short, they would fashion a "New South."

The Conservatives, who would soon begin calling themselves Democrats again, gained large majorities in both chambers of the legislature in 1870. Two out of every three North Carolina counties that moved from the Republican to the Democratic camp had experienced substantial Klan activity since 1868. Also undermining popular support for the Republicans were exaggerated allegations of governmental corruption.

Bolstered by their victory at the ballot box, the Democrats called for another constitutional convention in 1875. The voters approved thirty amendments the following year, the general effect of which was to concentrate greater power in the legislature now that the Democrats controlled it. The most important of the amend-

Mecklenburg County, the Klan had its local admirers, especially among affluent and middle class whites. "The Ku Klux Klan was all that saved our country, our women, children and old men," proclaimed J. B. Alexander.

Affluent and middle class whites were determined to reverse the political tide and undermine white support for the Republican Party "by attacking racial equality as the weakest point in the Republican program." In addition to brutalizing blacks when necessary, the Conservatives

Above: An advertisement from an 1868 edition of The Land We Love *for the Charlotte Female Institute. Educational opportunities for girls were quite limited— placing heavy emphasis on domestic skills and arts rather than the more academic education their male peers received at male schools.*

SPECIAL COLLECTIONS, ATKINS LIBRARY,
UNIVERSITY OF NORTH CAROLINA AT CHARLOTTE.

Right: The Treloar House (ca. 1887). William Treloar, who came to Charlotte from Cornwall, England and was involved in gold mining. The house is a rare example of a "row house." The idea of urban, high-density living was not popular in Charlotte after the Civil War.

COURTESY BRUCE R. SCHULMAN.

Good Samaritan Hospital, Charlotte, N. C.   3

ments gave the general assembly "full power by statute to modify, change, or abrogate" the existing rules of county government. This meant that the Democrats could nullify the election of county officials, most notably African Americans in the eastern part of North Carolina, where blacks were most numerous.

Two events in 1876 signaled the end of Reconstruction in the Tar Heel State. Zebulon Vance, North Carolina's popular Civil War governor, was elected chief executive again, thereby demonstrating that the antebellum elite was predominant once more. Also, Rutherford B. Hayes became President of the United States and withdrew the last Federal troops from the South.

African Americans continued to run for political office in Mecklenburg County until the end of the nineteenth century, and several routinely served on the Charlotte Board of Aldermen. But white Democrats invariably held the majority on the twelve-member Board of Aldermen, and Republicans never succeeded in electing a mayor. "While accommodating new economic growth, new business leaders, a vigorous Republican party, and black political participation, the town continued to be dominated by the secessionists of the Civil War," asserts historian Janette Greenwood.

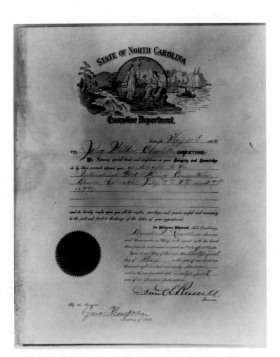

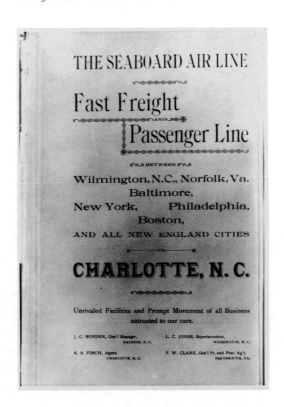

Cotton Mills
In New South Charlotte

The Democrats delivered on their promise of improving the economy of Charlotte and Mecklenburg County. The 1870s and 1880s witnessed vigorous commercial and industrial growth in Charlotte. "Everything about Charlotte seems to be on a big boom," observed a visitor in the 1880s, "and everybody seems to be in good spirits at the prospects." As in the 1850s, effective leadership was fundamental to this process. During the final quarter of the nineteenth century a talented assortment of ambitious entrepreneurs moved to Charlotte to join local businesspeople in taking advantage of the town's strategic location and its excellent railroad connections.

Two South Carolinians were paramount in making Charlotte the major commercial and industrial center of the two Carolinas. They were Edward Dilworth Latta and Daniel Augustus Tompkins.

Edward Dilworth Latta moved from New York City to Charlotte and established a men's clothing store in October 1876. Latta's impact on this community, however, was to go far beyond his clothing business. Until his departure in May 1923, when he moved to Asheville, Latta played a pivotal role in the transformation of the city from a modest commercial center of 7,094 inhabitants in 1880 into an industrial and financial center of the Piedmont in 1920, boasting a population of 46,338. In large measure, Latta was typical of the new class of investors, industrialists, and businessmen who arose in North Carolina and the South following the Civil War. As exponents of a "New South," such men became convinced that future wealth in the region lay not in traditional farming methods but in industrialization, urbanization, and scientific agriculture; and they took

advantage of the new economic opportunities afforded by the growth of manufacturing and the rise of sizable urban areas.

Daniel Augustus Tompkins was an ardent participant in the New South movement. He arrived in Charlotte in March 1883. A native of South Carolina, Tompkins had earned a degree in civil engineering from Rensselaer Polytechnic Institute in Troy, New York in 1873, had been a chief machinist for the Bethlehem Iron Works in Bethlehem, Pennsylvania, and had decided to return to his native region so that he might encourage and assist the development of industry and the diversification of agriculture.

Having secured a franchise from the Westinghouse Machine Company of Pittsburgh, Pennsylvania for the selling and installing of steam engines and other machinery, Tompkins selected Charlotte as the loca-

THE CHARLOTTE COTTON MILLS.

tion for his sales office, which opened on March 27, 1883. Tompkins chose Charlotte because of its railroads. On May 17, 1873, the Carolina Central Railroad Company had acquired the right of way and had undertaken the task of completing a continuous track from Wilmington to Rutherfordton. This job had been completed on December 15, 1874. By 1873 the Atlanta and Charlotte Airline Railroad had finished laying track between Charlotte and Spartanburg, South Carolina and on to Atlanta.

In 1884 Tompkins established the D. A. Tompkins Company. This enterprise was "at the forefront of machinery manufacturing for the southern textile mills," writes historian Brent Glass. D. A. Tompkins remained in Charlotte until his death in 1914 and helped build a virtual cotton mill empire in the Tar Heel State. As were the other powerful industrialists of his type and time, Tompkins was committed to laissez-faire capitalism and opposed public reforms for better industrial working conditions including the regulation of child labor. He was also a devoted defender of what he called "Anglo Saxon values," a code name for White Supremacy.

The first factory in Mecklenburg County devoted exclusively to the spinning of cotton fiber was the Glenroy Cotton Mill. Founded by

E. C. Grier and his son, G. S. Grier, the mill was located about halfway between Matthews and Providence Presbyterian Church, in southeastern Mecklenburg County. It contained 350 spindles and produced bale yarn. It was established in 1874 and operated for approximately eighteen months. The building was demolished in 1899.

The founder of the first cotton mill in Charlotte was Robert Marcus Oates, a native of Cleveland County and a Confederate veteran who also served on both the County Commission and the Charlotte Board of Aldermen. "He was strong in his convictions, conservative in his ideas, and these two characteristics together with his mental ability and correctness of life made him a tower of strength to the community," declared a Charlotte newspaper. Named the Charlotte Cotton Mills, the plant opened in December 1880 and went into full operation the next year. "The opening of the Charlotte Cotton Mill represented the beginning of a new industrial era in Charlotte's history," writes historian Janette Greenwood. Parts of the Charlotte Cotton Mills still stand at West Fifth and North Graham Streets.

D. A. Tompkins built and equipped three cotton mills in Charlotte in 1889 – the Victor, the Ada, and the Alpha. Called "hummers" because of the noise produced by the spinning and weaving machines, the new mills appeared at the edges of town along railroad lines. Tompkins did not like sites in the hearts of cities. "The proximity of lawyers...promotes law suits," he declared, and a "mill in the country can operate its own store and thereby get back some of money paid for wages." It is important to note that Northern capital played no direct role in financing the great majority of Charlotte's first cotton mills. They were home owned and home operated.

In 1892 Tompkins joined with three other local industrialists, R. M. Miller, R. M. Miller, Jr., and E. A. Smith, in picking the southern end of Dilworth, Charlotte's first trolley suburb, as the place to erect the only cotton mill in Mecklenburg County that he owned and ran, although he did operate a cottonseed oil plant nearby. The Atherton Mills began operations in January 1893, with 5,000 spindles manufacturing yarn goods. "There's no doubt about it, things are 'humming' in the Queen City, and 'humming' to the tune of lively progress," declared Tompkins's *Charlotte Observer.*

After 1900 entire mill villages containing more than one factory began to appear on the outskirts of Charlotte. E. A. Smith, a native of Baltimore and part owner of the Atherton Mills, organized the Chadwick and Hoskins Mills in Charlotte near Rozzelles Ferry Road, and by 1907, was head of the Chadwick, Hoskins, Calvine (formerly Alpha), and Louise Mills, and the Dover Cotton Mill in nearby Pineville. When these factories consolidated into the Chadwick-Hoskins Company in 1908, it was the largest textile firm in North Carolina.

Charlotte's biggest textile mill village was North Charlotte, the centerpiece of which was the Highland Park Manufacturing Company Plant No 3, designed by Stuart W. Cramer, who had first come to Charlotte as an engineer for the D. A. Tompkins Company. Erected at the former site of the municipal water works, the imposing brick, electric-powered mill, containing 30,000 spindles, 1000 looms, and employing 800 workers, opened in 1904. The Mecklenburg Mill (1904) and the Johnston Manufacturing Company (1913) were also located in North

✧

Above: Stuart W. Cramer.
COURTESY OF CAROLINA ROOM, PUBLIC LIBRARY OF CHARLOTTE AND MECKLENBURG COUNTY.

Below: Stuart Cramer's Highland Park Mill #3 was used as a model of modern mill design, emulated extensively after Cramer used it in his book Useful Information for Cotton Manufacturers.
SPECIAL COLLECTIONS, ATKINS LIBRARY, UNIVERSITY OF NORTH CAROLINA AT CHARLOTTE.

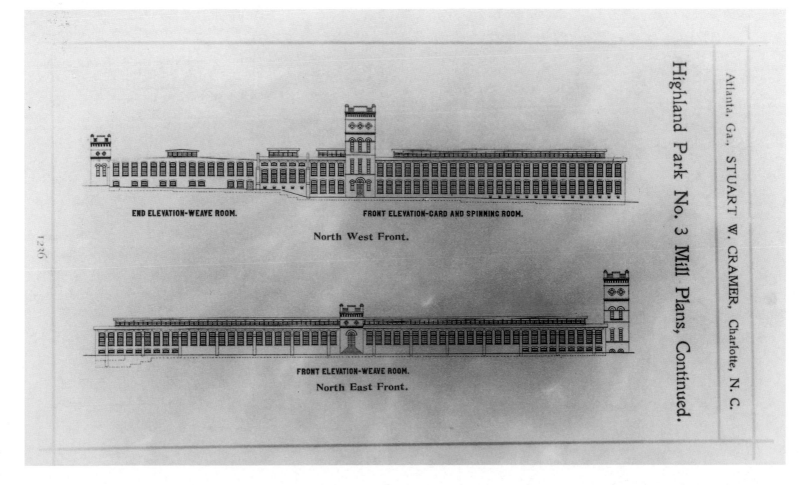

END ELEVATION-WEAVE ROOM.

FRONT ELEVATION-CARD AND SPINNING ROOM.

North West Front.

FRONT ELEVATION-WEAVE ROOM.
North East Front.

Atlanta, Ga., STUART W. CRAMER, Charlotte, N. C.

Highland Park No. 3 Mill Plans, Continued.

Charlotte, as were houses for the workers. All three mill buildings are still standing.

Textile employees, mostly white yeomen farmers and their families who had migrated to the city in search of jobs, typically labored ten to twelve house a day Monday to Friday and five hours on Saturday. When asked about books, one Mecklenburg mill hand answered that he had no time to read. "We have to go to work at fifteen minutes to six and work till seven in the evening," he explained.

New South industrialists opposed any efforts by outside groups to improve the lot of textile workers. A particularly dramatic encounter arose between Tompkins and Methodist minister J. A. Baldwin. Baldwin visited the Atherton Mill Village in 1898 and was appalled by the disease, malnutrition, and overall poverty that he insisted existed there. Tompkins responded by telling the preacher that the plight of textile workers was of their own making. They are "of roving dispositions, are shiftless, and improvident," he insisted.

D. A. Tompkins took advantage of the fact that it was not until 1903 that the General Assembly of North Carolina enacted a child labor law, prohibiting the employment of children less than twelve years of age. He did build a school, the Atherton Lyceum, to teach fundamental quantitative and verbal skills to the mill children and their parents. Despite his patriotic pronouncements, Tompkins compelled his workers to labor on the Fourth

of July, at least until July 4, 1907, when he acquiesced to the suggestion advanced by the superintendent of the Atherton Mills and sponsored a picnic at the Catawba River, where his employees were served sandwiches and lemonade.

A series of momentous developments in the physical evolution of Charlotte occurred in 1890-91. Edward Dilworth Latta joined with five associates on July 8, 1890, to create the Charlotte Consolidated Construction Company, locally known as the Four C's. Like Tompkins, Latta was an enthusiastic advocate of what historian Paul M. Gaston has termed "the New South Creed." Accordingly, like many Southern leaders who attained adulthood following the Civil War, Latta insisted that his native region must discard the past and seek to emulate much of the industrial and urban society of the North. Grounded philosophically in the tenets of Social Darwinism, Latta believed that the South should marshal its talents and resources and

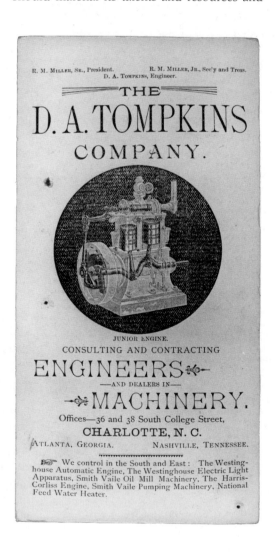

beat the Yankees at their own game. "We must go forward or retrograde—there is no resting place with progress," he contended.

As president of the Four C's, Latta superintended the activities preparatory to the opening of Dilworth, a suburb containing 1635 lots and located on the former fairgrounds and adjacent parcels to the immediate south of the city. Uppermost on his agenda was the installation of an electric streetcar or trolley system. Charlotte had obtained a horse-drawn or mule-drawn streetcar system in January 1887, but Latta became convinced that only the new-fangled electric streetcar could provide the kind of reliable service Dilworth would require.

The Edison Electric Company was awarded the contract on February 11, 1891 to construct the electric streetcar system for the Four C's. Work began in March and terminated on May 18, 1891, when the first trolley departed from the intersection of Trade and Tryon Streets and headed toward Dilworth. The *Charlotte News* reported that a "great and jolly crowd" assembled to witness the event. The *Morning Star* of Wilmington described the reaction of the public to the placement of the entire system into operation on May 20, 1891, the opening day of the land sale in Dilworth. "The streets and yards fairly swarmed with people, each hurrahing and waving as the car passed along. Bouquets were sent to adorn the cars with," the newspaper continued, "and every one was wild with joy."

One cannot discount the beneficent impact that D. A. Tompkins and Edward Dilworth Latta had upon the economy of Charlotte and its environs. Both men had their admirers. One biographer, George Winston, calls Tompkins "a Southern Franklin, growing in poor soil and enriching the soil he grew in." He was, says Winston, "full of zeal to help mankind by teaching men to help themselves, he was a rare combination of worker and philosopher, of student and teacher, of economist and philanthropist." The drive, foresight and ambition of Tompkins and Latta changed forever the nature of Charlotte. The *Charlotte Observer* was correct in its 1925 eulogy when it characterized Latta as the "builder of a city...He gave the town its first impetus, and

he kept it going until the day it went forward on its own accord." Still, at least in this writer's opinion, some aspects of the legacy that men such as Tompkins and Latta left behind is troubling, especially with respect to racial attitudes. That truth was to become painfully obvious in the 1890s.

White women began to play a more conspicuous role in community affairs during the

❖

Above: A typical mill house. This one was built for employees of the Mecklenburg Mill in North Charlotte.
COURTESY OF CHARLOTTE-MECKLENBURG HISTORIC LANDMARKS COMMISSION.

Below: St. Peter's Episcopal Church.
COURTESY BRUCE R. SCHULMAN.

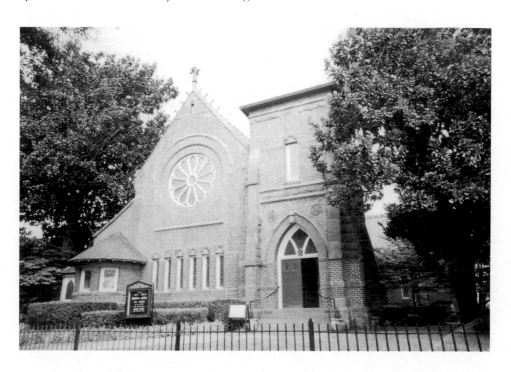

New South years. Most notable in this regard was Jane Renwick Smedburg Wilkes, daughter of a Swedish industrialist, native of New York City, and wife of John Wilkes, owner of the Mecklenburg Iron Works. Wilkes became the leader of the St. Peter's Church Aid Society on January 25, 1875, and headed the campaign to raise money to create Charlotte's first civilian hospital, the Charlotte Home and Hospital,

which opened on January 20, 1876. It served white people only. On May 30, 1878, the hospital, appropriately named St. Peter's Hospital, moved into its permanent home at North Poplar Street and West Sixth Street. Enlarged over the years, the building still stands and has been converted into condominiums.

Jane Wilkes was also determined to provide professional medical care for the African American citizens of Charlotte and Mecklenburg County. In 1882, at the instigation of Reverend Joseph Blount Cheshire, then rector of St. Peter's Episcopal Church and subsequently Bishop of the North Carolina Diocese, a mission chapel, St. Michael and All Angels Episcopal Church, was started to serve the black population of the city, and for that purpose a lot was purchased by the Diocese at the northeast corner of Mint and Hill Streets in Third Ward. Jane Wilkes lost no time in beginning to raise money for a companion hospital to be located nearby. On December 18, 1888, the cornerstone was laid for the Good Samaritan Hospital.

Jane Wilkes was an atypical woman in Charlotte in the late 1800s. Throughout the New South era, social mores and customs dictated that wealthier and more educated females restrict their activities to the home. To participate in public affairs was viewed as unfeminine. In April 1899 this pattern began to change when six prominent white women met and formed the Charlotte Mothers' Club. It changed its name in 1901 to the Charlotte Woman's Club and invited twenty-five additional women to join. While retaining the refinement and grace associated with womanhood, the members of the club committed themselves to public advocacy. Mrs. F. C. Abbot, the initial President of the Charlotte Woman's Club, forcefully expressed these sentiments. "You should broaden your club," she wrote, "to include civic activities for the sake of your children. There are health laws, school matters and social influences which you should investigate and discuss."

Many homes survive from the New South era in Charlotte-Mecklenburg. Two elegant Queen Anne style Victorian houses come immediately to mind. The Liddell-McNinch House at 511 North Church Street was con-

struck in 1892 by Vinton Liddell, whose father, W. J. F. Liddell, had moved to Charlotte in 1875. The second is the R. M. Miller, Jr. House, locally known as "Victoria." Cotton and grain merchant R. M. Miller, Jr., one of Tompkins's partners at the Atherton Mills, had the house constructed in 1891. Originally located at North Tryon and Seventh Streets, the R. M. Miller, Jr. House was sold in the early twentieth century and moved to 1600 The Plaza in Chatham Estates where it has been lovingly restored.

The Newcomb-Berryhill House at 324 West Ninth Street was built in 1884 by John H. Newcomb, who had journeyed from White Plains, New York to Charlotte in 1879 with his brother George to establish a bellows factory. Their wives, Annie Augusta, nicknamed "Gussie," and Susie A. Newcomb, ran a fancy hat shop on West Trade Street. Just a block east of the Newcomb-Berryhill House stands the John W. Sheppard House, at 601 North Poplar Street. This was the home of druggist John W. Sheppard, another Yankee who came to Charlotte in the late 1800's to seek his fortune. He and his partner, J. P. Woodall, opened Woodall and Sheppard Drug Store on the Square.

Dilworth has several graceful homes that date from the New South era. Many were designed in the Colonial Revival style by architect Charles Christian Hook (1870-1932), a native of Wheeling, West Virginia, and graduate of Washington College in St. Louis, Missouri. Hook had come to Charlotte in 1891 to teach mechanical drawing in the Charlotte Graded School, which was situated

in the building at the northern edge of Dilworth that had formerly housed D. H. Hill's North Carolina Military Institute. By 1892 Hook had entered private practice as an architect. Most of his early commissions were for houses in Dilworth.

On September 19, 1894 the *Charlotte Observer* reported that Hook had developed a specialty in the Colonial Revival style. The Gautier-Gilchrist House at 320 East Park Avenue (1897) is the oldest extant Colonial Revival style house that one can definitively attribute to C. C. Hook. Mrs. A. R. Gautier, the initial owner, was a wealthy widow in her 40s who moved from New York City to Charlotte in September 1895 to be close to her son. She held exquisite teas in her home and superin-

✧

Above: The John W. Sheppard House in Fourth Ward.

COURTESY BRUCE R. SCHULMAN.

Below: The Liddell-McNinch House.

COURTESY BRUCE R. SCHULMAN.

SCENES FROM TOMPKINS' TOWER.

*Above: Views of downtown Charlotte, 1904.
Top view features the spire of the 1891 City
Hall. Bottom view shows Fourth Ward at the
left. The views are from the Tompkins Tower.*
COURTESY OF CAROLINA ROOM, PUBLIC LIBRARY
OF CHARLOTTE AND MECKLENBURG COUNTY.

*Below: The D.A. Tompkins Machine Shop
in Dilworth.*
COURTESY BRUCE R. SCHULMAN.

tended a luncheon every Thursday. She was also active in the world of business.

Dilworth had a large factory district. In addition to Tompkins's Atherton Mills, it contained the Charlotte Trouser Company, which produced between 150,000 and 175,000 pairs of men trousers per year. In 1895, six factories were built in Dilworth: James Leslie and Company of Montreal, Canada, makers of card clothing, loom reeds, leather belting, and other textile supplies;

a sash cord factory owned by O. A. Robbins of Sumter, South Carolina; Gautier's Mecklenburg Flour Mill, which produced three brands of flour – Princess Charlotte, Royal Family, and Dilworth; a spoke and handle plant; a shirt factory; and the Park Manufacturing Company, producer of pumps, heaters, and elevators. By October 1895 Tompkins's *Charlotte Observer* was calling Dilworth the "Manchester of Charlotte."

Sometime shortly after 1900, Isaac Erwin Avery, city editor of the *Charlotte Observer*, went to the top of what was then the tallest building in town. It was the Tompkins Tower, a brick edifice that was the equivalent of a fourteen-story skyscraper. It soared above the main plant of the D. A. Tompkins Company on South Church Street. Avery described the New South city that lay before him. "Out over the town on all sides the range of vision extends for distances, varying according to the topography, from twelve to thirty miles," he began. Avery heard the "clatter of horses' hoofs and the exhaust of steam engines." He listened to the "rattle of a loaded truck passing in the street below." "The charm of the view," he continued, "is the picture of moving life, the living current of people and vehicles, the smoke from the factories and the exhaust of the railroad engines on the four sides of the town." Avery became almost rhapsodic in his description of the industrial and commercial vitality of Charlotte. "A beautiful picture of a busy and thrifty city is framed in the white and black of the steam and smoke of industry," he proclaimed.

Merchant David Ovens remembered a Charlotte that was less glamorous. Shortly after arriving here in 1903, Ovens was shocked to learn that a storekeeper had been shot and killed right on Tryon Street by a "one-armed man named Biggers." Ovens soon came to realize that the New South did not provide a "better life" for everybody. "Important people," he said, had grand homes on Tryon Street and Trade Street and rode around in fine surries, while the "poorer white class" lived in dwellings "beyond the homes of the aristocracy....Still further back were the homes (if they could be called such) of the colored folks." "I imagine," Ovens admitted, "that, if one wanted to stand in well with the elder statesmen of Charlotte, the least said of these the better; still, you couldn't beat an investment at twenty per cent."

The culminating symbol of New South Charlotte was the twelve-story Realty Building (1909), later Independence Building, the first steel-framed skyscraper in the two Carolinas. The construction contract was awarded in 1908 to the J. A. Jones Construction Company, and the architect was Frank Milburn. James Addison Jones, a native of Randolph County, had come to Charlotte in the 1880s to work as a common laborer for a Mr. Cecil, a contractor from Lexington who built several of Charlotte's textile mills, including the Victor, the Alpha, and the Ada. Jones established his own firm in the early 1890s.

On June 8, 1908, the *Charlotte Observer* reported that "pedestrians on the street are beginning to develop into a set of 'rubber necks' in their attempt to see, every morning, whether or not it (the skyscraper) has climbed during the night and, every night, how high it has leaped since morning." Two reporters visited the top of the still-unfinished skyscraper on the northwestern corner of the Square in October 1908. "Appreciation of what the city is," they asserted, "comes only to those who view it from this aerial spot." Only from the top of "the most magnificent building of the Carolinas" could one appreciate that "Charlotte assumes the nature of a mining-town in western Pennsylvania, everlastingly enwrapped in clouds of smoke."

So proud were the local residents of the emerging skyscraper that they persuaded J. A. Jones to "shove the towering structure 30 feet further up" by putting the first column of the final portion of the steel frame into place, thereby letting the delegates who were arriving for the Democratic Party State Convention in June 1908 see the extra height of the building. Tenants began to occupy the upper floors of the building in late 1908. It was not until May 18, 1909, however, that the banking facility opened on the first floor, just two days before President William Howard Taft was scheduled to visit the city.

✧

The Realty (later, Independence) Building. The first steel-framed skyscraper in the Carolinas stood on The Square until its 1981 demolition.
COURTESY OF CHARLOTTE-MECKLENBURG HISTORIC LANDMARKS COMMISSION.

JIM CROW AND THE DEFEAT
OF POPULISM

The 1890s and the first decade of the twentieth century were tragic years for African Americans and for working class whites in Charlotte and Mecklenburg County and throughout the entire South. Events occurred during those years that intensified racial and class antipathies that persist until the present day.

"If the psychologists are correct in their hypothesis that aggression is always the result of frustration, then the South toward the end of the 'nineties was the perfect cultural seedbed for aggression against the minority race," asserts historian C. Vann Woodward. Woodward contends that prejudice, hatred, and fanaticism have always existed in America, as they have in practically any human society. What allowed feelings of "extreme racism" to become dominant in the South at the end of the nineteenth century, he argues, "was not so much cleverness or ingenuity as it was a general weakening and discrediting of the numerous forces that had hitherto kept them in check."

According to Woodward, Northern liberals became more interested in the late 1800s in fostering sectional reconciliation than in continuing to champion the civil rights of African Americans. "Just as the Negro gained his emancipation and new rights through a falling out between white men, he now stood to lose his rights through the reconciliation of white men," explains Woodward. Wealthy Southerners abandoned their accommodating stance on race when they came to believe that fanning the flames of racial bigotry would be useful once more in holding onto white support for a continuation of the elite's political dominance of the South and for the New South agenda of unending economic growth.

Many educated African Americans were still hopeful about the future in the 1870s and 1880s. Fraud was rampant in elections, and registrars were often capricious in performing their official duties. But affluent whites did not hold a monopoly on political power in North Carolina in those years. "It is perfectly true that Negroes were often coerced, defrauded, or intimidated," writes Woodward, "but they continued to vote in large numbers in most parts of the South for more than two decades after Reconstruction." Tar Heel voters, for example, elected 52 African Americans to the North Carolina House of Representatives between 1876 and 1894.

It is true that Charlotte, like most Southern cities, was largely segregated along racial lines except for housing, but blacks and whites commingled during the routine acts of daily living in much the same way as people did in the North. Nobody can deny that there were blatant examples of discrimination, such as at the Charlotte Opera House, where African Americans had to sit in the balcony. But whites routinely attended concerts in black churches and listened to guest lecturers at Biddle Institute. Black camp meetings in Dilworth's Latta Park attracted "the best white and colored people."

William C. Smith, editor of Charlotte's first African American newspaper, the *Charlotte Messenger*, shared the belief of many citizens that blacks could gain acceptance by the majority community if they demonstrated their commitment to such values as good manners, self-discipline, hard work, and financial responsibility. African Americans, he declared, must "stop smoking cigars, drinking whiskey, pleasure riding" and joining in other ungentlemanly activities.

In her engrossing book *Bittersweet Legacy*, Janette Greenwood describes how affluent whites and upper class blacks in Charlotte did cooperate in the 1880s in a concerted effort to close saloons and other venues for obtaining alcoholic beverages. Prohibition was particularly well suited as a political issue that could bridge the racial divide in New South

W. C. SMITH

✧

Above: William C. Smith, founder and publisher of Charlotte and North Carolina's first black newspaper. Smith also worked with whites in favor of Prohibition.
COURTESY OF CHARLOTTE-MECKLENBURG HISTORIC LANDMARKS COMMISSION.

Below: Biddle University theological graduates and students, 1892.
COURTESY OF CAROLINA ROOM, PUBLIC LIBRARY OF CHARLOTTE AND MECKLENBURG COUNTY.

Charlotte. Wealthy whites, who were becoming increasingly disgusted with the reckless and flagrant disregard for common decency exhibited by many drunks, were willing to form alliances with supporters wherever they could find them, even if they were black. African Americans, especially those who had been educated in freedmen's schools or taught by Northern missionaries, were likewise eager to join hands with the majority community.

In 1881 white prohibitionists in Charlotte established the Prohibition Association to lobby the State legislature to pass a law outlawing whiskey anywhere and everywhere. Women, including Jane Renwick Smedburg Wilkes, were the backbone of the organization. During anti-whiskey municipal election campaigns in April, and again in State-wide elections held later that year and in 1886 and 1888, the Prohibition Association invited blacks to share the rostrum and platform with whites at public rallies. Not to be outdone, the pro-liquor crowd was also biracial.

Although the "wets" eventually succeeded in keeping the saloons open, prohibitionists like W. C. Smith and white lawyer E. K. P. Osborne had demonstrated that both sides of the color line could cooperate politically in Charlotte during the 1880s. "Exploitation there was in that period," says Woodward. "Subordination

there was also, unmistakable subordination; but it was not yet an accepted corollary that the subordinates had to be totally segregated and needlessly humiliated by a thousand daily reminders of their subordination."

It was in the 1890s that extreme racism gained the upper hand in Charlotte and throughout the South. New South boosters like D. A. Tompkins and Edward Dilworth Latta became deeply concerned about the course of political events and feared that their influence over governmental affairs in Mecklenburg County and North Carolina might diminish or even end. They and their compatriots decided to marshal their considerable resources and destroy this threat to their privileged positions.

There were three groups involved in attacking the political status quo in the 1890s — impoverished farmers, disgruntled mill workers, and unhappy blacks. They formed a political alliance that sought to topple the political dominance of the Democrat Party and its affluent leaders. The issues were essentially power and money. "Small farmers felt themselves losing power to the upstart railroad towns," says historian Thomas Hanchett. Factory workers, mostly tenant farmers who had been forced off the land, grieved over their loss of status and the diminution of their sense of personal independence. Blacks, explains Hanchett, "looked for a way to finally attain the respect and influence due them as free citizens."

The impetus for a political unrest arose in the countryside. Times were hard for farmers. Cotton prices plummeted in the 1870s and 1880s, putting many Mecklenburg County farmers in dire economic straits. By 1880, 43 percent of the agriculturists in Mecklenburg County were tenant farmers. Country people were angry and felt impotent. They blamed townspeople, especially bankers, storekeepers, and industrialists like D. A. Tompkins and Edward Dilworth Latta, for their plight. "When we farmers are in the fields working hard in the summer, with the drops of sweat falling from our brow," complained one rural resident, "the merchants are sitting around the store doors with their linen shirts and black neckties on, waiting for us to bring in our first bale of cotton."

Mecklenburg farmers established a local branch of the Farmers' Alliance in 1888. The Alliance sponsored picnics where rural families gathered to eat such "rural delicacies" as collard greens, cornbread, black-eyed peas, and pork chops while listening to speakers who would rail against the "enemies of the countryside." In 1892 disgruntled farmers gave up on their efforts to gain control of the Democrat Party and decided to establish a separate People's or Populist Party.

Country folks were further embittered by the Panic of 1893, the most severe economic downturn the country had experienced up until that time. Determined to sweep the Democrats aside and take command in North Carolina and other agricultural states, the Populists set out to unite rank-and-file whites, including those who worked in the factories and the mills of the cities, with the Republican Party, which was overwhelmingly black, to achieve a majority coalition in upcoming elections.

The prospects that the Populists could win broad support among industrial workers looked promising, because they too were dissatisfied with their station in life. Textile mills were dangerous places. Accidents at D. A. Tompkins's Atherton Mills were frequent, such as the mangling of a worker's hands in June 1893, or the death of an overseer who became entangled in a belting apparatus in October 1902. Having come to town in hopes of finding steady work, the mill hands soon learned that they could be let go at the whim of the owners. "Last week night work shut down at the mill on account of a dullness in the market," reported the *Charlotte Observer* in March 1896. "It throws about 15 families out of work."

The Knights of Labor did organize a local union in 1886, but it was largely ineffectual in its efforts to protect blue-collar workers from the actions of their employers. According to histori-

CHAPTER VIII

an Thomas Hanchett, skilled millhands in Charlotte earned between $1.00 and $1.40 per day in 1890, while unskilled men made between 65 cents and 75 cents. Women and children made even less—40 cents to 65 cents per day.

By the early 1890s blacks were becoming increasingly frustrated by the lack of on-going progress in race relations. J. C. Price, president of Livingstone College in Salisbury, spoke to a biracial audience at the Charlotte City Hall in April 1893. He described "the Southern race problem from the Negro's point of view." African Americans, said Price, were "denied equal accommodation for the money on the railroad trains; he cannot get justice in the courts; he is lynched on slight provocation; he is denied equal participation with the white man in the affairs of government."

"The pent-up frustrations of farmers, blacks, and ordinary North Carolinans whose interests had been ignored by the Democrat party exploded in the 1894 state elections," writes historian Paul Escott. The so-called "Fusionists" elected 74 members to the North Carolina legislature and sent two of their backers to the United States Senate. The insurgents controlled 62 percent of the seats in the General Assembly in 1894 and 78 percent in 1896.

It did not take long for the defenders of the status quo to realize that the Populists and their Republican allies represented a grave

threat to the economic and political hegemony traditionally held by the New South elite. The Fusionists passed legislation that put elected county commissions back in charge of local government. They capped the interest rate banks and merchants could charge at 6 percent. They increased funding for public schools in hopes that education would improve the economic standing of the masses. They made it easier for rank-and-file citizens to vote by reducing the discretionary power of local registrars to exclude them from the polls. They distributed ballots that even the illiterate could understand. The Fusionists elected Daniel L. Russell as governor in 1896 and backed his attacks against corporate privilege. The first Republican governor since Reconstruction, Russell lashed out at the "railroad kings, bank barons, and money princes" and called for much higher taxes on business.

The New South upper class decided it had to fight back and regain control of the State legislature in 1898. What they needed to succeed was a way to convince rank-and-file whites, mainly tenant farmers and mill workers, to quit cooperating with the Republicans, the majority of whom were black. The answer was for wealthy whites to "play the race card" just as they had in the late 1860s and early 1870s.

Most of the local leaders of the campaign to intimidate and disenfranchise African Americans were members of the Young Democrats Club. Composed mainly of middle class professionals in their thirties or early forties, such as attorneys Heriot Clarkson and Charles W. Tillett, the "Young Democrats" organized torchlight parades and held mass rallies to demonstrate their "bare-knuckle style" of determination to subdue the Populists and terrorize black voters. As many as 1500 "Young Democrats," bedecked in flamboyant red shirts, rode periodically down Tryon Street at night on horseback, brandishing their weapons, thrusting their chests defiantly toward onlookers, and proclaiming the superiority of the white race.

The *Charlotte Observer* enthusiastically endorsed the campaign to wrest the vote away from blacks and accordingly called upon the people of Charlotte-Mecklenburg to cast their ballots for the Democrats. The ballot, wrote a

✧

Myers Street School, c. 1915. This was the first public graded school for blacks. Founded in 1882, this structure, the only school for blacks in Charlotte until 1907, was built in 1886.

COURTESY OF CHARLOTTE-MECKLENBURG HISTORIC LANDMARKS COMMISSION.

reporter in January 1898, "becomes in the hands of the ignorant and the vicious classes a most destructive and dangerous element." The *Charlotte Observer* claimed that the Populists and their Republican allies had established a regime in Raleigh "as corrupt as the crypt of Hades" and predicted that on Election Day, November 8, 1898, the people would "bury its corrupters beneath an avalanche of ballots."

The Democrats understood that the support of factory workers would be crucial in the upcoming election. Consequently, they established the Workingmen's Democratic Club and dispatched speakers to preach the mantra of white racial unity. John D. Bellamy, a Democrat candidate for Congress, spoke to the laborers at Highland Park Manufacturing Plant No. 1 on September 27th. He told the mill hands that the election would determine whether the affairs of North Carolina would "be controlled by the vicious, or whether they shall be put in the hands of the intelligent people of the State—the white people."

The Populists and the Republicans attempted to stem the tidal wave of white racial antipathy that was running against African Americans. On March 31, 1898, a lecturer at Biddle Institute told his audience that politicians "should guard and protect" the interests of black citizens. Oliver H. Dockery, a Republican candidate for Congress, speaking at a political meeting at the old courthouse on West Trade Street, was even more direct in his denunciation of what he believed the Democrats were attempting to accomplish. According to a newspaper reporter who covered the event, Dockery insisted that his opponents "tried to narrow the issues down to one—the miserable cry of n.....! n.....!"

The Democrats assured all who would listen that they really had African Americans' best interests at heart. Indeed, to their way of thinking, all citizens, including blacks, would benefit from orderly government. What historian Paul Escott derisively calls the privileged "better half" claimed that it alone was fit to rule. "Be it our work, the work of all of us, to hasten the day when the dream of Southern supremacy through Southern prosperity shall be realized in all its fullness," declared the *Charlotte Observer* on March 6, 1898.

The *Charlotte Observer* appealed directly to the racial prejudices of white voters as Election Day neared. On October 22, 1898, the newspaper claimed that "the eyes of the nation" were upon North Carolina. " . . . unless the State rights itself at the coming election we are likely to fall under that contempt which is always visited upon cravens," the editors proclaimed. Calling Governor Russell "vicious and vindictive beyond any man in the State," the newspaper insisted that the governor had "appointed rascals to office, knowing them to be rascals." "No one has written or told what momentous consequences are involved in the result of the balloting of Tuesday," the editor wrote, "because no one can."

The Democrat Party emerged victorious from the balloting on November 8th. Predictably, the *Charlotte Observer* was overjoyed by the outcome. "The white people got together and won the election," the newspaper declared. The shift in votes by precinct was actually relatively small, but Democrat totals did rise in every box in Charlotte Township, including the two mill boxes and the three rural boxes. Just enough whites had abandoned the Populists and the Republicans to produce a Democrat victory. Statewide, the balloting put 134 Democrats in the General Assembly and only 36 Fusionists. "Being in power again," said the *Charlotte Observer* about the Democrats, "the real people of North

❖

Dr. J.T. Williams was the U.S Ambassador to Sierra Leone from 1898-1907. One of the leaders of the black community, Williams owned a house on Brevard Street, a farm south of town, and invested in businesses despite a hostile political climate.

COURTESY OF CAROLINA ROOM, PUBLIC LIBRARY OF CHARLOTTE AND MECKLENBURG COUNTY.

Carolina will proceed to enact laws which will be for the well being of all of our people, and we know that hereafter there will be peace and good government in our borders."

The consequences of putting Democrats in control of both houses of the General Assembly were not long in coming. The majority party moved quickly to change the election laws so that most African Americans would not be able to continue to cast ballots. On February 18, 1899, the General Assembly proposed a constitutional amendment that would establish literacy requirements for voting except for those whites whose grandfathers had been able to vote. If approved by a referendum of the people, these new requirements for exercising the franchise would render the Republican Party politically impotent. Charles B. Aycock, who would become the Democrat candidate for governor in 1900, knew exactly what was going on. The amendment, he maintained, would be "the final settlement of the Negro problem as related to the politics of the state."

The Democratic Party mounted another aggressive White Supremacy campaign during the months preceding August 2, 1900, the day set aside for the referendum on the disenfranchisement amendment. Red Shirts rode the streets again, and huge rallies were held to embolden whites and to intimidate blacks. Thousands of Democrats gathered on July 31st to witness a parade that wound through the streets of Charlotte and eventually ended at Latta Park, where "leaders of the community" addressed the crowd. Charlotte lawyer Hamilton C. Jones was the first speaker. "Another and the last great crisis to the State is reached," he proclaimed. "North Carolina proposes to lift up the cloud that has rested upon her for 30 years, and it is determined that North Carolinians shall take their rightful place in the world — freemen among freemen, Anglo-Saxon among Anglo-Saxon." The constitutional amendment was approved by a margin of 59 percent to 41 percent Statewide.

The future electoral impact of the disenfranchisement amendment of August 1900 was profound. "North Carolina had returned to an undemocratic political system that guaranteed the powerful in society effective means of protecting their power," writes Paul Escott. "The state's elite minority was secure against democratic challenges once more." The Republican Party was divested of its largest group of supporters, and the Populists faded into obscurity. Rich white men and their "allies" were in charge. An early consequence of this circumstance, especially since racial prejudice against blacks had been a fundamental component of elite's campaign to regain power, was the enactment by the Democrats of so-called "Jim Crow Laws."

"Jim Crow" was a derogatory nickname for African Americans. Mostly enacted by city ordinances and other local regulations, Jim Crow laws appeared across the South in the early 1900s as a principal means to guarantee racial separation. Charlotte was no exception. Imagine how the black citizens felt when the all-white Board of Aldermen passed an ordinance in 1907 instituting racial segregation on Charlotte's streetcars. Fancy how they reacted emotionally to the announcement that the owners of Lakewood Park, a popular amusement complex, would not extend the fall season for a week in 1910, so the black residents of Charlotte could visit the facility, because the "fear existed that such a course might injure the resort in some manner, or might lesson the prestige."

Clearly, the behavior of elite whites toward the black citizens of Charlotte at the turn of the last century was in direct opposition to today's sense of equity and fairness. Nothing can mitigate the essential wrongness of White

VIEW OF
LAKEWOOD PARK,
CHARLOTTE, N. C.

Supremacy. However, just as in the case of apologists for slavery, the defenders of "Jim Crow" laws believed that disenfranchisement and racial segregation would work ultimately for the benefit of society as a whole. Fundamental to the thinking of New South leaders like D. A. Tompkins and Heriot Clarkson was the belief that blacks should focus their attention upon educational and economic advancement, not the attainment of political prerogatives.

The message of the White Supremacists was unmistakable. They contended that what they called Anglo Saxon values must reign supreme because in their minds such beliefs alone would assure the advancement of all Southerners. Tompkins maintained that any man, black or white, could succeed in achieving the American Dream if he worked hard enough. By practicing self-discipline and becoming educated, African Americans might one day demonstrate their worthiness to participate on an equal footing with whites in the political realm; but for now they must be subservient to whites in governmental affairs.

Factory workers also suffered discrimination at the hands of the New South leaders in the opening decades of the twentieth century. Unlike most of Charlotte's earlier manufacturing establishments, which had had relatively few workers, factories like Latta's Charlotte Trouser Company (1883) and the Alpha, Ada, and Victor Cotton Mills (1889) attracted hundreds of laborers to town. Most were newcomers who had little, if any, loyalties to local elites. It became increasingly difficult within this cultural milieu to maintain the feelings of cordiality that had characterized social relationships between classes in pre-industrial Charlotte. For the first time residential enclaves filled exclusively with cottages for mill workers began to appear on the outskirts of Charlotte. To quote Hanchett, "The close-knit relationships of the small workplace were giving way to less personal interactions between the factory owner and his numerous and interchangeable employees."

The disenfranchisement amendment approved in 1900 stipulated that the infamous "Grandfather Clause" would last for only seven years and that thereafter illiterate whites would also be prevented from voting unless they had already registered. This provision resulted from the elite's skepticism concerning the likelihood that industrial workers would remain loyal to the Democrat Party. Strikes, such as that by streetcar conductors and motormen in 1903, reinforced these feelings of distrust. In 1905, typographical workers struck the local newspapers, machinists walked off their jobs at D. A. Tompkins Company, and messengers vacated Western Union. It was not uncommon for prosperous Charlotteans to refer to mill hands and their families as "white trash" or the "ignorant factory set," says Hanchett.

THE SORTED OUT CITY

A view of downtown Charlotte in 1904,

looking down East Trade Street.

COURTESY OF CAROLINA ROOM, PUBLIC LIBRARY
OF CHARLOTTE AND MECKLENBURG COUNTY.

There is a certain monotony to the history of Charlotte and Mecklenburg County in the first half of the twentieth century. There were consequential developments, not the least being an increase in Charlotte's population from 55,268 in 1900 to 197,052 in 1950. The essential dullness of Charlotte-Mecklenburg's history during these years arises from the fact that wealthy white businessmen were in virtual control of all public affairs. "Most major urban decisions in the early twentieth century," writes historian Blaine A. Brownell in his study of New South cities, "and the conceptual context within which these decisions were made, can be traced directly to the socio-economic elite group." Men like David Ovens, James B. Duke, Cameron Morrison, and Ben Douglas succeeded in suppressing all alternatives to their program of continuous economic growth. "Watch Charlotte Grow" became the catch phrase of the chieftains of local industry and commerce.

Seeing themselves as defenders of order against unruly blacks and unreliable mill workers, the "commercial civic-elite," says historian Thomas Hanchett, used their political preeminence to reshape the physical form of Charlotte into a network of homogenous districts, including immaculate neighborhoods like Myers Park, Eastover, and the curvilinear section of Dilworth. In 1875, Charlotte, like most Southern urban centers, "looked like a scattering of salt and pepper." Rich and poor, black and white, storeowner and day laborer frequently lived side by side in the same block. Homes, craft shops, stores, and livery stables were all mixed in together. The idea that Charlotte would have one district exclusively devoted to business, another to manufacturing, another for laborers, and another for blacks would have been unthinkable in 1875.

"By the end of the 1920s," Hanchett contends, "Charlotteans had undergone a conceptual shift in their definition of a desirable urban landscape." Hanchett singles out Piedmont Park, which opened soon after 1900, as the suburb that led the way in showing how to keep "undesirable" elements away. Situated on both sides of Central Avenue between Kings Drive and Louise Avenue, Piedmont Park was the brainchild of two of Charlotte's most influential developers , F. C. Abbott and George Stephens.

Deed covenants were the most innovative tools that Abbott and Stephens introduced to exclude people of the "wrong" race or poor whites from Piedmont Park. "The covenants provided a bulwark against a society that seemed to be growing more and more topsy-turvy," Hanchett contends. "In such a district the 'best population' would suffer no intrusions from people who did not 'know their place.'" Deed covenants, explains Hanchett, "hammered home three essentials of the sorted-out city." First, Piedmont Park would be exclusively residential, meaning that workplace and domicile could no longer exist side by side. Second, deed covenants stipulated that African Americans could not own or rent homes in Piedmont Park. Finally, houses had

to cost at least $1500, a substantial sum in that day. This meant that poor whites could not afford to own homes in Piedmont Park.

The same principles of exclusion governed the character of Charlotte's other streetcar suburbs, including Elizabeth, Chatham Estates, Wilmore, Dilworth, and Myers Park, and its first automobile suburb, Eastover. Clearly, the underlying desire of the New South leaders was to seal themselves off in homogenous, secure enclaves to which they could retreat after working hard all day to advance the economy of Charlotte and its environs and thereby justify their control of local politics. Edward Dilworth Latta, for example, built an elegant Neo Colonial Revival style mansion on East Boulevard in Dilworth. Cotton broker Ralph VanLandingham and his rich wife Susie had architect C. C. Hook design an Arts and Crafts style residence for them on The Plaza in Chatham Estates.

Sometimes owners went as far as to take their houses with them. In 1916 Dr. Charles R. McManaway had his elegant Italianate style

✧

Another view of downtown Charlotte in 1904, looking up North Tryon Street.

tually acquired the family home on Selwyn Avenue, and from 1909 until his retirement in 1956 he headed a department store empire that at its height contained over 50 stores.

Merchants played a significant role in Charlotte's economic growth in the early 1900s. William Henry Belk, a South Carolinian, established a store here on September 25, 1895, in a rented building just off the Square on East Trade Street. Belk acquired his own building in 1905 and by the time of his death in 1952 headed the largest and most successful chain of department stores in the two Carolinas. "He enjoyed the very scent of quality merchandise freshly unpacked and shelved and stacked," says Belk's biographer.

The third of Charlotte's major turn-of-the-century merchants was George Ivey. Joseph Benjamin Ivey, the handsome son of a Methodist preacher, opened a small storeroom in rented space near the Square on February 18, 1900. Among Ivey's early employees was David Ovens, who joined J. B. Ivey & Company in 1904. "I would probably have been satisfied with a moderate business that would make something over a living," said Ivey, "but Mr. Ovens was ambitious to make J. B. Ivey & Company a big store and the business grew rapidly under our combined efforts."

mansion moved from West Trade Street to Queens Road in Myers Park. Ten years later Benjamin Withers, founder of a building supply business, moved his imposing home from East Trade Street to Selwyn Avenue, also in Myers Park. Joseph Efird became Withers's son-in-law when he married Elizabeth Withers in 1917. A native of Anson County, Efird even-

Above: The home of Mr. And Mrs. Ralph VanLandingham.
COURTESY OF CHARLOTTE-MECKLENBURG HISTORIC LANDMARKS COMMISSION.

Right: Early development of the Myers Park neighborhood. The curving streets of Myers Park were designed to accommodate streetcars. The poles seen in the photo would carry the electric wires that powered the streetcars.
COURTESY OF CAROLINA ROOM, PUBLIC LIBRARY OF CHARLOTTE AND MECKLENBURG COUNTY.

Ivey insisted that the curtains be drawn in his store windows on Sundays, so that the pedestrians would not be tempted to consider matters of *this* world on the Lord's day. The Ivey's Department Store at Fifth and North Tryon Streets was designed by English architect William H. Peeps and opened as the new home of J. B. Ivey & Company in 1924. The store was renovated and enlarged in 1939. On May 4, 1990, Ivey's was purchased by Dillard's, another department store chain. The building has recently been converted into luxury condominiums.

Myers Park is the most historically significant of Charlotte's streetcar suburbs.

Thomas Hanchett and Mary Norton Kratt ably tell the neighborhood's history in their

❖

Above: The McManaway House relocated to Myers Park in 1916.

COURTESY BRUCE R. SCHULMAN.

Below: The Morgan School (1925) is the work of an important regional architect, Louis Asbury. John Springs Myers and Mary Rawlinson Myers laid out the Cherry neighborhood as a "model Negro housing development" in the 1890s and early 1900s. Its purpose was to provide good, low cost housing for black laborers.

COURTESY BRUCE R. SCHULMAN.

book, *Legacy: The Myers Park Story*. The events leading up to the founding of Myers Park in 1912 bear dramatic testimony to the positive consequences of New South leadership.

The individual most responsible for the creation of Myers Park was George Stephens, the co-developer of Piedmont Park. A native of Guilford County and an 1896 graduate of the University of North Carolina, Stephens had come to Charlotte to join the insurance agency headed by Walter Brem, the father of

Stephens's roommate at Chapel Hill. In 1899, Stephens became a partner with F. C. Abbott in the real estate firm of Abbott and Stephens, the first seller of homes to use "For Sale" signs in the city. "George was ten years my junior in age," Abbott remembered, "a fine genial fellow . . . a great athlete . . . and very popular with his many friends." Abbott and Stephens also organized the Southern States Trust Company, which has evolved into the Bank of America of today.

In 1902 Stephens married Sophie Myers, daughter of John Springs Myers, whose father had donated the land for Biddle Memorial Institute. Myers had inherited a large farm on Providence Road about three miles southeast of Charlotte. He sold it to his son-in-law's new company, the Stephens Company, on July 15, 1911. This land and adjoining parcels that Stephens had purchased would become the location for Myers Park.

To design his new subdivision Stephens hired a young landscape architect named John Nolen, whom Stephens had met while serving on Charlotte's Park and Tree Commission during the planning and construction of Independence Park. John Nolen came to Charlotte in 1905 to supervise the implementation of his plan for Independence Park. During his sojourn in this community, Nolen

explained the theories and concepts which underlay modern landscape architecture. "It is a pleasure to talk with Mr. Nolen," the *Charlotte Observer* asserted. "He lives close to nature. His ideas and ideals are fresh and clean."

Stephens recognized that a high-quality planned community would lure Charlotte's affluent residents from their center city estates. Nolen later wrote that Myers Park was "designed right from the first, and influenced only by the best practice in modern town planning." In keeping with his philosophy that the fashioning of neighborhoods should be approached holistically, Nolen oversaw every detail of planning, including the layout of streets, the selection of trees and shrubs for street plantings, and even the drafting of individual landscaping schemes for the buyers of houses. "It is the painstaking work of this pioneer city planner and his successor Earle Sumner Draper that sets this area off from others where the wealthy lived in the same period, and that has made Myers Park Charlotte's most lastingly successful early suburb," writes Hanchett.

Although some streets in Myers Park were reserved for moderate price homes, most of the neighborhood had houses for the affluent. As in Piedmont Park, deeds contained covenants setting forth a wide range of regulations, including the kind of fences, the minimum allowable home prices, and the exclu-

sion of all people except members of the white race. Houses in Myers Park mirror "the changing national fashions in architecture from the 1910s to the present," explain Mary Norton Kratt and Thomas Hanchett. Most prevalent in the neighborhood are examples of Colonial Revival, Tudor Revival, Bungalow, and Rectilinear or Four Square.

According to Kratt and Hanchett, the best example of the Rectilinear or Four Square style in Myers Park is the David Ovens House built in 1916 at 825 Ardsley Road. Houses of this genre retain Victorian-like floor plans but have box-like, unadorned exteriors. The original landscaping was by Earle Sumner Draper for the John Nolen firm. The home and its surroundings are suggestive of the straightforward pragmatism that formed the core of David Ovens's being. This man, now forgotten by most Charlotteans, is one of many individuals who have demonstrated the pivotal importance of leadership in making Charlotte the city that it is today.

THE NEW SOUTH ELITE IN CONTROL

David Ovens exhibited the best qualities of Charlotte's New South upper class. As early as 1912, when he had headed a fundraising campaign to build a new YWCA, Ovens had begun to establish himself as a prominent local philanthropist. Ovens was president of the Charlotte Chamber of Commerce, which was established in 1915 as the successor to the Greater Charlotte Club. He was president of the Good Fellows Club, a charitable organization that had its origins in Second Presbyterian Church. Ovens headed Charlotte's first Community Chest Drive, forerunner of today's United Way. He was the local chairman of the American Red Cross during World War II and served on the boards of several other prestigious Charlotte-Mecklenburg institutions, including Queens College, Davidson College, and Presbyterian Hospital.

Ovens was a member of the delegation that traveled to Washington, D.C. in July 1917 to lobby for the establishment of a World War One military training camp in Charlotte. Much as Dr. Charles J. Fox, James W. Osborne, and William Johnston had done in the late 1840s, Ovens and his compatriots were seeking to stimulate the local economy through the introduction of new infrastructure. They too were successful. General Leonard Wood, commander of the Army's Department of the Southeast, visited Charlotte on July 5, 1917. Wood toured "the site offered on the southwest of the city."

The Charlotte Chamber of Commerce raised thousands of dollars of private money to purchase a sufficient amount of land to accommodate the needs of the U. S. Army. Named Camp Greene in honor of Nathanael Greene of Revolutionary War fame, the massive facility, containing approximately 2000 buildings on 2340 acres of land, opened just to the southwest of town by the end of

✧

The Duke Mansion in Myers Park. Duke's house impressed not only because of its size, but also its huge fountain, which pumped water directly from the Catawba River several miles to the west.

COURTESY BRUCE R. SCHULMAN.

❖

Right: James B. Duke.
COURTESY OF CAROLINA ROOM, PUBLIC LIBRARY OF
CHARLOTTE AND MECKLENBURG COUNTY.

*Below: The Egyptian Revival style Masonic
Temple was a distinctive Charlotte
landmark until its 1987 demolition. Built
during the long growth period before the
Great Depression, the Masonic Temple was
an anchor of the South Tryon streetscape.
Its demolition helped spur the County
Commission to establish a revolving fund to
save historic landmarks.*
COURTESY OF CHARLOTTE-MECKLENBURG HISTORIC
LANDMARKS COMMISSION.

August 1917. Some 60,000 soldiers, many from New England, would eventually train at Camp Greene — about as many people as then resided in Charlotte.

The initial headquarters for Camp Greene were located in the James C. Dowd House, which still stands on Monument Avenue off Wilkinson Boulevard. The most tragic events at Camp Greene occurred during the Winter of 1918-1919, when a worldwide Spanish Influenza epidemic swept into Charlotte. Susie Harwood VanLandingham received a personal commendation from President Woodrow Wilson for her supervision of the Red Cross Canteen at Camp Greene.

David Ovens is best remembered as a lover of the arts. He served for eighteen years, from 1934 until 1952, as president of the Community Concert Association. His job was to bring excellent professional actors and

musicians to perform in Charlotte. The problem was that the city had no building that could meet even the minimum performance requirements of artists during the 1930's and 1940's. Founded in 1932, the Charlotte Symphony Orchestra played its initial concerts at Alexander Graham Junior High School on East Morehead Street before moving to the auditorium at Piedmont High School and then to the Armory Auditorium on Cecil Street, later Kings Drive. "There was a time," remembered Ovens, "when the old Armory was becoming so shabby that people didn't want to go to artistic events there, and the attendance fell off." Ovens played the pivotal role in securing public backing for Ovens Auditorium, originally called the Civic Center, and the Charlotte Coliseum, now Independence Arena. Charlotte architect A. G. Odell, Jr. designed both buildings, which opened in 1955.

Myers Park's most powerful and influential resident was James Buchanan Duke. On March 8, 1919, Duke purchased the Colonial Revival style home that architect C. C. Hook had designed in 1915 for utilities executive Z. V. Taylor. Duke transformed the already-substantial house into a majestic mansion of 45 rooms and 12 baths between 1919 and 1922. Two considerations were uppermost in causing Duke to purchase the property. First, business

activities compelled him to spend extended periods of time in the city. Second, he wanted to expose his one and only child, Doris Duke, to the "ins and outs" of Southern life.

In 1904, James B. Duke met Dr. W. Gill Wylie, a physician in New York City, who had joined with his brother in 1899 in launching the Catawba Power Company of Fort Mill, South Carolina, the first hydroelectric production venture on the Catawba River. Duke suggested that he form a partnership with the

Wylie Brothers to provide capital for expansion. The financially beleaguered Wylie Brothers readily accepted, thereby assuring the establishment of the Southern Power Company, later Duke Power Company. Duke believed that the economy of North Carolina would achieve its potential only if sufficient power was available to sustain an expanding textile manufacturing component. The early history of the Southern Power Company proved that Duke was correct. The harnessing of the Catawba River allowed the textile industry to prosper in the Piedmont and was the single most important factor in stimulating the industrial growth of this region in the first half of the twentieth century.

The most significant event in Lynnwood's history occurred in December 1924. A series of meetings in the sunroom in the west wing of the house culminated in the establishment of the Duke Endowment, a philanthropic enterprise of enormous importance to the people of North Carolina and South Carolina. Local institutions such as Johnson C. Smith University, formerly Biddle Memorial Institute, and Davidson College received substantial bequests James Buchanan Duke died at his home in Somerville, New Jersey in 1925.

Cameron Morrison was another prominent and influential resident of Myers Park. He lived on Queens Road until he and his second wife,

Left: Governor Cameron Morrison.
COURTESY OF CAROLINA ROOM, PUBLIC LIBRARY OF CHARLOTTE AND MECKLENBURG COUNTY.

Below: Cameron Morrison owned this house on Queens Road in Myers Park. After marrying his second wife, the Morrisons moved into the stately Morrocroft Mansion.
COURTESY BRUCE R. SCHULMAN.

Charlotte, N.C. North Tryon Street.

Sara Eckerd Watts Morrison, moved to their suburban farm named Morrcroft in 1927. A native of Richmond County, Morrison was an adroit and flamboyant politician. Morrison moved his law practice to Charlotte in 1905. The *Charlotte Observer* described him as a young man of ability who possessed a clear, musical voice. On December 6, 1905, Morrison married Lottie May Tomlinson of Durham, North Carolina, who was to be the mother of an only child, Aphelia Lawrence Morrison.

In 1920, Morrison opposed O. Max Gardner, Lieutenant Governor of North Carolina, in the Democratic primary for Governor. A principal ally of Morrison's in this campaign was Senator Furnifold Simmons,

✧

Above: Looking south on Tryon Street.

Right: March 14, 1938. A ceremony at The Square as the last streetcar finished its final trip. Buses replaced streetcars and have been used ever since.
COURTESY OF CAROLINA ROOM, PUBLIC LIBRARY OF CHARLOTTE AND MECKLENBURG COUNTY.

Below: Charlotte's passenger service began in 1930. Aviation's role remained comparatively small until the 1941 development of Morris Field.
COURTESY OF CAROLINA ROOM, PUBLIC LIBRARY OF CHARLOTTE AND MECKLENBURG COUNTY.

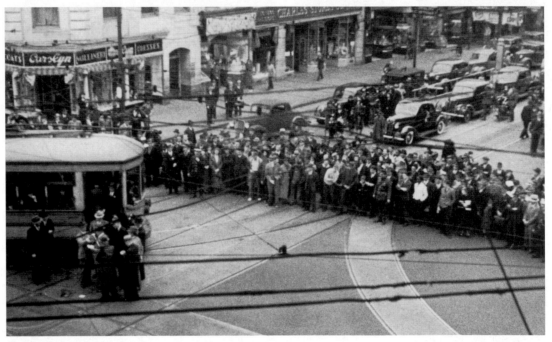

long-time leader of the Democrat Party. Morrison was victorious; and in January 1921, he became the Governor of North Carolina. He is remembered best as the "Good Roads Governor." To bring North Carolina "out of the mud," Morrison secured funds for a massive road-building program. His objective was to construct paved highways to every county seat in the state. Governor Morrison also labored to upgrade the educational system throughout North Carolina. Another of Morrison's major accomplishments was the improvement of medical facilities, especially those involved in the treatment of the mentally and emotionally infirm.

On December 13, 1930, Governor O. Max Gardner surprised many political pundits by appointing Morrison to the United States Senate to serve out the term of Senator Lee S. Overman, who had recently died. In 1932, however, Morrison was unsuccessful in his Senate campaign against Robert R. Reynolds, an Asheville attorney. Reynolds used his opponent's wealth as an effective political and oratorical weapon, accusing Governor Morrison of eating caviar and using a gold spittoon. In 1942 the voters of the Tenth Congressional District elected Morrison to the House of Representatives. He did not run for reelection. Instead, he campaigned in 1944 to return to the United States Senate. Again, he

Right: Harry Dalton, on left, at age 75.
COURTESY OF DAN AND MARY LYNN MORRILL.

Below: Downtown Charlotte, 1940. In this Chamber of Commerce map, it is noteworthy both how Charlotte promoted itself as a distribution center and the impact of rail and air connections on the city and its growth. U.S. 29/74, Wilkinson Boulevard, was Charlotte's first modern highway.
COURTESY BRUCE R. SCHULMAN.

was unsuccessful, this time losing to Clyde R. Hoey of Shelby, North Carolina. Governor Morrison did not run for public office again.

Mayor Ben Douglas had a house on Malvern Road in Myers Park. Like so many other New South leaders of Charlotte in the first half of the twentieth century, including Ovens, Duke, and Morrison, and for that matter Tompkins and Latta of an earlier generation, Douglas was not a native. Born in Iredell County, Douglas moved to Charlotte from Gastonia in the mid-1920s and established a funeral home at the corner of Fox Street and Elizabeth Avenue, now Independence Boulevard and Elizabeth Avenue.

Douglas was Mayor from 1935 until 1941. He earned the reputation of being the "Builder of Modern Day Charlotte." Douglas's greatest and most enduring contribution to the build-

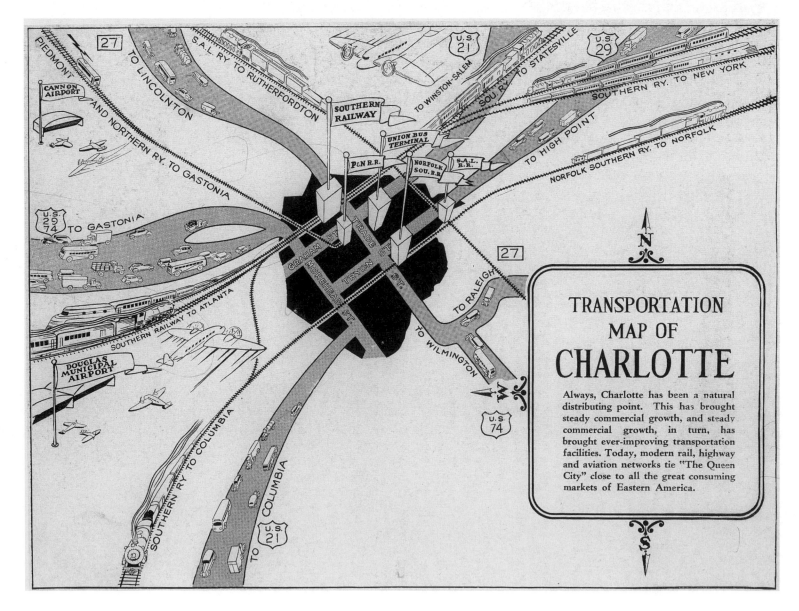

TRANSPORTATION MAP OF CHARLOTTE

Always, Charlotte has been a natural distributing point. This has brought steady commercial growth, and steady commercial growth, in turn, has brought ever-improving transportation facilities. Today, modern rail, highway and aviation networks tie "The Queen City" close to all the great consuming markets of Eastern America.

ing up of Charlotte was his commitment to the establishment of a municipal airport, which still bears his name. Passenger air service began here on December 10, 1930, but the Curtis Condor airplane had to land at a private field. At Mayor Douglas's insistence, the Charlotte City Council voted on September 3, 1935, to apply for Federal funds from the Works Progress Administration to build an airport for Charlotte. When Washington approved the request on November 13th, the City decided to use the money for land acquisition. Voter-approved bonds were sold on March 1, 1936, to pay for the improvements, including the terminal and the hangar.

Douglas was a prime mover in persuading the War Department to establish an air station at Charlotte shortly before World War Two. Dedicated on April 21, 1941, and named Morris Field in honor of William Colb Morris, a World War One aviator from Concord, North Carolina, the air station was devoted primarily to the training of pilots and the

maintenance of aircraft. Like Camp Greene during World War One, Morris Field was a boost to the local economy. "The Army Air Base at Morris Field became a $6 million government investment," boasted the *Charlotte Observer* many years later. Charlotte architect W. R. Marsh designed the buildings, and Blythe Brothers Construction Company and Goode Construction Company, both local firms, built Morris Field.

Charlotte and Mecklenburg County had two other large military installations during World War Two. The former Ford Motor Company Plant on Statesville Avenue became the home of a U. S. Army Quartermaster Depot on May 16, 1941. Lastly, a committee of Charlotte businessmen, including Mayor E. M. Currie, R. S. Dickson, W. Carey Dowd, Jr., and Edwin Jones, orchestrated a successful campaign to bring a large Naval Ammunition Depot to Mecklenburg County in 1942. Located in what is now the Arrowood Industrial Park and operated by the U. S. Rubber Company, the facility

✧

Charlotte Memorial Hospital. This facility, which replaced St. Peter's Hospital, has grown to become Carolina's Medical Center today. The original structure is shown in the background and a new addition in the foreground of this 1968 photo.

COURTESY OF CHARLOTTE-MECKLENBURG HISTORIC LANDMARKS COMMISSION.

Right: The Dowd House, initial headquarters for Camp Greene.

COURTESY BRUCE R. SCHULMAN.

Below: Colonel Macomb and staff at Camp Greene, 1919.

COURTESY OF CAROLINA ROOM, PUBLIC LIBRARY OF CHARLOTTE AND MECKLENBURG COUNTY.

covered over 2200 acres and employed about 10,000 people.

The substantial record of accomplishment by Charlotte's New South leaders is undeniable. It is difficult to imagine how Charlotte could have become the economic capital of the two Carolinas without the contributions of men like David Ovens, James Buchanan Duke, Cameron Morrison, and Ben Douglas. But just as incontestable is the fact that their power rested upon a narrow base and that Charlotte's upper class expected the rank-and-file citizens of Mecklenburg County to be deferential and obedient.

Textile executive and philanthropist Harry Dalton kept a dairy during World War Two. The 1942 volume survives, providing a fascinating glimpse into the lifestyles and attitudes of Charlotte's New South leaders of that era. Dalton had first come to Charlotte from his native Forsyth County as a young Army private at Camp Greene.

In October 1941 Dalton became the head of the rayon and nylon division of the War Production Board, which was headquartered in the nation's capital. Dalton would routinely leave Charlotte by train for Washington, D.C. on Sunday nights and return the next Friday mornings and spend the weekends with his wife and two children at the family home in Myers Park. Sometimes the trip was arduous. "The trains are crowded these days with people going to & from Washington," he wrote on January 4, 1942. "There is hardly any standing room in the club cars."

Harry Dalton belonged to the small group of white men who virtually controlled Charlotte during World War Two. Known as the "Round Table," these privileged gentlemen gathered most weekdays at noon for lunch at the restaurant in Ivey's Department Store. "I had lunch with the 'Round Table' group at Iveys," Dalton declared on January 2nd.

One of the important bonding rituals for upper-class males in Charlotte was playing golf. It still is. Dalton was an avid golfer and played most of his rounds at the exclusive Charlotte County Club, of which he was a member. "I had an 83 today," he wrote on November 14th. Another elitist ritual was traveling together to Chapel Hill or Durham to attend college football games. Dalton and about thirty of his friends boarded a bus at the Charlotte County Club on New Years Day 1942 for a trip to Duke Stadium, where the Rose Bowl was being held because of apprehension over a possible Japanese air attack against California. Duke was playing Oregon State. "We got home about midnight," said Dalton. "It was an interesting day."

The prominent white men of Charlotte would also gather at the Charlotte County Club on special occasions to celebrate and pay tribute to one another. One such event was a banquet honoring David Ovens on his seventieth birthday. "Attended dinner tonite (sic.)

to surprise David Ovens on his seventieth birthday," Dalton wrote on December 4th. George Ivey read a poem satirizing Eleanor Roosevelt. "Mr. Ovens does not like the Roosevelts," said Dalton.

Harry Dalton, like most wealthy white males of his time, was a man of substantial accomplishment. On the last pages of his 1942 dairy he meticulously listed all the business, philanthropic, and cultural organizations in which he held leadership positions. Dalton was on the Board of Directors of nine corporations. He belonged to the Board of Directors of the Charlotte Country Club, Charlotte Memorial Hospital, Charlotte Chamber of Commerce, Goodfellows Club, and the Mint Museum of Art. He was on the Board of Trustees of Queens College and a Deacon at Second Presbyterian Church.

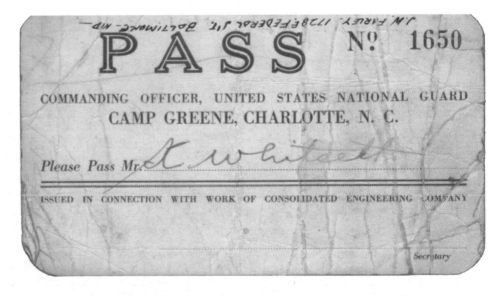

Dalton received no pay for his work for the War Production Board in Washington, D.C., which regularly took him away from his home and family.

However impressive or magnanimous his attainments might have been, Harry Dalton demonstrated little awareness of the advantages that might accrue from sharing power with rank-and-file Charlotteans, especially African Americans. Like D. A. Tompkins and Edward Dilworth Latta or James B. Duke or the great majority of Charlotte's New South upper class, Dalton believed that everyone would ultimately benefit from the leadership that only he and his "golf-playing buddies" could provide. Especially enlightening in this

✧

A pass from Camp Greene.

FROM THE DOWD HOUSE COLLECTION.

regard was Dalton's treatment of the black servants who worked in his Myers Park home. African American women prepared the meals for his family, not always successfully. "We have no cook: as Cora Young we let go," he declared on September 25th. Dalton was peeved when Cora's successor did not come to work even on Christmas Day. "Our cook...did not show up — sick I guess." In true paternalistic manner, however, Dalton went out of his way to assist a substitute cook whom he respected. He wrote on June 28th:

> The cook (Cora Young) has been on vacation. Julia McKnight, the nurse and Johnson C. Smith graduate is cooking. She teaches next year. We are trying to get her located. Mary called Dr. Harding, Superintendent of Schools. She is ever a conscientious girl. We hate to lose her but want to encourage her in bettering herself.

Julia, of course, taught in a racially segregated school.

Anyone who wonders what happened when someone defied Charlotte's New South leaders need only examine the events surrounding the bloody streetcar strike that erupted in Charlotte in August 1919. The behavior of the executives of the Southern Public Utilities Company might be compared to a fist in a velvet glove—warm and soft on the outside but tough and resolute at the core.

Trouble began shortly after midnight on Sunday, August 10, 1919. The motormen and conductors parked the streetcars in the car barn in Dilworth and voted unanimously to go on strike. Their aims were to secure a pay increase and to gain recognition of their union. The motormen and conductors were anxious to continue negotiating. "The street car operators of the town will meet the company officials in conference at any time the

Charlotte has been an auto-racing center since the beginning of the sport. In this 1919 photo, a racecar stops in front of the Charlotte Observer *office on South Church Street.*

company expresses the desire," union organizer Albert E. Jones announced.

The president of the Southern Public Utilities Company, which operated Charlotte's streetcars after 1911, was Z. V. Taylor, the same man who had just sold his Myers Park Colonial Revival style home to James B. Duke and one of the men who had persuaded the U.S Army to locate Camp Greene in Charlotte. Taylor's position remained unchanged throughout the strike. He refused to submit to the workers' demands and accused Albert Jones of being an outside agitator.

Taylor was condescending in his characterization of the strikers. "We know our 'boys' too well," he proclaimed on August 12th. "They are of our blood. They were raised by the same kind of mother as our mothers." Taylor called the labor unrest "dastardly, cunning, unfeeling" and insisted that the compa-

ny could not afford to raise the pay of the strikers. As for the union, he agreed to recognize a local union but not one affiliated with the Amalgamated Association of Street & Electrical Railway Employees.

The situation worsened when a large, boisterous crowd, composed mostly of mill workers from North Charlotte, gathered outside the electric substation on Elizabeth Avenue at Sugar Creek around midnight on August 12th. The demonstrators had come to give their support to the local electrical workers who had also gone out on strike. Two electricians had pulled the switches inside the Elizabeth Avenue substation in the afternoon and had cut off power to the entire city for a brief period. The police had arrested the pair for trespassing. Z. V. Taylor feared that the mill workers who had assembled that night on Elizabeth Avenue would try to seize the substation and cut the power again. He there-

✧

The original Charlotte Speedway located in Pineville near South Boulevard and the Southern Railway tracks.

COURTESY OF CAROLINA ROOM, PUBLIC LIBRARY OF CHARLOTTE AND MECKLENBURG COUNTY.

fore summoned the police. Chief Walter B. Orr spoke to the crowd, and the mill workers went home without further incident.

Mayor Frank R. McNinch called the unauthorized interruption of electrical power an outrage. "If any men or set of men challenge the forces of law and order, let them take notice that they do so at their personal peril," McNinch warned. Z. V. Taylor insisted that his company was "standing between the community and the forces of disorder." According to Taylor, "foreign and dastardly influences" had caused otherwise "good men" to cut off electrical service, thereby "jeopardizing the lives of the suffering in the hospitals." Taylor proclaimed that it was "high time that this people be aroused as never before in a century."

Mayor McNinch summoned representatives of the strikers and Z. V. Taylor to City Hall on North Tryon Street in an effort to settle the escalating dispute. Several sessions were held, but no agreement was reached on the issue of the recognition of the union. Meanwhile, the Southern Public Utilities Company escalated tensions by continuing to place advertisements in the newspaper soliciting applications for new streetcar workers. "Applications will be received at my office, beginning Saturday morning," said streetcar superintendent R. L. Wommack.

By August 15th the *Charlotte Observer* was growing impatient with the absence of streetcar service and blamed the strike mainly on the workers, who, the newspaper claimed, were being coached by a "strike agitator." The supposed villain was Albert Jones. In a moment of ill-advised candor, Jones responded to this criticism by saying: "I have long since learned that the capitalists who employ Mr. Taylor own the major part of Charlotte, but only recently I learned that they control the city hall, the banks, the newspaper, etc." Jones later retracted his statement and apologized.

A meeting attended by some 2000 people was held at the Mecklenburg County Courthouse on the night of August 19th to hear the workers' side of the issue. The principal speaker was Marvin Ritch, a Charlotte attorney who was active in attempting to organize local mill hands. Ritch extolled the virtues of unionism and assured the crowd that textile workers were solidly allied with the streetcar conductors and motormen. He proceeded to issue a threat to the Southern Public Utilities Company if it attempted to operate the trolleys with replacement crews. "Let them run," he declared. "The textile workers are so strongly organized that they will not ride cars by 'scabs' and other people will not take a chance."

The Charlotte Coliseum, as seen in this 1973 postcard. When built, the Coliseum was considered an engineering marvel, noted worldwide for its huge dome.

FROM THE COLLECTION OF DAVID T. RITCH.

Ovens Auditorium and the Charlotte Coliseum   Photo by Jim Dunn

Motormen and conductors began picketing in front of the car barn on South Boulevard. They were on the lookout for strikebreakers. The Federal government sent an official of the Department of Labor to town to try to mediate the dispute. On August 21st, Mayor McNinch and a citizens committee chaired by Clarence O. Kuester, nicknamed "Booster Kuester," urged President Taylor to recognize the Amalgamated Association of Street & Electrical Railway Employees and the national union of the electricians. "Mr. Taylor announced that he could not acquiesce in the agreement," reported the *Charlotte Observer*.

On Saturday, August 23rd, President Taylor, in direct defiance of the recommendations of Mayor McNinch and the citizens committee, stated that the Southern Public Utilities Company would resume streetcar service on Monday, August 25th with replacement crews. He also withdrew his earlier offer to give the former motormen and conductors priority in hiring. The *Charlotte Observer* announced that service would not begin immediately to the mill villages of North Charlotte and Chadwick-Hoskins "because of open threats that have been heard of disorders, destruction of company property and possible violence to passengers in these sections."

Mayor McNinch dispatched a body of policemen to the car barn in Dilworth on the morning of August 25th to maintain order. A large crowd of mill workers and strikers gathered along South Boulevard and hurled insults throughout the day at the replacement motormen and conductors. The frustration of the crowd grew minute by minute. The working class whites must have realized the utter hopelessness of their situation. Gunfire erupted outside the car barn about 3 a.m. on August 26th between the police and the demonstrators. About 100 shots were exchanged. "When the smoke of battle had cleared away," said the *Charlotte Observer*, "14 wounded were picked up and rushed to various hospitals, while Walter F. Pope, the first man found dead, was sent to the Hovis undertaking establishment." Four demonstrators were killed, including a machinist and a railroad engineer. One was mortally wounded in

the abdomen. Fourteen others were injured, some seriously.

The local press showed no sympathy for the strikers. "The business organizations of the city have gone on record against the sort of unionism that has been imported into the city and there is a determination that this character of agitation shall be suppressed," declared the editors of the *Charlotte Observer*. Z. V. Taylor and the Southern Public Utilities Company had won the day. The New South leaders remained firmly in control. Some of the former motormen and conductors were rehired.

✧

The Charlotte Trolley is a popular attraction in the Dilworth area today. But, in 1919, things were not so cheerful during a violent and bloody strike. This is the same streetcar that was retired from service in March 1938.
COURTESY CHARLOTTE TROLLEY, INC.

THE EMERGENCE OF DIVERSITY: WOMEN AND DISTRICT REPRESENTATION

The thirty years following the end of World War Two in Charlotte and Mecklenburg County were anything but dull. These three decades are rivaled in importance in terms of fundamental social and political modification only by the arrival of white settlers in the 1740s, the defeat of the Confederacy and the end of slavery in the 1860s, and the overpowering of Populism and the enactment of Jim Crow laws at the turn of the last century. Change occurred on many fronts, but all shared the common result of increasing participation by a broader spectrum of society in influencing and making decisions about the future of Charlotte and Mecklenburg County.

Nobody was predicting profound change when World War Two came to an end. Everybody assumed that it would be "business as usual." Indeed, during the immediate post-war years it looked as if Charlotte's white male business upper-class would continue to monopolize local power. The process by which Independence Boulevard came into being seemed to affirm this truth.

Hundreds of Chantilly, Elizabeth, and Piedmont Park residents gathered at Midwood School on Central Avenue on September 8, 1946. They had just learned that Mayor Herbert Baxter and the City Council wanted to use $200,000 of local bond money to help build a massive "cross-town boulevard." The protestors called it a "foolish scheme" that could "throttle traffic between downtown and the eastern residential districts." One irate resident suggested that the route had been chosen because it would increase the value of the property that Ben Douglas, District Highway Commissioner and former Mayor, owned at what is now the intersection of Independence Boulevard and Elizabeth Avenue.

"Somebody's toes are bound to be stepped on." That's how Councilman John P. White, the 67-year-old production manager and mechanical superintendent of the *Charlotte Observer*, responded to the protestors. A native of Alabama, White lived on Grandin Road in the Wesley Heights neigh-

PRESBYTERIAN COLLEGE, CHARLOTTE, N. C.

borhood off West Trade Street. Like the majority of Charlotte businessmen of that era, he was caught up in the euphoria and optimism that gripped the country in the years immediately after World War Two.

"You only look back for reasons to move ahead, and by golly nobody can say that we lacked ideas," Mayor Baxter told journalist Kays Gary in 1964. A handsome and personable Bostonian, Herbert Baxter had come to Charlotte during World War One to train at

Camp Greene, had settled here, had prospered in the lumber business, and had moved to a fine home on Queens Road in Myers Park.

The real brain behind the building of Independence Boulevard was James B. Marshall. He was a brilliant engineer who had served as Mayor Ben Douglas's City Manager. Born in Anderson, South Carolina in the early 1890s, Marshall graduated from the College of Charleston and settled in Charlotte in the 1920s. He left City govern-

ment in 1941 and joined J. N. Pease as an engineer and contact man with City Hall.

In 1946 the Charlotte Planning Board hired Marshall as a consultant to prepare a master plan for Charlotte's streets. Several month earlier, the North Carolina Highway Department had conducted a comprehensive survey of local traffic trends and had determined that Charlotte needed "cross-town boulevards" to relieve congestion on uptown streets. Mayor Baxter knew that Charlotte had become a major trucking and distribution center in the first half of the twentieth century and that highways were essential to the local economy. Buildings such as the Charlotte Supply Company Building and the Textile Mill Supply Company Building attested to Charlotte's service to the regional textile industry.

Word leaked out in September 1946 that the expressway would split the Chantilly, Elizabeth, and Piedmont Park neighborhoods. A throng of infuriated citizens packed the City Council meeting on September 10th, and their spokesman, attorney Frank K. Sims, Jr., accused the City of being secretive and manipulative. On October 8, 1946, the City Council gathered for an informal dinner at the Myers Park County Club, where Mayor Baxter was president. There in the midst of Myers Park, with fine china, cut crystal, and sumptuous food on the table, the representatives of the people endorsed the route through

Chantilly, Elizabeth, and Piedmont Park. That's how deals were struck in those days.

On October 21, 1946, the residents of the affected neighborhoods descended upon City Hall for a public hearing. The atmosphere was tense and electric. "Isn't it a little absurd," Frank Sims remarked, "to build a highway that winds and twists and turns across a park and baseball diamond and over a rose garden and through a thickly populated residential section just to reach Ben Douglas' property?"

Mayor Baxter and the Councilmen did modify their position in the face of this fierce public opposition, at least in terms of the preferred route. But this route was never built, because the Federal government, the principal financier of the project, rejected it outright as unsuitable for an expressway. On December 5, 1946, the Councilmen took up the issue again. For a while it looked like Charlotte would never decide the issue of where to build Independence Boulevard. The members of City Council seemed to be hopelessly divided.

City Councilman John P. White saved the day. He persuaded Ross Puette and Henry Newson to abandon Hawthorne Lane and back the original route. "By jingo, at one point there, I thought I was going to have to switch to Hawthorne Lane myself," White laughed. Such were the fickle ways of politics in those days. The battle was not over. City Council approved the contract with the Federal government on March 11, 1947.

Few Charlotteans noticed when Bonnie E. Cone, a mathematics teacher at Central High School, was named the director of the Charlotte Center of the University of North Carolina at Chapel Hill in 1947. The school was a temporary facility created to educate veterans. Cone's appointment to head the institution turned out to be a momentous event and a harbinger of significant change. A woman of indomitable will and determination, Cone began almost immediately laying plans to make the school a permanent institution of higher education. "It is doubtful that city leaders fully anticipated at the beginning the ramifications of having a major university in their midst," writes Ken Sanford in his history of Charlotte College and UNCC. "However,"

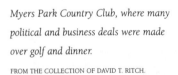

✧

Myers Park Country Club, where many political and business deals were made over golf and dinner.

FROM THE COLLECTION OF DAVID T. RITCH.

Sanford continues, "the coming of state-supported higher education to Charlotte set in motion a sequence of events that would forever change Charlotte and its greater region."

The creation of Charlotte College in 1949 as a municipally-financed institution and its eventual transformation into the University of North Carolina at Charlotte in 1965 was a seminal development in the history of this community, perhaps as notable as the arrival of Alexander Craighead in 1758, the coming of the first railroad to town in 1852, and the opening of the Charlotte Cotton Mills in 1881. So profound was the impact of Cone's attainments that one must place her accomplishments even above those of Jane Renwick Smedburg Wilkes, in this writer's opinion the second most important woman in Charlotte-Mecklenburg history.

"Charlotte College wouldn't be where it is now if it hadn't been for her," said Board chairperson J. Murrey Atkins about Bonnie Cone. Born on June 22, 1907, in Lodge, South Carolina, Cone earned an M.A. in mathematics from Duke University and moved to Charlotte in 1941 to teach the same subject at Central High School. In 1943 Cone returned to Duke to work as a statistician for a U.S. Naval Ordnance Laboratory. After a brief stint in Washington, D.C., she returned to Central High School in 1946 and resumed her career as a high school mathematics instructor. Elmer Garinger recruited Bonnie Cone also to be a part-time teacher in the newly-opened Charlotte Center of the University of North Carolina.

In August 1947 Garinger summoned Cone to his office and asked her to become the Director of the Charlotte Center. Everybody assumed that Cone had taken a dead-end job. "People told me I was out on a limb, that I couldn't last. They said I should look for another job." Cone worked up to eighteen hours a day. She taught classes. She recruited faculty. "I can't say anything but good about her," proclaimed Mary Denny, a long-time associate.

Cone decided to fight to keep the Charlotte Center open because of the educational opportunities the institution provided for students who otherwise would have had little hope of attending college. "I saw what was

happening to the young people," she explained. Governor James Holshouser summed up Cone's achievements best at the time of her retirement. "Some people devote their lives to building monuments to themselves. She has devoted hers to building educational opportunities for others."

Cone's first major victory came in 1949. She and her supporters won permission from the North Carolina General Assembly to continue the two-year college under the auspices of the Charlotte public school system of which Garinger had just become Superintendent. Named Charlotte College, the institution ran on a shoestring. It operated with part-time faculty in part-time classrooms and had to depend almost solely upon student tuitions for its financial survival.

Except for the tenacity of Bonnie Cone and others, including W. A. "Woody" Kennedy, Charlotte College would never have moved beyond being a two-year community college. "Miss Cone has provided the faith on which the college many times found its primary ability to exist," commented J. Murrey Atkins. "She has stuck with it and never even thought of giving up when sometimes the sledding seemed pretty hard." Support among the business executives of Charlotte for the school was lukewarm at best. "Charlotte has never

✧

Sallie Davidson. "Miss Sallie," descendent of General William Davidson, was legendary in Charlotte–and the richest woman in town. She would cross streets whenever she pleased, raising her arm and commanding cars to stop as she crossed. She was very frugal, having her water cutoff when she thought the bill was too high. When she died, she left her cousin a clematis vine in her will.
COURTESY OF CHARLOTTE-MECKLENBURG
HISTORIC LANDMARKS COMMISSION

been short on pride," said the *Charlotte News* on May 11, 1956, "but with the chips down, it has often exhibited distressingly little interest in higher education in the past."

Dramatic breakthroughs for Charlotte College did occur in 1957 and 1958. The school began holding its first day classes; it acquired an independent Board of Trustees; local property tax revenues in support of the school increased; and Charlotte College secured options on land for its own campus. On August 12, 1957, the Charlotte College Board of Trustees voted to buy land on Highway 49. Businessman Oliver Rowe remembered going to the site with Bonnie Cone when the only buildings on the tract were a barn and a silo left from farming days. "She reached down and grasped a handful of earth, let it sift through her fingers and said, 'This is the place. This is the place.'"

Charlotte College moved to its suburban campus in 1961. On May 8, 1962, the Board of Trustees voted to request the addition of the junior year in 1963 and the senior year in 1964. The North Carolina General Assembly did approve four-year, state-supported status for Charlotte College in 1963. Victory came on March 2, 1965, when the General Assembly approved the transformation of Charlotte College into the University of North Carolina at Charlotte, effective July 1, 1965. A spontaneous celebration erupted on campus when word reached Charlotte from Raleigh. "Miss Cone, can you hear the victory bell ringing?" exclaimed her secretary into the telephone.

Certainly, there were influential women in this community before Bonnie Cone. Not the least among them was Gladys Avery Tillett. Tillett labored tirelessly for the ratification of the 19th Amendment in 1920, even using a handkerchief embroidered "Votes for Women." She helped found the Mecklenburg League of Women Voters and was an active Democrat until her death in 1984.

It was in the 1950s, 1960s, and 1970s that substantial numbers of women began to assume positions of political influence in Charlotte and Mecklenburg County. In 1954, Martha Evans, an exuberant redhead, became the first female member of the Charlotte City Council. She twice ran for mayor, against James Smith in 1959 and against Stan Brookshire and James Smith in 1961. In 1972 Myers Park resident Elizabeth or "Liz" Hair won a seat on the Board of County Commissioners and became chairperson of that body in 1974. A founding member of the Charlotte Women's Political Caucus, Hair was determined to advance issues that were especially important to women. She was instrumental in establishing the Mecklenburg County Women's Commission, the Council

The beginnings of the University of North Carolina at Charlotte campus, 1962. At this time, it was Charlotte College— a two-year school.

SPECIAL COLLECTIONS, ATKINS LIBRARY, UNIVERSITY OF NORTH CAROLINA AT CHARLOTTE.

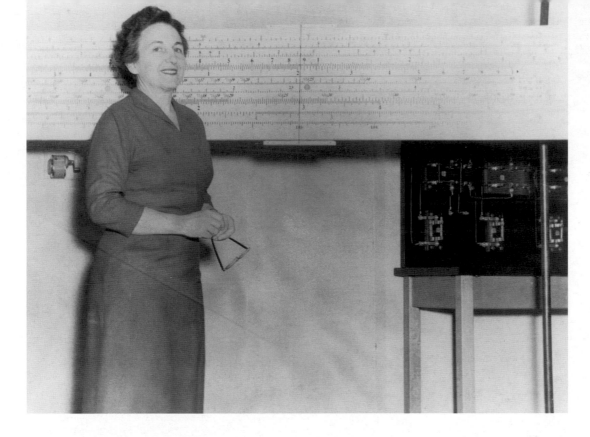

on Aging, and the adoption of the county's first affirmative action plan. She was responsible for the County's initial greenway master plan and was pivotal in saving the historic First Baptist Church in 1977 as the home of Spirit Square.

Betty Chafin, now Betty Chafin Rash, was elected to City Council in 1975 and championed the abolishment of the totally at-large system for electing members. That arrangement, enacted in 1917, had assured that white males would dominate local government. "Almost the whole council lived in one quadrant of the city," declared one of Chafin's allies.

Sam Smith, a computer software developer, called it "as pure grass-roots an effort as you'll ever see." Smith insisted that Charlotte's Westside was the "stepchild" of the city and would never receive just treatment until it was more adequately represented on City Council and on other elected and appointed committees and agencies. Smith recruited other Westsiders, including truck driver Marvin Smith, and leaders of Charlotte's emerging neighborhood movement to back his efforts.

John Belk, son of New South retailer William Henry Belk, was mayor from 1969 until 1977. He opposed district representation. On October 11, 1976, Belk vetoed a resolution calling for a referendum on the issue. According to Belk, a specific scheme had to be presented to the voters. "Being for district representation is like being for motherhood," he declared. "In my opinion, you've got to find out who your mother is before you come out for motherhood."

Much like his father, Belk believed that corporate executives and their lieutenants provided the best government. "When you've got a winning team," he maintained, "you ought to leave it alone." Mayor Belk contended that "district representation would impede growth of the city, create 'horse trading' among council members and mean that the district council members would not represent the city at large on some issues," writes Alex Coffin in his book, *Brookshire & Belk*.

Sam Smith and his allies overcame Belk's veto by gathering thousands of names on petitions to force a referendum. The voters of Charlotte narrowly approved district representation for City Council on April 19, 1977. Blacks broke their traditional alliance with southeast Charlotte and sided instead with middle class and lower middle class white precincts in west, north, and east Charlotte and with neighborhoods such as Dilworth. A reporter for the *Charlotte Observer* understood the import of what had occurred. "When neighborhood groups in north, west, and east Charlotte combined with a substantial majority of black voters to pass district representation Tuesday, they said goodbye to a long tradition in city government—the domination of City Hall by well-to-do business leaders from southeast Charlotte."

✧

SouthPark Mall, 1971. Suburbanization led to a massive growth in the physical size of the City of Charlotte. Dependence in automobiles led to large shopping centers at the city's edge. Businesses left the Center City to move closer to their customers–a trend which is continuing as Interstate 485 is built.

Aerial view of the University of North Carolina at Charlotte, 1975.

THE EMERGENCE OF DIVERSITY:

AFRICAN AMERICANS

The significance of the creation of the University of North Carolina at Charlotte, the concurrent rise of female influence on local elected governmental bodies, and the enactment of district representation notwithstanding, it was the persistent struggle of African Americans to gain the full rights of citizenship that occupied center stage in Charlotte-Mecklenburg during the years following World War Two.

In 1965 Fred D. Alexander became the first African American elected to the Charlotte City Council and the first black to hold elected public office in Mecklenburg County since the 1890s. He served for nine years. Frederick Douglas Alexander was named for Frederick Douglass, the Great Emancipator of the nineteenth century. Born in Charlotte in 1910, Alexander had a soft-spoken, diplomatic demeanor, which assisted him in winning white support for the improvement of the African American community. Alexander's father was Zachariah Alexander, who, after graduating from Biddle Memorial Institute, established Alexander Funeral Home in the Second Ward or Brooklyn neighborhood.

Even before Fred Alexander graduated from Lincoln University in Chester County, Pennsylvania in 1931, he had decided that access to the ballot box was the only way that black Charlotteans could improve their lot. "Fred came back to Charlotte with one thing in mind—political action," said noted local author and newspaperman Harry Golden.

Beginning in the 1930s, Fred Alexander started registering African Americans to vote. New Deal programs assisted him in this endeavor. Alexander was a founding member and executive secretary of the Citizens' Committee for Political Action, an organization established in 1932 to increase political participation by African Americans. In 1949 the group sponsored two candidates for public office. Bishop Dale, a lanky Texan who operated an insurance and real estate business in Second Ward, ran unsuccessfully for City Council; and James Wertz, pastor of St. Paul's Baptist Church on East Second Street, failed in his bid for a seat on the Charlotte City School Board. Their defeats

were virtually guaranteed, because an at-large voting and representation system for municipal offices had been instituted after Dale had almost won a seat on City Council in 1934.

Fred Alexander carefully built the political base from which he would launch his campaign for City Council. "There has been no Negro in public office in my lifetime," he proclaimed. "If there had been, we would have seen a different type of community human relations." Knowing that he would have to win a city-wide race, Alexander sought appointments to high profile institutions so he could

become better known in the white community. He became the first African American member of the Charlotte Chamber of Commerce in 1962 and of the Mecklenburg County Board of Public Welfare in 1963. He was picked to serve on the Mayor's Community Relations Committee and became a member of the Executive Committee of the Mecklenburg County Democrat Party in 1964.

Fred Douglas Alexander announced his candidacy for the Charlotte City Council on February 4, 1965. "Alexander stresses his desire not to be considered 'the Negro candidate,' but rather as a man who will work for the good of the entire community," proclaimed the *Charlotte Observer* on April 24, 1965. Although regarded by some blacks as overly cautious, especially by Civil Rights advocate Dr. Reginald Hawkins, Alexander received an outpouring of support from the African American precincts and was able to garner just enough white support to win the last contested seat. On May 11, 1965, Fred Alexander took the oath of office as the first black City Councilman in twentieth century Charlotte.

Alexander's most significant symbolic victory on the Charlotte City Council was the removal of a fence that separated Elmwood Cemetery and Pinewood Cemetery, the former for whites and the latter for blacks. "It's cheaper to take it down than to maintain it. Plus the insult that comes with it," said Alexander on April 30, 1968. City Council voted on January 6, 1969, to remove this galling vestige of Charlotte's Jim Crow past.

The greatest challenge to the continuation of the status quo in Charlotte and Mecklenburg County in the years following World War Two arose in the area of public education. On September 4, 1957, the local public schools became racially integrated for the first time in their history. With the backing of School Superintendent Elmer Garinger, Dorothy Counts enrolled that day at Harding High School; Gus Roberts entered Central High School; his sister, Girvaud Roberts, became a seventh grader at Piedmont Junior High School; and Delores Maxine Huntley matriculated at Alexander Graham Junior High School.

In this writer's opinion, the gradual abandonment of rigid racial segregation in the

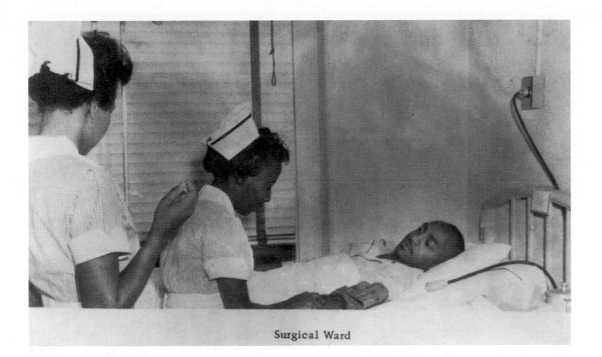

Surgical Ward

1950s and 1960s in Charlotte and Mecklenburg County occurred essentially for the same reason that it had been put into place in the 1890s. Jim Crow had now become *bad* for business. Men like D. A. Tompkins, Hamilton C. Jones, and Cameron Morrison, had looked upon Populism and black Republicanism as threats to unremitting economic development and growth at the turn of the last century. By the 1950s, however, the racial arrangements of the South were becoming increasingly anachronistic, even embarrassing, and were isolating the region from the rest of the county and the world.

Tensions were running high between the races in September 1957. Robed and hooded members of the Ku Klux Klan picketed the Visulite Theater on Elizabeth Avenue on September 1st. They were protesting the showing of the movie, "Island in the Sun," which depicted interracial romances. The Klansmen dispersed without incident when they were ordered to do so by Police Chief Frank Littlejohn.

Even more provocative were comments made by a racist rabble-rouser named John Kasper. Kasper came to Charlotte on September 1st and signed up members for what he called the White Citizens Council. He delivered a inflammatory speech to about 300 white people who had gathered on the steps of the Mecklenburg County Courthouse. He called upon the white citizens of Charlotte to rise up against the school board. "We want a heart attack, we want nervous breakdowns, we want suicides, we want flight from persecution," Kasper declared.

The culmination of the crisis occurred shortly after 9:30 a.m. on Wednesday September 4th at Harding High School. 15-year-old Dorothy Counts left her parents' home on Beatties Ford Road just across from Johnson C. Smith University, where her father taught theology. A crowd of upperclassmen, who had registered earlier that morning, congregated in front of the school to listen to John Z. Warlick and his wife, leaders of the White Citizens Council. "It's up to you to keep her out," shouted Mrs. Warlick. Dorothy Counts remained stoical throughout this anxious encounter. "I do remember something hitting me in the back," she told a newspaper reporter, "but I don't think they were throwing at me, just in front and at my feet." Dorothy Counts exhibited remarkable poise that day. When asked if any whites spat upon her, Counts answered: "Yes. Many. A good many times, mostly on the back."

Dorothy Counts soon succumbed to the harassment and scorn she experienced. She withdrew from Harding High School after four days, but the other three African Americans who had enrolled with little or no fanfare at other schools on September 4th remained for the entire year. Gus Roberts would eventually graduate from Central High School. Progress, however, was slow. "Not a lot happened in the schools for the next several years," writes historian Frye Gaillard. The number of blacks attending integrated classrooms increased but only gradually. Charlotte remained mostly a segregated city.

The greatest legacy of the stirring events that transpired at Harding High School on September 4, 1957, was the determination of Charlotte's white business leaders that such events would never happen again. The man who best exemplified the accommodating attitude of

Charlotte's white business upper-class on racial issues was Stan Brookshire, Mayor of Charlotte from 1961 until 1969. Brookshire "always considered himself the Chamber of Commerce's choice for mayor and he ran the city from that perspective," stated City Councilman John Thrower. Having served as president of the Chamber of Commerce, Brookshire sought to avoid a repeat of the embarrassing events of 1957. "Brookshire identified himself with Atlanta Mayor Ivan Allen, Jr.," explains Alex Coffin. Unlike Mayor Arthur Hanes of Birmingham, Alabama, who championed the continuation of segregation, Brookshire, like

Segregation made way for the pursuit of profit. In this 1971 photo, Kits Jones scores the first run of the game for minor league baseball's Charlotte Hornets. The town's ability to cheer on an integrated sports team mirrors its desire to look forward and focus on success.
COURTESY OF CHARLOTTE-MECKLENBURG HISTORIC LANDMARKS COMMISSION.

Central High School

Allen, favored peaceful reconciliation and looked upon moderates in the African American community as his principal allies.

Charlotte teetered on the edge of racial conflict in the early 1960s. There were sit-in demonstrations at eight local lunch counters on February 9, 1960. Store managers refused to serve the African Americans and closed down. Seven did resume operations on an integrated basis the following July. Black dentist and Presbyterian minister Reginald Hawkins was the most strident voice in the local African American community.

On May 20, 1963, Hawkins led hundreds of Johnson C. Smith students on a protest march against racial segregation in business establishments that served the general public. "We shall not be satisfied with gradualism," Hawkins proclaimed. "We want freedom and we want it now." As the students began to disperse, Hawkins issued a threat to the white leadership of Charlotte. "Any day might be D Day . . . . They can either make this an open or democratic city or there is going to be a long siege. They can choose which way it's going to be."

C. A. "Pete" McKnight, editor of the *Charlotte Observer*, telephoned Brookshire and suggested that decisive action was needed to maintain the peace. Brookshire agreed. He asked Ed Burnside, president of the Chamber of Commerce, to call a meeting of the

Chamber's executive committee. These actions culminated in the Chamber of Commerce's approving a resolution on May 23rd calling upon businesses in the community to open their doors voluntarily to African Americans. Legal racial segregation ended in Charlotte and Mecklenburg County in 1963. "I positively think that this voluntary action enabled us to avoid the violence of murder, riots, arson, and looting, which plagued many of our cities," declared Brookshire shortly before his death from lung cancer in 1990.

The struggle for full integration of the public schools was not yet over. On January 19, 1965, Julius Chambers, acting on behalf of Vera and Darius Swann, whose son had been assigned to all-black Biddleville Elementary School near Johnson C. Smith University, filed legal briefs in Federal District Court in Charlotte. Chambers argued that the pupil assignment plan of the Charlotte-Mecklenburg Schools violated the United States Constitution and that the School Board was obligated to take more resolute action to eliminate the vestiges of racial segregation in the public schools.

Many Charlotteans, including School Board Chairman William Poe, believed that this community had a sterling record with respect to race relations and that some in the African American community were pressing

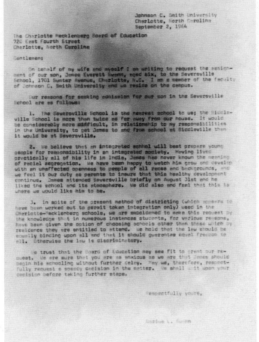

their demands for more comprehensive school integration too assertively. "I never knew of any occasion when he even wrote a letter," Poe stated many years later when discussing Chambers. "He never came in and said, 'let's talk about these things.'" Such behavior frustrated and angered Poe.

Anger of a more sinister kind erupted in Charlotte during the early morning hours of November 22, 1965. Sticks of dynamite

exploded with dramatic suddenness in the yards of the homes of Fred Alexander, Kelly Alexander, Reginald Hawkins, and Julius Chambers. It was as if a compressed coil of racial hatred suddenly sprang forward. Luckily, nobody was hurt. The perpetrators were never identified. According to Alex Coffin, Brookshire regarded these bombings as the "low point in his time in office." Mayor Brookshire himself would experience the barbs of racial retaliation. A burning cross was found in his yard on August 26, 1966.

Charlotte experienced another round of intense racial stress in the days following the tragic assassination of Dr. Martin Luther King, Jr. on April 4, 1968. Mayor Brookshire and County Commission Chairman Jim Martin declared a citywide day of mourning and scheduled a memorial service for noon on April 6th at Ovens Auditorium. George Leake, the minister of Little Rock A.M.E. Zion Church, alarmed Mayor Brookshire and other civic leaders during a meeting of the Committee on Community Relations on April 6th. Leake spoke with uncharacteristic candor to representatives of the white elite. He warned that Charlotte could experience "long hot summers" and even "chaos" unless it curbed racist behavior. Leake invited whites to come to a memorial service on April 8th where "men of color will honor one of their own."

This writer attended the Dr. Martin Luther King, Jr. Memorial Service held at St. Paul's Baptist Church on the evening of April 8, 1968. Mayor Brookshire was there. County Commission Chairman Jim Martin was there. "I didn't believe you would come," proclaimed Reverend Leake. "I am encouraged that at last you did come down and share with us." Kelly Alexander, Fred Alexander's brother, agreed. "I'm glad to see so many people here," he declared. "I'm sorry it took Martin Luther King's death to bring us together."

The service ended with black people and white people singing "We Shall Overcome," the anthem of the civil rights movement. This writer realized that he was witnessing a watershed moment in the history of Charlotte and Mecklenburg County. Dr. Raymond Wheeler of the Southern Regional Council appreciated its meaning. "I tell all of you, black and white, racial separation is not the answer."

✧

Above: The letter that started it all: Darius Swann's request to the Charlotte-Mecklenburg Schools to allow their son to attend a white school. This 1964 letter triggered the eventual Supreme Court ruling, which initiated thirty years of busing for school integration.
SPECIAL COLLECTIONS, ATKINS LIBRARY, UNIVERSITY OF NORTH CAROLINA AT CHARLOTTE.

Right: The Supreme Court ruling, which mandated school integration, has now been challenged. The schools are defending the original ruling while working to develop a less race-conscience districting plan.
SPECIAL COLLECTIONS, ATKINS LIBRARY, UNIVERSITY OF NORTH CAROLINA AT CHARLOTTE.

Banks will lead Charlotte into the new century. Financial institutions have long occupied a vital place in the history of this community. The significance of financial institutions in Charlotte's economy leaped forward in the 1980s. Thomas Storrs ordered Hugh McColl, a feisty ex-Marine and president from 1983 until 2001 of what is now the Bank of America, to take advantage of opportunities to expand the operations of local banks across state lines. In 1982 Congress approved the Garn-St. Germain Act that officially permitted out-of-state emergency takeovers and encouraged other forms of interstate banking. Because it already owned a small trust company in Orlando, North Carolina National Bank, the predecessor of Bank of America, made its first full service acquisition in Florida in 1982.

The pace of interstate banking quickened after the Supreme Court ruled on June 10, 1985, that states could band together in regional compacts to permit reciprocal interstate banking without having to open their doors to banks from all states. Within months McColl's bank purchased Pan American Banks Inc. of Miami, Florida, Bankers Trust of South Carolina, and Southern National Bankshares Inc. of Atlanta. "If you don't grow, you do the opposite. You die," said McColl in 1987. No less aggressive than McColl in expanding Charlotte's role in interstate banking was Edward Crutchfield, Jr., president of First Union Corporation. The beat goes on.

Left: The Commercial National Bank. By means of mergers and acquisitions, the bank is now the Bank of America, largest bank in the United States.
FROM THE COLLECTION OF DAVID T. RITCH.

Below, left: Corporate headquarters of the Bank of America.
COURTESY BRUCE R. SCHULMAN.

Below, right: First Union National Bank's headquarters. When built, it was the tallest building in the Carolinas.
COURTESY BRUCE R. SCHULMAN.

BIBLIOGRAPHY

BOOKS AND ARTICLES

Alexander, J. B. *The History of Mecklenburg County (NC) 1740-1900*. Bowie: Heritage Books, Inc., 1996.

Avery, Isaac Erwin, *Idle Comments*. Charlotte: Stone Publishing Company, 1912.

Barringer, Paul B. *The Natural Bent. The Memoirs of Dr. Paul B. Barringer*. Chapel Hill: The University of North Carolina Press, 1949.

Bisher, Catherine W. and Brown, Charlotte V. and Lounsbury, Carl R. and Wood, Ernest H., III. *Architects and Builders in North Carolina. A History of the Practice of Building*. Chapel Hill and London. The University of North Carolina Press, 1990.

Bisher, Catherine W. and Earley, Lawrence S., eds. *Early Twentieth-Century Suburbs in North Carolina*. Lillington: Edwards Brothers, Inc., 1985.

Blythe, LeGette and Brockman, Charles Raven. *Hornets' Nest. The Story of Charlotte and Mecklenburg County*. Charlotte: McNally of Charlotte. 1961.

_____. *William Henry Belk. Merchant Of The South*. Chapel Hill. The University of North Carolina Press, 1950.

Boyte, Jack O. *Houses of Charlotte and Mecklenburg County*. Charlotte: Delmar Printing, 1992.

Bradbury, Tom. *Dilworth: The First 100 Years*. Charlotte: Dilworth Community Association, 1992.

Bridges, Hal. *Lee's Maverick General. Daniel Harvey Hill*. New York, Toronto, London: McGraw-Hill Book Company, Inc. 1961.

Brownell, Blaine E. and Goldfield, David R. *The Growth of Urban Civilization in the South*. Port Washington: Kennikat Press, 1977.

Claiborne, Jack. *The Charlotte Observer. Its Time and Place, 1869-1986*. Chapel Hill and London, The University of North Carolina Press, 1986.

Clay, James W. and Orr, Douglas M., Jr. *Metrolina Atlas*. Chapel Hill. The University of North Carolina Press, 1972.

Coffin, Alex. *Brookshire & Belk. Businessmen In City Hall*. Charlotte. The University of North Carolina at Charlotte, 1994.

Craig, Wilma Ratchford, *Ratchfords . . . I Reckon*. Baltimore: Gateway Press, 1971.

Crow, Jeffrey J. and Escott, Paul D. and Hatley, Flora J. *A History Of African Americans In North Carolina*. The North Carolina Division of Archives and History, 1992.

Current, Richard N. "That Other Declaration: May 20, 1775 - May 20, 1995." *North Carolina Historical Review* (April 1977): 169-191.

Davidson, Chalmers Gaston. *The Plantation World Around Davidson*. Davidson: Davidson Printing Company, 1973.

Durden, Robert F. *The Dukes of Durham, 1865-1929*. Durham: Duke University Press, 1975.

Escott, Paul D. *Many Excellent People. Power and Privilege in North Carolina, 1850-1900*. Chapel Hill and London: The University of North Carolina Press, 1985.

Folk, Edgar Estes and Shaw, Bynum. *William Woods Holden*. Winston-Salem: John F. Blair, 1982.

Gaillard, Frye. *The Dream Long Deferred*. Chapel Hill and London. The University of North Carolina Press, 1988.

Gaston, Paul M. *The New South Creed. A Study in Southern Mythmaking*. New York: Alfred A. Knopf, 1970.

Glass, Brent D., *The Textile Industry In North Carolina: A History*. Raleigh: Division of Archives and History North Carolina Department of Cultural Resources, 1992.

Green, Fletcher Melvin. "Gold Mining: A Forgotten Industry Of Ante-Bellum North Carolina." *North Carolina Historical Review* (January 1937): 169-191.

Greenberg, Kenneth S. *Masters and Statesmen. The Political Culture of American Slavery*. Baltimore: The Johns Hopkins University Press, 1985.

Greenwood, Janette Thomas. *Bittersweet Legacy. The Black and White "Better Classes in Charlotte, 1850-1910*. Chapel Hill and London: The University of North Carolina Press, 1994.

_____. *On the home front: Charlotte during the Civil War*. Charlotte: History Department Mint Museum of Art, 1982.

Hanchett, Thomas W. *Sorting Out The New South City. Race, Class, And Urban Development In Charlotte 1875-1975*. Chapel Hill and London: The University of North Carolina Press, 1998.

Harding, Barbara, *The Boy, the Man, and The Bishop. A Biography of the Everyday Counselor, Bishop Herbert Spaugh*. Charlotte: Barnhardt Brothers Company, 1970.

Henderson, Cornelia Wearn. *Early Charlotte and Mecklenburg County for Children*. Charlotte: Crabtree Press, Publishers, 1968.

Ivey, J. B. *My Memoirs*. Greensboro: The Piedmont Press, 1940.

Kolchin, Peter. *American Slavery 1619-1877*. New York: Hill and Wang, 1993.

Kratt, Mary and Boyer, Mary Manning. *Remembering Charlotte. Postcards From A New South City, 1905-1950*. Chapel Hill and London: The University of North Carolina Press, 2000.

Kratt, Mary Norton and Hanchett, Thomas W. *Legacy: The Myers Park Story*. Charlotte: Myers Park Foundation, 1986.

Kratt, Mary Norton. *Charlotte. Spirit of the New South*. Tulsa: Continental Heritage Press, Inc., 1980.

Lefler, Hugh T. and Newsome, Albert R. *North Carolina: The History of a Southern State*. 3rd ed. Chapel Hill: The University of North Carolina Press, 1973.

McEwen, Mildred Morse. *Growing Up In Fourth Ward*. Charlotte: Heritage Printers, 1987.

Mitchell, Miriam Grace and Perzel, Edward Spaulding. *The Echo of the Bugle Call*. Charlotte: Dowd House Preservation Committee and Citizens For Preservation Inc., 1979.

Morison, Samuel Eliot. *The Oxford History Of The American People*. New York: Oxford University Press, 1965.

Morrill, Dan L. "Edward Dilworth Latta and the Charlotte Consolidated Construction Company." *North Carolina Historical Review* (July 1985): 293-316.

Ovens, David. *If This Be Treason. A Look At His Town And Times*. Charlotte: Heritage House, 1957.

Parker, Inez Moore. *The Biddle-Johnson C. Smith University Story*. Charlotte: Charlotte Publishing, 1975.

Rabinowitz, Howard. *Race Relations in the Urban South, 1865-1900*. New York: Oxford University Press, 1978.

Reynolds, D. R., ed. *Charlotte Remembers*. Charlotte: Don D. Reid, 1972.

Rieke, Robert. *A Retrospective Vision. The University Of North Carolina At Charlotte 1965-1975*. Charlotte: The University of North Carolina At Charlotte, 1977.

Rogers, John R. and Amy T. *Images of America. Charlotte Its Historic Neighborhoods*. Dover: Arcadia Publishing, 1996.

Romine, Dannye. *Mecklenburg: A Bicentennial Story*. Charlotte: Independence Square Associates, 1975.

Sanford, Ken. *Charlotte and UNC Charlotte. Growing Up Together*. Charlotte:

The University of North Carolina at Charlotte, 1996.

Shaw, Cornelia Rebekah. *Davidson College*. New York: Fleming H. Revell Press, 1923.

Sommerville, Charles William. *The History Of Hopewell Presbyterian Church For 175 Years From The Assigned Date Of its Organization 1762*. Mecklenburg County: Hopewell
     Presbyterian Church, 1987.

Tompkins, D. A. *Cotton Mill: Commercial Features*. Charlotte: Observer Job Print, 1899.

_____. *History of Mecklenburg County and the City of Charlotte, from 1740 to 1903*. 2 vols. Charlotte: Observer Printing House, 1903.

Wilkinson, Henrietta H. *The Mint Museum Of Art at Charlotte*. Charlotte: Heritage Printers, 1973.

Winston, George Tayloe. *A Builder Of The New South. Being The Story Of The Life Work Of Daniel Augustus Tompkins*. Freeport: Books For Libraries Press, 1972.

Woodward, C. Vann. *The Strange Career Of Jim Crow*. London, Oxford, New York: Oxford University Press, 1968.

Wright, Christina and Morrill, Dr. Dan. *Charlotte-Mecklenburg Historic Tours.Driving and Walking*. Charlotte: Charlotte-Mecklenburg Historic Preservation Fund, Inc., 1994.

Yockey, Ross. *McColl: The Man With America's Money*. Atlanta: Longstreet, 1999.

DISSERTATIONS AND THESES

Bowers, H. Beau. "'Government Under Which We Fund Most Liberty: The Political and Religious Culture Of Colonial Mecklenburg County, 1755-1775." M. A. Thesis,
     University of North Carolina at Charlotte, 1993.

Clay, Henry B. "Daniel Augustus Tompkins: An American Bourbon." Ph. D. diss., University of North Carolina, Chapel Hill, 1951.

Forret, Jeffrey Paul. "' . . . Promises To Be Very Rich': The Development of The Gold Mining Industry In the Agrarian Society Of Western North Carolina, 1825-1837." M. A.
     Thesis, University of North Carolina at Charlotte, 1998.

Penninger, Randy. "The Emergence of Black Political Power in Charlotte, North Carolina: The City Council Tenure of Frederick Douglas Alexander, 1965- 1974." M.A. Thesis,
     University of North Carolina at Charlotte, 1989.

UNPUBLISHED MANUSCRIPTS

Dalton, Harry. "Deluxe Diary 1942."

Davidson College Archives.

Hanchett, Thomas W. "Design Through Time." Charlotte: Charlotte-Mecklenburg Historic Landmarks Commission.

Robinson-Spangler Room. Charlotte Mecklenburg Public Library.

"Survey and Research Reports." Charlotte: Charlotte-Mecklenburg Historic Landmarks Commission.

NEWSPAPERS

Charlotte Democrat

Charlotte News

Charlotte Observer

Morning Star

Raleigh Register

✧

A Christmas reception at the home of Bishop and Mrs. Clinton on Myers Street, c. 1918. Bishop Clinton is standing in the foreground center, with his wife behind his left shoulder. The reception at the Clinton home was a top social event in Charlotte's black community.

SHARING THE HERITAGE

historic profiles of businesses, organizations, and families that have contributed to the development and economic base of Charlotte and Mecklenburg County

SPECIAL THANKS TO

CIStech Incorporated

General Bonded Warehouse

Industrial Sign & Graphics

McCoy Holdings, LLC

Robinson, Bradshaw & Hinson, P.A.

The Charlotte Police Department, 1900.

QUALITY OF LIFE

healthcare companies, educational institutions,

local governments, churches, and civic and

historical organizations contribute to the

quality of life in Mecklenburg County

✧

The Charlotte Police Department, 1900.

PRESBYTERIAN HOSPITAL

❖

Presbyterian Hospital has improved the quality of life in the Charlotte community for nearly a century by offering compassionate patient care, along with the latest in medical innovation and knowledge.

Just as Charlotte grew from a sleepy Southern town to a major metropolitan U.S. city, Charlotte's oldest hospital expanded from its quarters in a cramped hotel to a major regional healthcare institution.

Repeatedly named Charlotte's most preferred hospital as it entered the twenty-first century, Presbyterian Hospital today is the flagship hospital of Presbyterian Healthcare. Presbyterian Hospital Matthews, Presbyterian Orthopaedic Hospital, SameDay Surgery Center, Wesley Care Center, and a network of physician practices help broaden Presbyterian's services in the region.

But long before growth became a driving force behind Charlotte and its historic institutions, Presbyterian Hospital's leaders focused on building a foundation both for its facilities and finances.

When the hospital's Board of Trustees first met in 1903, representatives from Charlotte's white Presbyterian churches were named to govern the hospital. Committee members were appointed to approach churches to find ways to support the hospital's wards. The board's rules covered who would be admitted to the charity ward; the hospital would receive "only such cases as are likely to be cured or improved by treatment."

Just months after the twenty-bed Presbyterian Hospital opened in a North Church Street building, the board leased the Arlington Hotel on West Trade Street for $1,200 a year. The hospital shared the three-story building with a barbershop, a fruit stand and the "Last Chance" saloon. As renovations got under way, the women of Charlotte's Presbyterian churches raised money to convert the former hotel dining room to the hospital's charity ward.

But the church support was not enough. Finances were a constant struggle during the hospital's first twelve years. With the help of several fraternal organizations and a loan, the hospital turned the road. The hospital's Ladies Auxiliary, formed in 1905, also helped with fundraising.

Another Presbyterian institution established in 1903 was the School of Nursing with its first class of three young women. Students staffed the hospital during twelve-hour shifts, plus scrubbed and cooked—all for $5 a month.

The early 1900s were a time when unsanitary living conditions contributed to public health problems. Contaminated well water led to a variety of illnesses, including typhoid fever, malaria and an outbreak of hookworm in 1909. Local doctors, including one of the South's first female physicians Dr. Annie Alexander from Presbyterian Hospital, worked with civic clubs to improve public health.

By the end of 1916, trustees convinced local churches to support fundraising efforts for a new hospital. A community fundraising campaign to support the hospital's growth started in February 1917, the same week the U.S. was on the verge of entering World War I. But with the nation's future so uncertain, citizens were hesitant to contribute.

Despite falling short of the $100,000 goal, the board proceeded with plans to build. But materials were in short supply, so the hospital instead bought the twenty-acre Elizabeth College grounds and buildings, just outside the city limits, for $225,000.

Presbyterian moved to its new home on Hawthorne Lane in February 1918 and more than doubled its size, from 50 to 100 beds, making it Charlotte's largest hospital. People from all over the Carolinas streamed to Presbyterian for medical care.

In November that year, the hospital faced its greatest challenge as a deadly worldwide influenza epidemic hit Charlotte. One source said that half the city's population was infected. Nursing classes were suspended while nurses and doctors worked long stretches. One nursing student caught pneumonia and died on graduation day.

Presbyterian faced a record number of patients that fall and was dangerously overcrowded at times. When the war was over and by the early 1920s, the hospital was again in dire financial straits with a large mortgage and numerous flu patients who were treated without paying. Neglect by the Presbyterian churches led to another dark period for the hospital. Dr. J. R. Alexander, who had served as the hospital's superintendent since 1905, announced his resignation, leaving W. E. Price, president of the board of trustees, as the interim administrator. Price convinced the churches to come to the rescue, and community-spirited bankers and businessmen also responded. With help from the women's auxiliary, funds were raised for revitalizing the hospital.

Department store founder William Henry Belk became president of the board, a position he held for more than twenty years. In 1924 the Reverend Dr. C. C. Beam took over the role of superintendent, a job he also kept for twenty years.

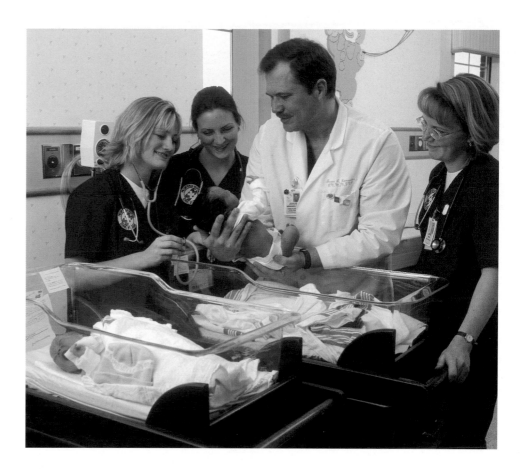

The 1920s also marked the beginning of the hospital's relationship with The Duke Endowment, which has provided millions of dollars, along with professional expertise.

The 1930s were a time when many distinguished local physicians served on Presbyterian's staff. But modern medicine was still decades away. The hospital was not air-conditioned. Most of the surgeons didn't have assistants. Laboratory and pathology

✧

Above: Presbyterian's nurses and its School of Nursing are a key element in the hospital's focus on patient care. The School of Nursing opened in 1903.

Below: In the mid-1980s Presbyterian met the continuing demand for outpatient surgery with the opening of SameDay Surgery Center.

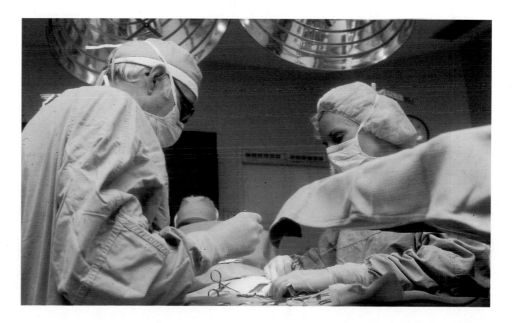

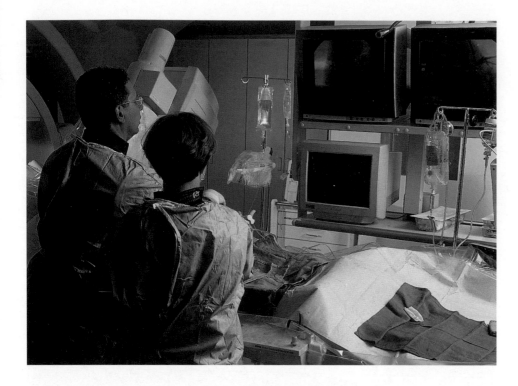

✧

Above: Presbyterian's Belk Heart Center opened in 1986 with its state-of-the-art catheterization labs.

Below: Presbyterian Hospital Matthews, a 102-bed hospital, opened in 1994.

departments were primitive by today's standards; blood from a ram that grazed behind the hospital was used to test for syphilis.

The Great Depression meant that many patients had no money to pay their bills, even though a single room cost only $7 a day. Charity care was taken for granted by many people.

But thanks to the groundwork laid in the mid 1920s, Presbyterian was debt free by 1939 and expansion plans resumed. Charlotte's booming population was causing a shortage of hospital beds, and nearly all of the 110 beds were always filled.

A new seven-story building opened in July 1940 in front of the old Elizabeth College building. Built and furnished at a cost of $560,000, the new hospital added operating

rooms and recovery rooms, an obstetrics area, children's wards and charity facilities.

During the next three decades, Presbyterian embarked on eight major building projects and tripled in size from 188 beds in 1940 to 502 beds in 1972. The hospital led the way in Charlotte with the first intensive care unit, the first outpatient surgery unit and the first ambulatory unit for patients who needed minimal care. J. P. Richardson, who from 1944 to 1977 was Presbyterian's first professionally trained hospital administrator, spearheaded the innovations and expansions. By the 1950s the hospital was no longer staffed primarily by student nurses. Graduate nurses took charge, and licensed practical nurses later took over chores, so registered nurses could concentrate on professional duties.

Massive advances in medical knowledge and technology marked the period from 1940 to 1972. Physicians and nurses returned from World War II with innovative ideas about medical care, and they now worked side by side as a team. One of the most important developments was the availability of new drugs, including penicillin and other antibiotics.

Spurred on by federal legislation, Presbyterian Hospital changed its admissions policy in the mid 1960s and opened its doors to black patients.

The 1970s brought a new Diagnostic and Treatment Center for more outpatient treatment and a new thirty-bed emergency room for around-the-clock medical coverage. In 1980, the Elizabeth College building was demolished and a new 119-bed patient tower opened, bringing the total number of beds to 554.

Presbyterian's Child Development Center also opened in 1980 and was one of the pioneers in offering on-site child care to employees.

The Presbyterian Hospital Foundation was formed in 1980 as the hospital's fundraising arm. One of its first successes resulted in a School of Nursing building designed and built for the school.

A new corporate structure based on a holding company concept was formed in 1983 to reflect changes in the healthcare industry. Called Presbyterian Health Services Corp., its purpose was to serve as the parent organization for all of the hospital's organizations and corporations except the Foundation.

One of the first projects under the corporate reorganization was an immediate care center in Matthews, about ten miles southeast of Presbyterian Hospital. It was the first venture away from the main Charlotte campus. Following its success, Presbyterian Hospital Matthews, a 102-bed hospital opened in 1994 with emergency care, inpatient and outpatient services and a family maternity center.

In the mid 1980s Presbyterian met the continuing demand for outpatient surgery with the opening of SameDay Surgery Center across from the main hospital and opened the Belk Heart Center, an intensive care nursery and a psychiatric unit. In the 1990s, the Presbyterian Hemby Children's Hospital, a hospital-within-a-hospital, opened to meet the unique needs of children and families. Programs serving businesses and providing care in patients' homes also started, along with a Parish Nurses program for nurses to work with church congregations.

Presbyterian formed a management services organization in 1992 to provide employees, facilities, equipment and other services to physicians. A year later, these physicians became employees of Presbyterian to help them negotiate managed care contracts and other contracts with large employers.

A leader in providing cancer services and hospice care in the region and the state, Presbyterian opened a new Cancer Center in 1996, with radiation oncology, clinical research, inpatient oncology and a bone marrow transplant unit. The Buddy Kemp Caring House, a unique facility offering counseling and educational support for cancer patients and their families, opened in a non-institutional setting several blocks from the hospital in 1999.

Presbyterian also reached outside the main hospital campus in 1996 to take over management of Wesley Care Center, a 289-bed, skilled nursing facility.

In 1997 Presbyterian Healthcare and Carolina Medicorp, Inc. of Winston-Salem announced a merger to form a new healthcare company, Novant Health. The two nonprofit companies serve an area of more than 3.4 million people in North Carolina, southern Virginia and northern

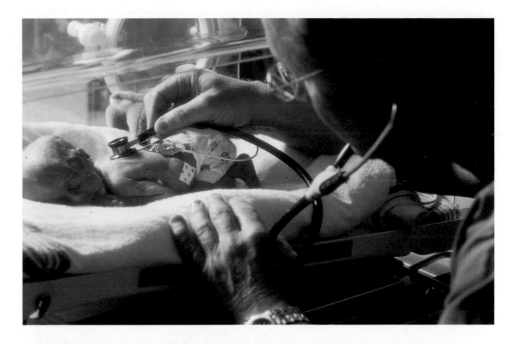

South Carolina. Carolina Medicorp, Inc. President and Chief Executive Officer Paul M. Wiles assumed leadership of the new company.

A year later, Novant Health acquired full ownership of Presbyterian Orthopaedic Hospital, one of six hospitals in the nation dedicated to the diagnosis, care and treatment of injuries and diseases of the bones and joints.

As Presbyterian Healthcare's fifty-five hundred employees prepare for the hospital's centennial in 2003, the healthcare provider continues to be a dynamic business with its mission to improve the health of communities in the Charlotte region.

✧

Top: Presbyterian Hospital's Neonatal Intensive Care Unit cares for more than four hundred infants each year.

Above: The colorful Blume Playroom in Presbyterian Hemby Children's Hospital provides activities for children.

CITY OF CHARLOTTE

As the largest city between Dallas, Texas, and Washington, D.C., Charlotte has a population of approximately 545,293. With more than 1.3 million people in its metropolitan area and another 6 million within a 100-mile radius, Charlotte is the country's second fastest growing city and the center of the fifth largest urban region.

Among Charlotte's many points of pride are its airport, banking industry and long tradition of public-private partnerships. In flights per day per capita, Charlotte-Douglas International Airport ranks first among the top thirty metro regions in the country. Charlotte is second only to New York as the largest banking/financial center in the U.S. And over the years, the City of Charlotte has developed partnerships with the private sector that have resulted in the successful completion of such projects as the North Carolina Blumenthal Performing Arts Center, Ericcson Stadium, home to the NFL's Carolina Panthers, and Discovery Place.

With the Charlotte-Mecklenburg property tax rate in the lowest quarter of one hundred metro areas nationwide, the City of Charlotte is one of just twenty-one in the country to attain the highest (AAA) credit rating from both Moody and Standard & Poor rating agencies, a factor that means savings for taxpayers.

Combining a rich history dating back to 1768 with the advantages of a modern, twenty-first century city, Charlotte has twice been chosen (in 1995 and 2000) by the National League of Cities as one of the most livable cities in the United States, fulfilling an

Above: Working together is key to addressing community issues effectively.
COURTESY OF KRIS SOLOW.

Below: Construction is underway to expand the trolley's service through the Center City.
COURTESY OF KRIS SOLOW.

1895 prediction by the influential *Harper's Weekly*, describing it as "a city with potential."

Charlotte adopted the council-manager form of government in 1928, creating a continuity of service and talent that supports the mayor and eleven-member city council, with four members elected at large and seven from districts. Over the years, city government has earned a national and international reputation as innovative, responsive and well managed. Through a combination of vision, cooperation and hard work, Charlotte has become known for:

• Encouraging citizen involvement in city government by creating substantial opportunities for individuals to participate in public meetings and serve on one of the more than thirty-five boards and commissions that advise the council on policy;

• Developing and implementing comprehensive plans for everything from community safety and transportation to neighborhood improvement;

• Being the first municipality to employ the Balanced Scorecard approach as a way to measure performance and establish strategic priorities and objectives;

• Effectively managing resources to support Council "Focus Areas," ranging from Community Safety, Transportation and Economic Development to Affordable Housing and Smart Growth;

• Establishing a City Within A City Focus Area initiative designed to comprehensively deal with economic development and quality of life issues in Charlotte's older urban neighborhoods and business areas. This effort has enabled the City to attract new residential and business development to the center city at a time when other cities are experiencing a deterioration of their urban core.

The City's priorities are reflected in its annual operating and capital budgets. Funded through a variety of user fees, sales taxes, federal agencies and other sources, the City relies on the property tax and special tax districts for approximately 34.5 percent of its overall annual income. The $997 million budget in 2000-01 includes not only operating costs for such services as police and fire protection and garbage collection, but the capital investment plan that funds major infrastructure projects such as road/sidewalk construction, fire stations and police facilities.

Focusing on outcome-based performance measures has enabled the City to streamline operations, cut costs and concentrate resources in priority service/project areas. These efforts coupled with strong growth and clear Council policy has allowed Charlotte to maintain a stable property tax rate for more than fourteen years.

For all its successes, Charlotte also recognizes the challenges ahead. Addressing issues of sprawl, traffic congestion, affordable housing and employment opportunities are central to the City's ability to remain economically viable and competitive with other cities. By taking a regional approach to problem solving and working with other governmental, corporate, civic, non-profit and neighborhood leaders, the City is well positioned to meet present and future challenges that will enable it to continue to be considered one of the country's best places to live, work and raise a family.

Above: The City focuses on building sidewalks to improve safety for pedestrians.
COURTESY OF KRIS SOLOW.

Below: The City Council meets weekly to conduct business.
COURTESY OF KRIS SOLOW.

THE UNIVERSITY OF NORTH CAROLINA AT CHARLOTTE

The University of North Carolina at Charlotte, the fourth-largest university in North Carolina, was founded as a junior college to ease an enrollment crisis created by returning World War II veterans. Its rapid development parallels the rise of many other urban universities across the United States, established in response to rising post-war demands for higher education.

Early in 1946, North Carolina Governor Gregg Cherry and other state officials moved to create temporary junior colleges called "college centers" to accommodate a tide of WWII veterans that threatened to overflow traditional colleges and universities. Operating under the Extension Division of The University of North Carolina at Chapel Hill, the centers offered credits transferable to any senior institution in the state.

The Charlotte Center opened on September 23, 1946, with an enrollment of 278 men and women, by far the largest of 14 such institutions organized across the state. It offered night classes on the third floor of Charlotte's Central High School. Its headquarters were in the high school's Lost and Found office. In its second year, the center's enrollment grew to 302, and it began fielding football, basketball and baseball teams.

In 1949, assuming the crisis had passed, state officials moved to close the emergency

Above: Students still ring the old bell to commemorate special events today, just as they did in the past.

Below: UNC Charlotte's 1,000-acre campus has changed dramatically in the last 40 years when it moved to its present-day site.

centers. But Charlotte residents, who had long sought a public institution of higher learning, arranged to have the city school board take over the center, support it with local revenues, and operate it as a municipal junior college named Charlotte College. This initiative is memorialized in the nickname of the school's athletic teams, which are called '49ers.

The person who most inspired public support for the institution was Bonnie Cone, a tireless Central High mathematics teacher who became director of the Charlotte Center in its second year and went on to become president of Charlotte College. A great favorite with students, Cone persuaded leaders of the business community that higher education was crucial to Charlotte's future success and pointed out that the nearest state college or university was ninety miles away. Many of the leading citizens agreed to serve on the college's board of trustees or to lobby for its support before local and state agencies.

Cone persuaded prominent Charlotteans such as author Harry Golden, newspaper editor C.A. "Pete" McKnight, and lawyer (later federal judge) Robert D. Potter to teach at the college. She also recruited a promising full-time faculty that made excellence in teaching a hallmark of the institution.

In 1958 Charlotte College gained state support as a member of the North Carolina community college system. In 1961 it moved from Central High to what would become a one-thousand-acre campus on North Carolina

Highway 49, about ten miles northeast of the center city. In 1964 it was expanded into a four-year institution.

In 1965, on the recommendation of Dr. Arnold K. King, assistant to UNC President William C. Friday, and with the support of Governor Dan K. Moore, it became the fourth campus of The University of North Carolina, with UNC Chapel Hill, North Carolina State and UNC Greensboro. That fall it enrolled 1,815 students.

Bonnie Cone served as its chief executive until April 1966 when Dean W. Colvard, former president of Mississippi State and previously dean of agriculture at North Carolina State, became the school's first chancellor. He organized its programs on a university scale and began planning its future. He also led efforts that converted thirty-four hundred acres near the campus into University Research Park. During his tenure, an underdog men's basketball team won the hearts of the community by advancing to the finals of the National Invitational Tournament and the NCAA finals in successive seasons.

UNC Charlotte's early mission was to serve the populous Charlotte metropolitan area by offering undergraduate programs. Initially a school for commuters, it opened its first residence halls in 1968. A year later, it began offering master's degree programs and, in 1993, began offering Ph.D. programs. In August 2000 the UNC Board of Governors reclassified it a doctoral/research university.

New Yorker E. K. Fretwell succeeded Dean Colvard as chancellor in 1979 and, through his leadership of national and international education organizations, greatly expanded the school's identity and reputation. During his tenure, the school also led efforts that resulted in the development of University Place, expanding the amenities available in the burgeoning area known as University City.

In 1989, James H. Woodward, an engineer/educator from the University of Alabama at Birmingham, succeeded Chancellor Fretwell. Encouraged by the support of the business and political leaders, he rapidly expanded the university's mission, led a campaign that increased its endowment, began a program that enhanced campus facilities, and

launched initiatives to expand the Charlotte economy by emphasizing research and the creation of intellectual capital.

The University is comprised of seven colleges: Architecture, Arts and Sciences, Business Administration, Education, Engineering, Information Technology and Nursing and Health Professions. It draws students from across North Carolina, the United States and around the world. In the fall of 2001 it enrolled 18,250. It has granted more than seventy thousand degrees, most of them to alumni who have chosen to live and work in the Charlotte region.

✧

Above: The Barnhardt Student Activity Center is home to Halton Arena where the Charlotte 49ers play in Conference USA.

Below: UNC Charlotte is achieving world-wide recognition for conducting leading-edge research in fields such as precision metrology in its C. C. Cameron Applied Research Center.

ROMAN CATHOLIC DIOCESE OF CHARLOTTE

The growth of the Roman Catholic Church can be traced to the early nineteenth century when Father Joseph Stokes, a missionary priest from Savannah, Georgia, began visits to the area. A permanent Catholic presence in Charlotte began in 1851 when Father Jeremiah O'Connell, after a two-day trip by stagecoach from Charleston, laid the cornerstone of the first church building.

Much of the money needed to construct this church was donated by non-Catholics who had been impressed by Father O'Connell's preaching. Bishop Ignatius Reynolds of Charleston, South Carolina, dedicated St. Peter Church in 1852. At the time of the dedication of St. Peter's, the population consisted of about one hundred Catholics.

The cornerstone of the present St. Peter Church at South Tryon and First Streets was laid on September 3, 1893, and was dedicated that same year by the Right Reverend Leo Haid, OSB, vicar apostolic of North Carolina and abbot of Belmont Abbey. St. Peter's Gothic style, including a tin-paneled ceiling, is representative of late-Victorian architecture in vogue at the time. An adjoining rectory was built in 1897, which continued to reflect the same architectural style.

One of the many benefactors who helped build the present structure was Saint Katharine Drexel, the Philadelphia-born heiress who devoted her life and wealth to the establishment of schools and missions for

Native Americans and African Americans. Her gift was contingent upon a promise to reserve pews in the church for black parishioners.

St. Peter's Parochial School was built in 1906 on the corner of Stonewall and Tryon Streets. The parish hall behind the church became the first Mercy Hospital, founded by the Sisters of Mercy of Belmont, and served the city until 1915, when the hospital was relocated to its present site.

Today, St. Peter Church is well known for a massive fresco, completed in 1993, by artist Ben Long that covers the entire rear wall of the sanctuary. The fresco is a triptych depicting the Agony in the Garden, the Resurrection and Pentecost.

Construction of St. Patrick Church began in March 1939, through the generosity of John Henry Phelan of Beaumont, Texas, who built the church in memory of his parents. Located at 1621 Dilworth Road East, St. Patrick Church is noted for its Old World style with a gray stucco face, 400-seat nave, balcony and 77-foot tall tower. A rectory and convent were built in 1941.

A Catholic grade school, known as O'Donohue School, was built on the property in 1930 and was expanded in 1943 to include high school grades. During the 1950s and early 1960s, with the founding of Charlotte Catholic High School, the school reverted to elementary grades and was named St. Patrick School.

St. Patrick Church was elevated to cathedral status in 1972 when His Holiness Pope Paul VI

Above: The Most Reverend Michael J. Begley, first bishop of the Diocese of Charlotte.

Right: St. Peter Catholic Church, c. 1950

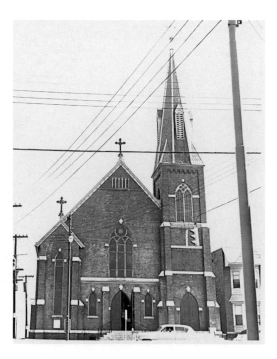

established the Diocese of Charlotte. The Reverend Michael J. Begley was installed as first Bishop of the Diocese of Charlotte in St. Patrick Cathedral. Bishop Begley had served the Catholic Church in North Carolina since his ordination to the priesthood in 1934. Bishop Begley retired in 1984 and was succeeded by the Reverend John F. Donoghue. The present Bishop of Charlotte is the Most Reverend William G. Curlin, D.D., who was installed as the third bishop of Charlotte on April 13, 1994.

The Diocese is composed of forty-six counties in Western North Carolina. While the non-Catholic population of western North Carolina has increased twenty-one percent in the past decade, the Catholic population has increased seventy-five percent. Since 1972, the number of Catholic households has increased from approximately 11,200 to 47,619 in the year 2000. In addition, the number of children in Catholic Schools and Faith Formation Programs also increased dramatically. Catholic school enrollment increased forty-three percent from 1972 to 2000. The increase of students in Faith Formation Programs was even more dramatic, rising 178 percent during the same

period. Those baptized and received into the faith have also shown major increases. When the Diocese was first formed in 1972, there were 880 infant baptisms and 170 adults received into full communion. The year 2000 saw a total of 3,733 infant baptisms and 638 received into full communion, an increase of 275 percent over 1972.

The twelve parishes located in the Charlotte area include: Our Lady of the Assumption, Our Lady of Consolation, St. Ann, St. Gabriel, St. John Neumann, St. Luke, St. Mark, St. Matthew, St. Patrick, St. Thomas Aquinas, and St. Vincent de Paul.

Our Lady of Consolation Parish was founded in 1955 as an African-American parish but its history traces back to 1941 when the Redemptorists came to minister to African-Americans in the area. The parish now serves over thirteen hundred individuals.

Bishop Curlin's policy of welcoming refugees has changed the ethnic diversity of the Church. Aside from the traditional African American, Native American, and European cultures, the Diocese, and particularly Charlotte, also has large numbers of individuals from Southeast Asia and an increasing number of families from Latin America and Mexico. Three new cultural centers have been established. The Hispanic Cultural Center was established in 1993 and has served the needs of the growing Hispanic community of Charlotte. The Center will be moving to larger facilities in 2001. St. John Lee Korean Catholic Church was established in 1994 and serves about three hundred members. In 1999 Bishop Curlin dedicated St. Joseph Vietnamese Church, which now serves fifteen hundred Vietnamese Catholics.

✧

Above: The Vietnamese community celebrates the establishment of St. Joseph Church.

Below: Mother Theresa of Calcutta and the Most Reverend William G. Curlin on the occasion of her 1996 visit to Charlotte.

PUBLIC LIBRARY OF CHARLOTTE & MECKLENBURG COUNTY

With a history of service that dates back well over a century, the Public Library of Charlotte & Mecklenburg County has earned the designation of "The University of the People." Charlotte's first library opened in 1891, when prominent citizens created a Literary and Library Association and charged 50 cents per month to residents who wanted to borrow books. This fledgling library, which offered a limited book collection, operated for nine years in rooms above a bookstore on South Tryon Street. Because of difficulties in collecting the fees directors of the association transferred control of the library to the city's schools in 1901. The library was moved to two rooms in the Charlotte City Hall, where it remained for the next two years, offering free service to anyone except African-Americans.

A $25,000 Andrew Carnegie grant to build a permanent public library stipulated that the city must provide a site for the building and finance its operation. On July 2, 1903, the Carnegie Free Library opened in a beautiful, freestanding, classical building located a few yards from the site of the present Main Library at 310 North Tryon Street. Two years later the Brevard Street Library for Negroes, the first public library of its kind in North Carolina, opened as an independent facility.

Branching out to other parts of the county began in 1919, first utilizing school libraries, and later with freestanding branches in towns around Charlotte, thanks to funding from the Julius Rosenwald Fund. The Brevard Street library became an official branch. A few years later even more widespread library service was added through service by bookmobiles.

But every change in the Library in this era was not positive. In 1938, during a long economic depression, the North Carolina Supreme Court ruled that a library was not a public necessity. This decision meant that voters must approve a public referendum if tax money was to be used for support of library service. The referendum, held in 1939, failed by a close margin, and on June 30 of that year, the library's doors were closed and locked. By the next year, however, voters apparently realized how vital library service is, and the library was reopened following a second referendum. In 1944 the official name of the institution was changed to the Public Library of Charlotte and Mecklenburg County.

The 1940s-1960s brought a host of modern innovations and improvements. Among these was the creation of a Business Information Bureau to provide timely statistical and financial information for business and industry. The library began offering educational films in 1942, with the growing demand leading to the loan of over 200 films per month by 1944. This evolved into the library's Film and Sound Division, one of the first programs of its type, which served as a national model.

By this time the system was in need of additional operating funds, a situation relieved in 1947, when voters approved a measure designating five percent of Alcohol Beverage Control sales profits for use by the library. Service was expanded, two bookmobiles were purchased, and both the Carnegie Library and Brevard Street Branch were refurbished. But increasing use of the library and the many expanded services had created a serious need for more space. Voters approved a $1.6 million bond issue in 1952 to construct a new Main Library and nine branch buildings.

The old building was razed, and in its place was built the new Main Library that opened November 19, 1956, containing more than twice the space of its predecessor. Desegregation of the library system in 1956 gave all people equal access to an exemplary facility.

Rapid growth of the city and county, along with additional library services, technological changes and ever-increasing use of the facility, meant more space was sorely needed by the 1980s. A $9.3-million package approved by Mecklenburg County voters in 1983 funded a three-story addition and complete remodeling that more than doubled the size of the Main Library and also provided additional branch library locations. Creation of the Carolina Room on the third floor of the new addition provides a home for archives, books and journals documenting regional history.

In the last years of the twentieth century, the library system grew to over twenty locations (including five regional libraries offering expanded services) serving people in neighborhoods and towns across the county.

From a grand total of 2,526 books when the Carnegie Library opened in 1903, today's library system contains over 1.5 million adult and children's classics, favorite paperbacks, modern best sellers, videos and CD's, with over five hundred employees county-wide helping to make information available to virtually anyone who wants it. Library staff present at least ten thousand programs to adults and children each year. Programs are as diverse as the people who attend them, drawing people of all ages and walks of life. The Novello Festival of Reading has been a fixture in the Charlotte region since the early 1990s and is known and admired nationally.

The Library uses technology to reach people too. Three hundred computers provide Internet links to information on topics ranging from business to health to history, with links leading to interactive—and often multi-lingual—sources of learning and fun. The Library's Family of Websites (www.plcmc.org) includes information and interactive content for children and adults.

Named as the National Library of the Year in 1995 and Library of the Future in 1996, the Public Library of Charlotte and Mecklenburg County continues to search for new and better ways to involve itself in the community, to make The University of the People the very best it can be.

✦

Above: The reading room of Charlotte's Carnegie Library. The Carnegie Library opened in 1903 and closed in 1954 to make way for a much larger building in 1956.

Bottom: Over three million users visit the Main Library and the system's 22 other branches each year. For more information about the Library and its activities, please call (704) 336-2725 or visit www.plcmc.org.

FIRST PRESBYTERIAN CHURCH

Although the early settlers of Mecklenburg County were predominantly Ulster-Scot Presbyterians, the little village of Charlotte had no church within its boundaries for nearly fifty years after its incorporation.

Instead, preaching was conducted whenever a minister was available, with services held in the courthouse at the crossroads of Trade and Tryon Streets.

In 1815, town commissioners set aside a plot of land on West Trade Street, a block from the Square, to be used for a town church. It was to be built by the townspeople and used by all denominations. Construction began about 1818, but the public venture failed, and the commissioners had to borrow $1,500 to complete the church.

The church, dedicated in 1823, was known as the Brick Church, the Town Church and, most often, the Presbyterian Church, since that denomination represented the majority of those meeting there.

Commissioner John Irwin, a Presbyterian, paid off the debt on the building and, in 1841, deeded a clear title to the "members of the Presbyterian Church in the Town of Charlotte."

The first building was outgrown and a second erected on the site in 1857 at a cost of about $13,000. Its Gothic Revival style of architecture has been retained through all subsequent additions. The facade, narthex and tower with a spire rebuilt in 1883-84 remain as part of the present First Presbyterian Church. In 1895 the sanctuary was enlarged to its present size.

Several additions have been made to the building over the years. A Sunday School building was added in 1894-95, and then doubled in size in 1916-17. A Fellowship Hall with additional classroom space was added in 1952. At that time a part of the old Sunday School building was remodeled into the Orr Memorial Chapel. An Office-Educational Building was constructed in 1960-61 on the site of the old church manse. The Jones Memorial windows were placed over the sanctuary entrance in 1970. In 1993 a building was constructed to house children's ministries and administrative offices.

A 1999 capital campaign provided funds for a new Fellowship Hall and Christian Education Building that blend with the existing facilities and maintain the historic sanctuary as the visual and spiritual focus of the First Presbyterian campus. A Ben Long fresco, completed in 2001, is located in the new Fellowship Hall and depicts the parable of the Good Samaritan.

For more than 175 years, First Presbyterian Church has been closely aligned with the history of Charlotte.

During the Civil War, the church once more opened its doors to all denominations and Presbyterians, Methodists, Baptists and Lutherans joined together each morning to pray for the Confederate cause. The steeple was used as a lookout around the clock and the bell was removed to save it from being melted down into ammunition. The bell was later used in the Methodist Church and at the courthouse, before being returned to First Presbyterian Church in 1942.

The church was the scene of several celebrations of the Mecklenburg Declaration of Independence and two women have been honored with military funerals in the church.

❖

Above: The facade, narthex, tower and spire of First Presbyterian Church remain much as they were in 1883.

Below: This pew deed, dated 1868, records that R.M. Miller paid $50 for the rights to pew number eight.

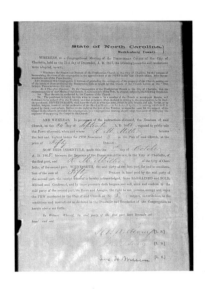

FIRST PRESBYTERIAN CHURCH
Charlotte, North Carolina
from History of Mecklenburg County
by D. A. Tompkins, Volume 1

They were Julia Jackson Christian and Mary Anna Morrison Jackson, the daughter and wife of Confederate General "Stonewall" Jackson. They were also the daughter and granddaughter of Dr. Robert Hall Morrison, first pastor of the church.

Relics of the church include the first bell, used from 1826-1861, a pulpit Bible given in 1853, a pew used from 1857-1894, and a communion set and baptismal bowl presented in 1857. Beautiful stained glass windows are located throughout the church and date back to the 1800s.

Sunday School classes for black students were begun in the 1850s and continued through the Civil War and into the 1880s. In the 1860s and '70s the present-day site of Ericksson Stadium was the location of a day school run by the church, as there were no public schools in Charlotte at the time. The church's outreach also included mission and Sunday schools in the various mill villages throughout the city.

Alexander Children's Home and Barium Springs Home, which today serve troubled youth, are the outgrowth of First Presbyterian programs. The church from as early as the 1870s also supported foreign missionary work.

In recent years, the church continued its outreach with the opening of the Child Development Center in 1947, a pioneering move at the time. As suburbanization forced several downtown churches to relocate from the center city, members of First Presbyterian decided to hold their ground, bearing witness to Christ and serving the needy as well as the more fortunate who live and work in the downtown area.

With the redevelopment of the downtown area, the church has continued to grow. Innovative ministries have included the Community School of the Arts, which brings training in the arts to disadvantaged children. Loaves and Fishes, a Child's Place, and the Weekday School are examples of other programs started by First Presbyterian Church to meet the needs of children and the hungry and homeless in the community.

As the church enters the twenty-first century, its newest projects—the Center for Urban Ministry, serving Charlotte's

homeless, and a preschool in the impoverished Lakewood community—join the many other outreach programs initiated over the past two centuries by members of First Presbyterian Church.

By remembering the past, members of First Presbyterian Church hope to inspire future generations to find their own ways to "serve Christ in the heart of Charlotte."

✧

Above: The church bell at First Presbyterian Church dates back to 1826. It was removed from the steeple during the Civil War to save it from being melted down for ammunition.

Below: The sanctuary of First Presbyterian Church was enlarged to its present size in 1895.

YMCA OF GREATER CHARLOTTE

On November 11, 1874, twenty-three young men gathered in a rented hall above a livery stable on the southeast corner of North Tryon and Sixth Streets to organize a local branch of the Young Men's Christian Association.

More than 125 years later, the YMCA continues to support Charlotte's spiritual and physical needs. "We put Christian principles into practice—principles which all people find valuable: caring, honesty, respect, responsibility and faith," explains Andy Calhoun, president and CEO of the YMCA of Greater Charlotte.

"We're a Christian organization but not just an organization for Christians. We're very inclusive."

Organization of the Charlotte YMCA came during the hard times that followed the Civil War. Federal occupation troops had been removed from the city only two years before and the small town of 4,500 citizens was struggling to survive.

The YMCA provided inspiration and spiritual instruction that helped the city endure that dismal period in its history.

Two newcomers to the city encouraged the Association's idea. William Phillips, a young architect from Scotland, had been impressed by the work of the Association there, and George Hanna, an assayer with the Federal Mint, had previously been active in the growing YMCA movement.

By the 1880s Charlotte had begun to pull out of the post-war depression and, after a

dozen years in rented space, the YMCA began a fund-raising campaign for its own building. The drive raised $14,000 and a turreted, brown stone building was erected on the southwest corner of Tryon and Fourth Streets.

Facilities included the city's first gymnasium, auditorium, library, meeting rooms, and resident rooms. Business rental space was available on the ground floor.

By 1908 the YMCA had outgrown its original building and members raised $80,000 for a larger structure at the northwest corner of South Tryon and Second Streets. The new building included the city's first swimming pool. This structure served the YMCA's needs until 1960 when a new facility, now the Dowd Branch, was opened at 400 East Morehead Street.

The Association first established programs for African-American boys in 1910 and the Second Street YMCA, the first YMCA for African Americans, opened in the old Brooklyn neighborhood in 1936. The Second Street YMCA was later renamed the McCrorey YMCA and, in 1969, was moved to its present location on Beatties Ford Road.

The YMCA opened its doors to female members in 1972.

True to its heritage, the YMCA of the twenty-first century still builds strong kids, strong families and strong communities. The structure and programs have changed over

❖

Above: The first YMCA-owned building stood on the southwest corner of Tryon and Fourth Streets.

Below: The YMCA is focused on building strong kids, strong families, and strong communities.

COURTESY OF PETER BRENTLINGER.

Young Men's Christian Association Building.

the decades, but the Association's mission remains the same.

"We accomplish our mission through people—from one person to another," says Eric Ellsworth, one of two senior vice presidents and COOs of the Greater Charlotte YMCA. "Everything centers on relationship building. When people come into our programs, they come into an atmosphere where they will meet caring people face-to-face."

Because of the Association's strong outreach program, membership and program financial assistance are available.

"Although many immediately think 'gym and swim' when they think of the YMCA, the Association's programs are much more diverse," says Eric Mann, senior vice president and COO. The YMCA builds healthy spirit, mind and body through leadership programs, prayer breakfasts, GED classes, summer camps, children's literacy programs, and group exercise classes. Older adults are served through programs ranging from aqua aerobics and learning sessions to planned outings and social activities. For teens, the YMCA provides fellowship, leadership development and hundreds of other activities.

To help families in need reach self-sufficiency, the YMCA partners with a number

of organizations, including United Way, Urban League, Junior League, Central Piedmont Community College and local healthcare providers.

In 2000 the Association served one out of every six and a half people in its service area, the highest market penetration of any urban YMCA in the country.

In 2001 the YMCA of Greater Charlotte opened its thirteenth branch. Each branch has its own volunteer board of directors so that programming and most decision-making may be customized to the community served by the branch. A volunteer metro board of directors supports and guides the Association.

The YMCA of Greater Charlotte has enjoyed phenomenal growth in recent years and is now one of the largest in North America. The YMCA employs 2,000 people and thousands of volunteers, including 450 board members, who assist with various activities.

With several new branches and a membership that is growing each year, the YMCA of Greater Charlotte puts its principles into practice each day. The YMCA has changed and grown since 1874 but it remains dedicated to putting Christian principles into practice through programs that build healthy spirit, mind and body for all.

✧

Above: Volunteers help children develop character values through YMCA programs.
COURTESY OF MITCHELL KEARNEY, 1997.

Below: Tens of thousands of YMCA members use its fitness facilities and participate in group exercise programs
COURTESY OF PETER BRENTLINGER, 1998

CHARLOTTE AUDITORIUM • COLISEUM • CONVENTION CENTER AUTHORITY

✧

Above: Charlotte Coliseum.

Below: Charlotte Convention Center.

For nearly fifty years, the Charlotte Auditorium•Coliseum•Convention Center Authority has managed Charlotte's publicly owned event facilities. Today, these facilities include Charlotte Coliseum, Charlotte Convention Center, Cricket Arena and Ovens Auditorium.

Annually, these four venues attract approximately 2.8 million people for major league sports events, top-drawer entertainment and important meetings and conferences.

Authority members are charged with overseeing the management of the four facilities. The Authority is composed of seven members; five members appointed by City Council and two members appointed by the Mayor. Each member serves a three-year term and can serve a second consecutive term if chosen to do so by the Mayor or City Council. Authority members, who receive no compensation, are charged with operating the facilities in a proper, efficient, economical and business-like manner. The Authority makes all reasonable rules and regulations necessary for the proper operation and maintenance of the facilities and appoints the managers who are responsible for day-to-day management.

The Charlotte Coliseum, located off Tyvola Road, first opened in 1988. It is one of the largest arenas in the nation, seating 24,000 spectators for concerts and 23,901 for basketball games.

The Coliseum is home to the Charlotte Hornets NBA professional basketball team as well as the WNBA's Charlotte Sting. The Coliseum has also hosted the NBA All Star Game, the NCAA Men's Final Four, the NCAA Women's Final Four and several ACC Basketball Tournaments.

The Coliseum has attracted such major entertainment figures as Garth Brooks, Eric Clapton, the Grateful Dead, and Janet Jackson. Other major events have included Jubilate, one of the premiere Christian New Year's Eve Celebrations in the United States, a visit by Mother Teresa, Ringling Brothers Barnum and Bailey Circus, and Walt Disney's World on Ice.

The Charlotte Convention Center, located at 501 South College Street, opened in 1995. As the perfect venue for trade shows, banquets, dances and theater style conferences, the Convention Center attracts tens of thousands of visitors each year.

From its gracefully arched entrances to the glass concourses beyond, the Convention Center was designed to be elegant and inviting. Flanked by art and spacious alcoves, the Grand Concourse welcomes visitors and provides easy orientation and access to all points in the Convention Center.

Soaring ceilings add volume to the 280,000-square feet of contiguous exhibit space which accommodates general session set-ups or up to 1,250 exhibit booths. This space may be sectioned into four halls with separate loading entrances for simultaneous shows. Twenty-two covered loading docks and direct drive-in access to each hall makes set up easy and efficient.

The Convention Center's ballroom spans 35,000 square feet with banquet seating for up to 2,500 guests. Pre-function areas extend the ballroom space by 15,000 square feet. More than 40 meeting rooms feature centralized audio recording and separate controls for podiums and lights.

In addition, the Business Center is equipped to support almost any business transaction needed to keep convention operations running smoothly.

Cricket Arena, located at 2700 East Independence Boulevard, was the original Charlotte Coliseum. The landmark dome opened in 1955 and was the city's major sports and entertainment facility until the new Coliseum was built in 1988. After extensive refurbishing and up fitting, the venue reopened in 1993 as Independence Arena. It was renamed Cricket Arena in 2001.

The renovation restored the arena's classic ambiance and visitors to Cricket Arena experience the true feeling of a 1950s and '60s-style building. Vibrant neon colors and checkerboard tile floors are featured throughout the facility along with numerous brightly lit, spacious concession areas.

Cricket Arena is home to the East Coast Hockey League Charlotte Checkers hockey team. The Arena is also the Charlotte location for world-class figure skating and rodeo and bull riding competitions. The Arena is also the site of the North Carolina State High School Championships in wrestling.

Ovens Auditorium, located adjacent to Cricket Arena on East Independence Boulevard, opened along with the original Coliseum in 1955.

For nearly half a century, world-greats and countless graduates alike have graced the stage of Ovens Auditorium. Ovens has hosted top events and performances from the Billy Graham Crusade to Bob Hope to Bruce Springsteen. The symphony, opera, dance recitals and nationally known speakers have also found a home at Ovens, along with countless thousands of

graduates who have walked across its stage to receive their diplomas.

With a seating capacity of approximately 2,600, Ovens has hosted more than 6,900 events, attended by 9.2 million people.

Ovens Auditorium is truly a Charlotte landmark and will shine brightly for years to come as one of the jewels in Charlotte's crown.

Charlotte Coliseum, the Convention Center, Cricket Arena and Ovens Auditorium have contributed immeasurably to the growth of the Charlotte region. Members of the Charlotte Auditorium•Coliseum•Convention Center Authority are determined that these outstanding event facilities will continue to meet the city's entertainment, cultural and convention needs for decades to come.

Above: Cricket Arena.

Below: Ovens Auditorium.
COURTESY OF DUSTIN PECK, KPC PHOTOGRAPHY C2000.

YWCA
CENTRAL
CAROLINAS

The YWCA, the oldest and largest women's membership organization in the world, was established locally in 1902. While the YWCA has grown and changed over the years, the focus has remained remarkably consistent: empowering women and families with a concern for justice and the dignity of all people.

The first decade of service focused on the needs of women arriving in the city to work in the textile mills. The YWCA provided safe and affordable shelter, recreational programs, and education. The young Association quickly spawned outreach programs. One of these organizations, Traveler's Aid, started placing cribs in railroad stations to assist traveling mothers as early as 1909. An extension program placed libraries in factories, and a night school was begun in North Charlotte in 1911.

By 1914 the YWCA had its own new building on East Trade Street. The Association offered classes in the city's clothing factories in addition to access to a gymnasium, a directory of local boarding houses, and limited boarding in the YWCA facility. During this period, lectures were offered on such diverse topics as law, banking, city government, nursing, salesmanship, and "Vocations Open to Women: Supply Vs. Demand." These classes led to the establishment of an employment bureau for women.

With the coming of World War I in 1917, the Business Women's Employment Council was conceived to assist women attracted to Charlotte for jobs created by the war effort.

YWCA Founding Mothers

Simultaneously, the YWCA opened the city's first childcare center at the Highland Park Mill.

A pool was added to the Association's building on East Trade Street in 1922 and swimming classes became a main feature. Through the years, thousands have learned to swim in YWCA pools, allowing parents to breathe easier during the outdoor swimming months because their children were able to swim.

The challenges of the Great Depression were met head-on by the YWCA, with such practical programs as unemployment counseling, a job bank and access to rooms where women could practice their typing.

By the end of World War II, the YWCA's thrust had changed to vocational counseling for women facing unemployment. Employment fairs showed women the opportunities available in personnel, public relations, business and medicine. One session was devoted to equal pay for equal work, an idea that would become a cornerstone of the Women's Movement of the 1970s.

In 1964 the YWCA began an after-school and summer enrichment program for children whose families were receiving public assistance. Efforts were expanded to include additional federally funded childcare so mothers could work, which became the first of its kind in the state.

From its very beginnings, the YWCA has worked toward the elimination of racism. As far back as 1917, in cooperation with local African-American leaders, the YWCA established one of the earliest YWCA facilities for African Americans in the United States and the first branch in the South. The Phyllis Wheatley

❖

Above: The founding mothers of the YWCA (clockwise from top right): Mrs. F. C. Abbott, Mrs. W. O. Nisbett, and Mrs. W. S. Liddell.

Below: The building that served as the YWCA headquarters in 1902 (left) and YWCA Park Road today (right).

Branch was a thriving YWCA component offering a wide range of community services until 1966, when the Association's programs were fully integrated.

The organization also worked to promote awareness of international affairs for Charlotteans, spawning the local World Affairs Council, and presenting lectures from visiting relief workers and dignitaries. In addition to raising money to assist the children of Beijing, the local YWCA provided refuge and employment for a a Jewish teacher from Poland, during the time that would later become known as the Holocaust.

The Association opened a new facility on Park Road in 1965, providing a sixty-six-bed residence for women in transition, along with an indoor pool, exercise and meeting rooms, a full-service kitchen, chapel, lighted tennis courts and corporate offices. A full-size gymnasium was added in 1977.

In 1970 a new facility was erected on the site of the Association's building on East Trade Street. In 1989 an anonymous gift of $1.3 million provided for demolition of this facility and construction of the first nationally accredited childcare center in uptown Charlotte. The Uptown Child Development Center continues as a great community success story.

A century after it's founding, the YWCA Central Carolinas continues to respond to the community's needs by providing comprehensive programs for women, children and families. For example, the Women in Transition Program provides safe and affordable housing and intensive support services to meet the needs of single women who might otherwise be homeless.

Children and youth, a critical priority of the YWCA, are served in nineteen centers throughout Charlotte and Monroe. YWCA childcare and after school enrichment programs serve over 800 children, aged six weeks through fifteen years, each day. Eighty-five percent of these children live in public housing or in fragile neighborhoods. Thousands of children and adults are strengthened each year through YWCA programs including: the early childhood Family Support Project and Bright Beginnings program; a Literacy Project pilot; specialized Support Our Students (SOS) programs for

middle-school youth; and after-school and camp programs that include science labs, cultural enrichment activities, recreation, academic support and mentoring.

In January 2001 the YWCA reopened its Health & Fitness Center on Park Road with a full range of offerings for children through seniors. As it approaches its Centennial Celebration, the YWCA continues to weave opportunities for women at all stages of life. Just as the courageous women who founded the organization intended, the YWCA has come to symbolize a refuge—a safe place to grow and be nurtured.

This publication was made possible by a contribution from The Harkey Foundation, Inc., in honor of Mrs. Elizabeth A. Harkey, YWCA president 1977 79.

✧

Above: Camp E. W. Young, c. 1948 (left) and the YWCA Youth Development Program today (right).

Below: Children benefiting from YWCA's Uptown Child Development Centers.

QUEENS
COLLEGE

Queens College traces its history back to 1857 when it was founded as a Presbyterian-affiliated women's college. But while it is still church-affiliated, the college has changed dramatically as society's and the area's, needs have changed.

Queens became coeducational through a series of steps. In the aftermath of World War II, Queens admitted its first male students in a non-residential status. A coeducational evening college was created in 1948 and a coed MBA program was started in 1980. The institution went fully coed in all of its programs in 1987.

The evening college has evolved into the Pauline Lewis Hayworth College, named after a Queens alumna, which now provides working adults the opportunity to earn both undergraduate and graduate degrees without giving up their jobs.

The graduate business school was named the McColl School of Business in 1993 in honor of Hugh L. McColl, Jr., CEO and chairman of Bank of America (from which he retired in April 2001) and chairman of the Queens College Board of Trustees. The McColl School has blossomed into the premier graduate business school in the region, offering both MBA and Executive MBA degrees. With these many changes, Queens College has gained university status.

But what gives Queens its special dimension is a liberal arts philosophy that imbues all of its programs.

"Our purpose here is threefold: to help students lead noble lives, to pursue productive careers, and to develop global awareness," says President Dr. Billy O. Wireman. "We ask our students to explore these questions: What are the characteristics of a noble life? What is a just society? What is a good citizen?"

Queens continues its tradition of changing in response to the community's changing needs. In fall 2000, Queens completed a $1-million new façade for the library and the twenty-eight-thousand-square-foot Sykes Learning Center. The $11-million Sykes building is the first newly constructed facility on campus in about twenty years. In fall 2001, Union Theological Seminary of Richmond, Virginia, opened a satellite degree program on the Queens campus. Its faculty members will be available to teach in Queens' programs, too. Also in the fall of 2001, the campus opened a brand new $12-million residence hall.

The reason for all this activity is clear: Queens College is on the move. "Queens has been a real gem in the history of the city, and we want to be a major factor in shaping Charlotte's entry into the twenty-first century," Dr. Wireman says.

✧

COURTESY OF STEPHANIE CHESSON.

✧

*Above: The Charlotte Trolley offers charm
and connectivity in one package. It will
link South End with the Center City and
set the stage for other neighborhoods to
connect with one another through the
new trolley stops.*

*Below: The Tryon Center for Visual Arts,
which is housed in a fire-damaged church,
is one of the many new attractions in
the growing arts, entertainment, and
cultural districts.*

Charlotte Center City Partners believes that historic preservation stimulates and is compatible with economic development. The two can, with a little imagination and creativity, enhance one another.

Compelling examples of the adaptive reuse of structural treasures that have recently catalyzed economic development in downtown include: the Mint Museum of Craft + Design, which occupies what once was an upscale women's clothing store; and, the Tryon Center for Visual Art, housed in what not long ago was an abandoned, fire-scarred church building.

Perhaps the most dramatic example of this trend is the Partners' spearheading the vision for extending the vintage trolley line into the Center City. The promise of bringing the trolley back to downtown has already been a tremendous generator of economic development, even before the first track has been laid.

The group's conviction stems from several articles of faith. For starters, Center City Partners believes that cities—vibrant cities, exciting cities—are made up of character, and that a critical component of a city's unique character is an understanding that it's the small things that count. Building on that philosophy, Center City Partners advocates

initiatives that add character, champions preserving things that have indigenous value, while facilitating public and private development in Charlotte's Center City.

Center City Partners never tires of asking the question, "What's missing here?" Then—having come up with an answer—the organization works hard to fill in the blank. That's how a vendor has come to sell fresh-cut flowers from a cart at the corner of Trade and Tryon Streets, the City's historic center. That's also how pizza-by-the-slice came to be available in the Center City, and a farmer's market came to be a weekend fixture during the market season. It's how the annual holiday tree lighting ceremony came to be a major event.

Business leaders, Center City residents and city government formed the organization in 1979. It is funded by a municipal service assessment self-imposed by Center City property owners. Oversight is provided by the City Council and a board of directors comprised of representatives from Center City neighborhoods, businesses, government, hospitality, arts and cultural organizations. For more information, log on to the organization's web site at **www.charlottecentercity.org**.

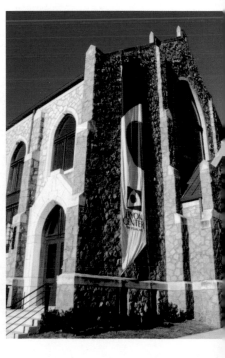

MINT MUSEUM OF ART/ MINT MUSEUM OF CRAFT + DESIGN

Founded in 1933 and opened to the public in 1936, the Mint Museum of Art is North Carolina's oldest art museum. The museum's name reflects the building's original use by the first branch of the United States Mint in Philadelphia. The original building, completed in 1836, was located in uptown Charlotte and operated as a mint until the Civil War. It was then used as a Confederate Headquarters and hospital, and later as an assay office. In 1933, when adjacent construction and expansion threatened its existence, a group of preservationists bought the building for $950 and moved it to its current site, where it has twice been expanded.

The cultures and artistic expressions of the Americas are featured in the museum's permanent collection. With a focus on art in the Americas, including influential art from other cultures, the Mint provides a unique perspective that spans from pre-Columbian through Colonial America to the present day. It provides a view of the Americas that opens windows to other cultures and times.

The collection includes American paintings and decorative arts, African art, North Carolina pottery and one of the country's most extensive displays of European ceramics and pre-Columbian art, providing a feast for the eyes, mind and soul.

Featured exhibitions at the museum include "On the Surface: Late 19th-Century Decorative Arts," May 26-August 12, 2001, followed by "The Sport of Life and Death: The Mesoamerican Ballgame," the first traveling exhibition on the ballgame in the United States. For more information about these and other exhibitions, check the Mint's Internet listings.

Bank of America gave the historic former Montaldo's department store building to the Mint in order to open a new museum devoted to the evolution of craft. The Mint Museum of Craft + Design, which opened in January 1999, focuses on the mediums of ceramic, fiber, glass, metal and wood.

In addition to outstanding exhibitions, programs and other activities, both museums boast unique museum shops with extensive selections of books, posters, jewelry and handmade crafts, many one-of-a-kind, which complement the exhibitions and permanent collections. The shops are open the same hours as the museums: Tuesday 10 a.m. to 10 p.m.; Wednesday through Saturday 10 a.m. to 5 p.m.; Sunday noon to 5 p.m. Both are closed Mondays and major holidays. Admission prices and operating schedules may vary, so call (704) 337-2000 for specific information. Visit www.mintmuseum.org for current exhibitions, programs, and more.

✧

Above: A piece of Charlotte's history still stands following the transformation of an upscale department store into the Mint Museum of Craft + Design.

Below: Visitors can still see the historic facade of the original Strickland design at the Mint Museum of Art on Randolph Road.

THE DUKE ENDOWMENT

The Duke Endowment was established December 11, 1924, when North Carolina industrialist and philanthropist James Buchanan "Buck" Duke created the trust that bears his name. But the roots of the foundation go much deeper.

When Washington Duke, Buck's father, returned to the family farm near Durham following service during the Civil War, his only material assets were two blind mules, fifty cents, and some tobacco that had been stored in a shed for several years. To survive, Washington Duke, along with Buck and his older brother, Benjamin, went on the road, selling small pouches of tobacco from the back of a wagon.

From this humble beginning, the small company eventually evolved into the mammoth American Tobacco Company. The family fortunes, however, were not dependent on tobacco. Long before an anti-trust decision split the tobacco company in 1911, the Dukes had invested in the textile industry and turned their attention to a new development, hydroelectric power. This led to the founding of Duke Power Company, now Duke Energy.

As their fortunes grew, the two brothers, Buck and Benjamin, worked together in business and philanthropy. Largely through the guidance of Benjamin Duke, the Duke family for many years contributed generously and privately to selected hospitals, orphanages, the Methodist Church, and Trinity College, a small Methodist-affiliated school. By the time Buck Duke signed the indenture creating The Duke Endowment in 1924, the general trends of the family's philanthropic interests were already established. The Endowment systematized and strengthened what already existed.

The Duke Endowment received its original assets from Buck Duke in the amount of $40 million, most of which consisted of stock in Duke Power Company. In accordance with his wishes, stock in Duke Energy remains the Endowment's largest single investment. The original asset base of $40 million was increased in 1925, when Buck Duke died and left the Endowment $67 million in his will.

A total of $17 million from these two gifts was designated for the construction of Duke University, formerly Trinity College. Thus, in 1925, the Endowment had $90 million on which to earn income and make grants. At the end of 2000, its assets were valued at more than $2.8 billion.

The Duke Endowment focuses its grant making on the areas specified in Buck Duke's indenture, healthcare and children's welfare in North and South Carolina, the rural United Methodist Church and its pastors in North Carolina, and four universities: Duke, Davidson, Furman, and Johnson C. Smith.

In 2000 the Endowment, which has its headquarters in Charlotte, appropriated almost $100 million for programs in North and South Carolina, ranking The Duke Endowment among the largest philanthropic foundations in the nation.

✧

Above: James Buchanan Duke.

Below: The statue of Buck Duke on the campus of Duke University.
COURTESY OF DUKE UNIVERSITY PHOTOGRAPHY. PHOTO BY LES TODD.

HISTORIC CHARLOTTE, INC.

We are proud to present *Historic Charlotte: An Illustrated History of Charlotte and Mecklenburg County* and hope you enjoy what Dr. Dan Morrill has written about our colorful past. Our mission is to advocate a greater appreciation of Charlotte-Mecklenburg's historic and architectural past. Established in 1991 as the Charlotte-Mecklenburg Preservation Foundation, our name was changed in August 1999, along with the focus of our organization. It is our hope to continue to raise awareness about our rich history through seminars and tours and by rewarding those in our community who have made a difference through their efforts in preservation.

Historic Charlotte's plans for the future include continuing our annual Preservation Celebration Awards and Blast for the Past. In 2001 we honored First Union National Bank for its efforts to save the Ratcliffe Florist Shop, the Keith Corporation for its efforts to save the Carolina Theatre, and David T. Ritch for Lifetime Achievement. Past honorees include Bank of America for its efforts to restore the Mint Museum of Craft and Design and the Tryon Center for Visual Art, John Crosland who generously donated the air rights to the Latta Arcade to our organization, Bruce Parker for his efforts to restore the Great Aunt Stella Center, and Dan Morrill for Lifetime Achievement.

It is our dream to establish a storefront along the Trolley line in the near future where we will be able to support all of our history and heritage organizations in this community, provide walking and driving tours, and have items for sale which are symbolic of our past.

Charlotte has a rich history, vivid heritage, exciting present, and immeasurable potential. What was once a wooded crossroads of Native American trading paths has become a vibrant, progressive, and unique city. As we embark on a new millennium, we are keenly aware of how Charlotte and Mecklenburg County are evolving and growing. Historic Charlotte is committed to preserving and celebrating our past.

We want to acknowledge our board of directors and staff who continue to work on behalf of Historic Charlotte, Inc.

Frank D. Whitney, president
Lisa Lee Morgan, vice president
James N. Reichard, treasurer
Cheryl L. Helden, secretary
Anthony T. Pressley, past president
Tiara Able
Tattie Bos
Jeffrey G. Doggett
Justin D. Faircloth
Rodger F. Hinton
Edwin R. McCoy III
John E. Misenheimer
Walter S. Price
Ross Richardson
David T. Ritch
Betty Seizinger
Jennie Sheppard
Mack Staton, Ph.D.
Fitzhugh L. Stout
Lynn Wheeler
Sally Billington, executive director

For more than a century, the tower of Biddle Memorial Hall at Johnson C. Smith University has been a major landmark in the City of Charlotte and a revered symbol of an institution rich in history and bright with promise for the future.

The beginnings of Johnson C. Smith University date from 1867 when two Presbyterian ministers, S. C. Alexander and W. L. Miller, persuaded the Catawba Presbytery to establish a school for the education of African-American men. With a donation by Colonel W. E. Myers of eight acres of land on Beatties Ford Road, the school, named the Freedmen's College of North Carolina, came into existence.

When Mrs. Mary D. Biddle of Philadelphia, Pennsylvania learned of the new school, she pledged $1,400 toward its development. In appreciation for this first generous contribution, the name was changed to Biddle Memorial Institute in honor of Mrs. Biddle's husband, Major Henry Biddle. In 1876 the North Carolina State Legislature changed the name to Biddle University.

In 1923, as a result of the generous gifts of Mrs. Jane Berry Smith of Pittsburgh, Pennsylvania, the institution received the name by which it is nationally and internationally known today, Johnson C. Smith University. In honor of her husband, Mrs. Smith provided funds for several buildings including a dormitory and science hall. Her gifts were augmented by

contributions from philanthropist James B. Duke and the school continues to receive support from The Duke Endowment. In 1932 Johnson C. Smith University opened its doors to both women and men.

Since then, the University has continued to make historical moves as the first historically black college or university to become an IBM ThinkPad University, distributing laptops to every full-time student.

Recently, the University invested $7 million in a renovation and expansion of the James B. Duke Memorial Library, $4 million in a state-of-the-art technology center, and $8 million in a new track and field academic sports complex. The University is currently completing a $6.6-million campaign to renovate historic Biddle Hall and beginning restoration of another University landmark, the Davis House. This is the home of the first African-American professor at Johnson C. Smith University and an economic spur for the northwest Charlotte community. A 1999 study conducted by John E. Connaughton showed Johnson C. Smith having a $60-million impact on the City of Charlotte.

Today, as a coeducational liberal arts institution, the University has an enrollment of approximately 1,580 students from cities across the nation and countries around the globe, a group of distinctive alumni, many of who are recognized as leaders in business, education and other professions, and a distinguished faculty, eighty percent of whom hold doctorates.

At its inception, the University was committed to academic excellence, leadership training and community service. That commitment, a gift from the past, has been threaded into its exceptional present and its promise for a more than exceptional future.

JOHNSON C. SMITH UNIVERSITY

✧

Above: Dr. Dorothy Cowser Yancy, president, Johnson C. Smith University.

Below: Biddle Memorial Hall on the campus of Johnson C. Smith University has been a Charlotte landmark for more than a century.

CHARLOTTE KNIGHTS

✧

Below: Crockett Park on Magnolia Avenue in Dilworth was professional baseball's home in Charlotte for forty-five years. The stadium burned to the ground in 1985.

Bottom: Knights Stadium in Fort Mill, with 10,002 seats, opened in 1990.

Professional baseball will celebrate its centennial season in Charlotte during the 2001 season when the Charlotte Knights take the field as one of the top teams in the Triple-A International League.

Professional baseball in Charlotte began in 1901 when the Portsmouth team of the Virginia-North Carolina League went broke halfway through the season and the players transferred to the Queen City.

Since that humble beginning, Charlotte's professional baseball teams have won 15 championships and made 30 post-season appearances, including one in the Triple-A World Series.

Charlotte teams have played in a number of leagues over the years—Southern, Tri-State, South-Atlantic and others—and have been farm clubs of several major league teams, including its current affiliation with the Chicago White Sox.

Charlotte fans have cheered for dozens of future major league stars, including Hall of Famer Early Wynn, Harmon Killebrew, Tony Oliva, Eddie Murray, and Carl Yastrzemski.

From 1901 until 1973, long before NBA basketball, Charlotte's professional baseball team was known as the Hornets. At one point, the Hornets, who played in Dilworth's Latta Park, won twenty-five consecutive games, a winning streak that remains the second longest in minor league history.

In 1940 the Hornets moved to a new ballpark on Magnolia Avenue, near South Boulevard. At the time, the team was a Washington Senators farm club and the stadium was named Calvin Griffith Park in honor of the Senators' owner.

Baseball left Charlotte in 1973 but sports promoter Frances Crockett brought it back in 1976 as a Double-A affiliate of the Minnesota Twins. Later the team became affiliated with the Baltimore Orioles and was renamed the O's. The stadium, known then as Crockett Park, burned to the ground in 1985, but the team continued to play in makeshift facilities until it was sold to George Shinn in 1987.

Shinn changed the team's name to the Knights and built Knights Stadium, a 10,002-seat, state-of-the art stadium just off I-77 in Fort Mill that opened in 1990. In 1993 Charlotte was awarded a new Triple-A expansion franchise and the Knights joined the International League. The team won the International League's Governors' Cup championship in its inaugural AAA season, Charlotte's first championship in any sport since the O's won the Southern League in '84.

In December 1997, Don Beaver, along with partners Bill Allen and Derick Close, purchased the team from Shinn. In 1999 the Knights again won the Governors' Cup Championship and advanced to the Triple-A World Series.

After a century, professional baseball still attracts hundreds of thousands of excited fans each year and the Knights are once again thinking expansion, perhaps a new stadium in Charlotte's South End...maybe even a major league franchise sometime soon.

CHARLOTTE MUSEUM OF HISTORY

Visitors to the Charlotte Museum of History can experience the echoes of 250 years of backcountry American life as they tour three national treasures—the spacious, $6.5 million new educational and research center, the Hezekiah Alexander Home and the American Freedom Bell.

The thirty-six-thousand-square-foot Museum building, which opened in late 1999, features a thirty-five-foot atrium and multiple-use hall to accommodate seminars, lectures, and receptions. This rotunda branches out to two exhibition corridors accessing 5 exhibition halls, 2 smaller rotundas, and 3 learning centers. An estimated fifty thousand visitors annually will tour exhibits including everything from a Charlotte gold mine to a facsimile of the Mecklenburg County Courthouse that once stood at The Square and was the site of the American Revolutionary Battle of Charlotte.

The Museum's primary focus is the two Carolinas, with emphasis on the Piedmont region. A core exhibit spans the Pre-Colonial Period to the twentieth century. Changing exhibits portray Early American history. Other features include craft demonstrations, public programs, a research library/reading room, archives, and a gift shop.

Docents dressed in authentic eighteenth century costumes lead tours of the historic Hezekiah Alexander home, built in 1774 and situated on its original site. Alexander, one of North Carolina's most venerated citizens, was among the twenty-seven signers of the Mecklenburg Declaration of Independence and also helped frame the North Carolina State Constitution and Bill of Rights.

The American Freedom Bell, a gift from the Belk Foundation to the people of America,

symbolizes the patriotic heritage of the people of Charlotte, Mecklenburg County, and the two Carolinas. It was created to honor all those who contributed their lifeblood, efforts, and passion to the cause of American freedom. This seven-and-a-half-ton bell, which has a hammer weighing three hundred pounds, tolls on key dates. These include the Fourth of July and May 20, when Charlotte celebrates the 1775 Mecklenburg Declaration of Independence from British rule. It is inscribed in Latin with the year of its installation, *Anno XX*. Below the words, "The American Freedom Bell" is an admonition: "Never Forget that You Are Free," and a two-inch hornet.

The grounds, themselves, are of historical interest. Thermal imaging is helping determine where formal buildings such as outbuildings and slave quarters may have been placed over two centuries ago. This aerial photography process utilizes an un-cooled sensor that can differentiate soil temperatures to detect differences between undisturbed and disturbed soils.

Administered by the independent, private and non-profit Hezekiah Alexander Foundation, the Museum, Homesite and Freedom Bell help make learning an enjoyable, lifelong pursuit.

✧

Above: The Charlotte Museum of History.

Below: The Hezekiah Alexander homesite in Charlotte, North Carolina.

CHARLOTTE COUNTRY DAY SCHOOL

Charlotte Country Day School, the oldest independent school in the city, also ranks as the tenth largest independent day school in the United States. Throughout its sixty-year history, the school has earned a stellar reputation for academic excellence in college preparatory education through superior teaching of a rigorous curriculum. Country Day's success is due in large part to its focus on the whole child, in the belief that education is not just about what a child learns, but also about what a child becomes.

Emphasizing five key values—individual potential, character, diversity, community, and vision—the school strives to:

- To develop the abilities, skills, and talents of each individual by promoting active participation in a broad range of academic, athletic, and extracurricular activities within a supportive, nurturing environment;
- To recognize the dignity and worth of each individual, while cultivating high standards of moral and ethical behavior consistent with the school's Judeo-Christian heritage;
- To cultivate a school community that reflects cultural, ethnic, racial, and socioeconomic diversity;
- To inspire service and leadership within the school and community and prepare students for stewardship, responsible citizenship, and global awareness;

- To equip students with the knowledge, skills, and confidence to shape and respond to the future;
- To heighten the sense of belonging and encourage self-discovery, the school has three divisions on two campuses–Lower School for junior kindergarten through fourth grade; Middle School, on its own campus, for fifth through eighth grades; and Upper School for grades nine through twelve. Each division has its own facilities and programs geared to the needs of that age group and its own carefully chosen faculty.

Charlotte Country Day School offers a nurturing community bound together by a shared commitment to academic and personal excellence and by shared values. With a strong traditional academic core, it has added innovative programs and teaching methods that foster a sound scholastic foundation and the critical-thinking skills needed to apply that knowledge to the real world. Experiential, hands-on learning is offered at every grade level and in every discipline.

Teachers and administrators, who help students handle their strengths with confidence and their weaknesses with dignity, believe that each child comes to the school already equipped with a distinct set of talents and abilities. Discovering those and helping students shape and develop them are hallmarks of this school. Alumni, who have made numerous and profound contributions to their professions and their communities, offer tangible evidence of the lasting value of a Charlotte Country Day School education.

✧

Above: Margaret Gragg, head of the Charlotte Country Day School, talks to students.

Below: In the 1950s, when most students lived in the city rather than the suburbs, Charlotte Country Day School acquired its first bus to get pupils to the school on Sardis Road.

THE ARTS & SCIENCE COUNCIL

The Arts & Science Council (ASC) is guided by a belief that the lives of the people in the Charlotte/Mecklenburg area are enriched by cultural experiences.

Organized in 1958, ASC combines resources from an Annual Fund Drive, allocations from local and state governments, and its endowment to support cultural organizations, cultural educational programs and creative individuals in Charlotte-Mecklenburg and throughout the region.

Nearly 34,000 individual donors contribute to the ASC Annual Fund Drive, which accounts for 70 percent of the total donations received. ASC's donors have made Charlotte number one in the nation among United Arts Funds in per-capita giving and worksite campaigns, and number two among the largest United Arts Funds in the nation.

Thanks to this generous support, ASC reached a new level of grant making in 2001. It distributed $14 million in grants to 28 arts, science, and history organizations and through the Community Cultural Connections grants program supported over 60 community and neighborhood organizations. More than fifty individuals were awarded fellowships or regional grants. Combined, the cultural community offers events and programming to enrich more than 2.8 million lives each year and provide more than 1.2 million cultural experiences to children.

Children of the Charlotte/Mecklenburg region are perhaps the most influenced by ASC programs. The ASC broadens cultural education within the schools by funding the Cultural Education Collaborative, a non-profit agency developed to increase partnerships between cultural organizations, creative individuals and the Charlotte-Mecklenburg Schools. In addition, ASC cultural partners provide meaningful experiences to children that increase their appreciation of culture.

To ensure that art is accessible throughout the community, the ASC also provides support for art in public places through ASC Public Art, Inc. Each year, the City of Charlotte and Mecklenburg County set aside up to one percent of funds used to construct or renovate public buildings to commission works of public art. ASC also coordinates public art projects for private corporations. These art works range from murals at the Charlotte Convention Center to a kinetic neon installation for Duke Energy's headquarters to an interactive sound installation at Bank of America's retail and parking center.

In addition to the intrinsic value of the arts, cultural activity generates jobs and economic prosperity. A recent economic impact study completed by the University of North Carolina at Charlotte clearly demonstrates that our cultural institutions enrich the region's economy.

The economic study revealed that ASC affiliates support more than seventeen hundred direct or indirect jobs to the local economy. In addition, ASC affiliates contributed more than $94 million in direct or indirect revenues through ticket sales and salaries as well as hotel, restaurant, automotive and retail spending.

Through the Arts & Science Council, more than 800 volunteers, 34,000 donors, nearly 600 companies, along with city, county, and state governments and the school system, support Charlotte's arts, science, cultural education and history community.

Looking to the future, ASC will continue to broaden support and access of Charlotte's cultural opportunities.

❖

The Arts & Science Council promotes arts, science, and history by supporting individual artists, organizations, and community groups throughout Charlotte-Mecklenburg. With the help of ASC's Community Cultural Connections program, George Wallace and the Grier Heights Economic Foundation are preserving the history of Grier Heights, one of the first African-American subdivisions in the area. The foundation is housed in the neighborhood's Billingsville School, where Wallace's former second-grade classroom now serves as his office. Built in 1927, the school was known as a "Rosenwald" school, one of several schools built throughout the South by Julius Rosenwald, a Jewish philanthropist, and Booker T. Washington for a new generation of free blacks. Progressively constructed, the Billingsville School was also the first school in Mecklenburg County to have a brick veneer, as opposed to the wooden clapboard typical of the time period.

COURTESY OF JEFF CRAVOTTA.

CHARLOTTE TECHNICAL HIGH SCHOOL

Around 1920 several prominent citizens, led by Justice Heriot Clarkson, saw the need for a Vocational School to serve children from the Belmont and North Charlotte communities. Cotton mills had come to the communities and the possibility of college for the children of the mill workers was slim.

Clarkson, aided by other citizens, convinced the members of the Junior Order of American Mechanics that industrial education was needed, especially for children of blue-collar parents.

Construction began following approval of a $750,000 bond issue, and the school known as Belmont Vocational School, was completed in September 1922. Harry K. Moore of Middleton, Ohio, became the principal of the school and the first class graduated in 1926.

✦

Above: Charlotte Tech High School served the Belmont and North Charlotte communities from 1922 until 1954.

Below: Teachers at Tech High in 1926.

When the school opened the high school classes did not fill all the rooms, so primary classes from the overcrowded Villa Heights School used them. The new school included the seventh, eighth and ninth grades that first year. As the school continued to grow, the junior and senior high school classes soon took over the rooms use by the primary grades.

Moore resigned in 1926 and Forest T. Selby became the second principal. Selby, a graduate of Miami University in Oxford, Ohio had served as instructor and counselor at North Carolina State College and as industrial arts teacher in the Durham, North Carolina, schools. He was also head of the adult education program in the Charlotte schools. Courses in diverse subjects were added to the curriculum and a

woodworking shop was built at the rear of the main building. Night classes were conducted for men and women, including classes for mill mechanics. In 1927 the school was renamed Charlotte Technical High School.

As classes graduated, Tech High students entered a wide variety of careers. These graduates give high priority to class reunions as a way to keep in touch with their classmates. When the Class of 1954 graduated and Tech became Hawthorne Junior High, reunions became even more important. As a result of a reunion that included classes of 1951–54, the Tech High Lunch Bunch was organized January 15, 1998, with Doug Dellinger, Class of '52, as chairman.

The group, which meets the third Thursday of each month, has become a huge success. Over seven hundred newsletters go out each month to former students, providing news and information about old friends.

Under the leadership of John R. Bradey, Class of '46, a scholarship fund was established to honor a beloved teacher, Lula Faye Clegg, for her dedication over forty-two years of teaching civics, American History, and world history. A steering committee of former students works with John to provide publicity and handle details of the fund, which now totals over $115,000. More than a dozen scholarships have been awarded.

Also, under the leadership of Lois Moore Yandle, Class of '46, twelve former Tech WWII veterans, who left school before graduating, received their diplomas in 2000.

According to the Reverend Grady Faulk, Class of '52, the Tech High Lunch Bunch participates in a number of community activities as a way of honoring their teachers of long ago who taught them love, discipline and self-reliance. These lessons, learned at their beloved Charlotte Technical High School, have served them well throughout life.

Festival in the Park, a colorful celebration of arts and crafts, performances, and great food, has been a Charlotte tradition since 1964.

Grant Whitney, an executive with Belk Stores Services, organized the first Festival at the suggestion of former Mayor John Belk, who was president of the Chamber of Commerce.

The initial Festival in the Park had a budget of $4,000, ten exhibit tents, an art exhibit, and a few stage performances. Festival in the Park has grown to over 100 tents, more than eighty panels of art, six performing arts stages, a children's 'hands-on' arts and crafts area, and various special activity and demonstration areas.

Festival in the Park, held each September in Freedom Park, has received the prestigious *Sunshine Artists Magazine* award as one of the "Top 200 Festivals in the United States."

Whitney, the guiding spirit behind the Festival's success, died in 1997, but his love and enthusiasm for the Festival was embraced by the leadership that now organizes Festival in the Park each year. Volunteers, private donors, and corporate sponsors, along with physical support from Mecklenburg County Park and Recreation Department, have kept the Festival alive.

Festival in the Park continues to serve the community by producing a wholesome, quality event that strives to carry out Grant Whitney's vision: "A completely free, family oriented event that brings arts, crafts, performing arts and just plain fun to all who attend."

FOUNDATION FOR THE CAROLINAS

The purpose of Foundation For The Carolinas is to advance philanthropy by serving donors, increasing charitable giving and improving communities, now and for all time.

The Foundation was established in 1958 by a group of community leaders with the vision to help plan for the area's charitable needs. Gordon Berg, who championed the community foundation concept in Charlotte and oversaw its operation until 1986, fostered this vision. From its first gift of $3,000 from the United Way, the Foundation has grown into a major philanthropic resource for the Piedmont region of the Carolinas.

The Foundation links donors to the charitable causes they care about. Donors recommend the majority of Foundation grants for specific charitable purposes through charitable gift funds they establish. Areas of giving are limitless and include everything from arts and education to environment and religion.

The Foundation also provides funding and convenes concerned citizens and groups to tackle significant regional issues. These efforts have resulted in many noteworthy programs including

the Regional HIV/AIDS Consortium, Voices & Choices, the Community Building Initiative and the Carolinas Land Conservation Network.

Gift by gift and donor by donor, Foundation For The Carolinas is building a legacy for generations to come.

✧

Foundation For The Carolinas—building a caring community for generations to come.

THE MARKETPLACE

Mecklenburg County's retail and commercial

establishments and manufacturing base

offer an impressive variety of choices for

North Carolinans and visitors alike

✧

The Mecklenburg County Courthouse at the corner of West Trade Street and Church Street. The courthouse is no longer standing.

BELK, INC.

✦

Top: Belk, Inc. founder William Henry Belk.

Above: Belk, Inc. founder Dr. John M. Belk.

Below: The Belk Brothers opened their fourth store in 1895 on East Trade Street in Charlotte.

Charlotte is the home of Belk, Inc., the nation's largest privately-owned department store organization, which operates more than 200 fashion stores in 13 states across the Southeast and Mid-Atlantic regions.

Belk has been an integral part of the Charlotte community since September 25, 1895, when the company's founder William Henry Belk and his brother, Dr. John M. Belk, opened their fourth store in a four-room building on the first block of East Trade Street.

William Henry Belk moved from Monroe, North Carolina, site of the first Belk store, to manage the Charlotte store, and the Queen City soon became the base of operations and heart of the rapidly growing retail enterprise.

The Belk store in downtown Charlotte was expanded and renovated numerous times over the years, and eventually became one of the South's largest department stores. Subsequently other Belk stores were opened to serve the Charlotte area at SouthPark Mall (1970), Eastland Mall (1975), and Carolina Place Mall in Pineville, North Carolina, (1991). A BelkExpress specialty store offering cosmetics and hosiery opened downtown in 1993.

When the original Charlotte Belk store was closed in 1987, the company donated the property to the City of Charlotte as the new site for the North Carolina Blumenthal Performing Arts Center, which opened in 1992 and includes the two-thousand-seat Belk Theater.

Belk established a corporate buying office in the Charlotte store in 1927. Relocated to a new building on East Fifth Street in 1949, it was incorporated as Belk Stores Services, Inc. in 1955. Belk Stores Services moved to a new 562,000-square-foot building on West Tyvola Road in 1988, the year of the company's hundredth anniversary.

Belk was founded on May 29, 1888, when twenty-six-year-old William Henry Belk opened a small bargain store in Monroe, North Carolina, with $750 in savings, a $500 ten-percent-interest loan from a local widow, and about $3,000 worth of goods taken on consignment from a bankrupt store. In less than seven months, he had paid off his debts and netted a $3,300 profit.

Belk introduced some radically new retailing ideas for the time. He bought and sold large quantities of goods for cash at a low mark-up. All merchandise was clearly marked with its retail price—there was no haggling over prices. If customers were not completely satisfied, they could return merchandise for a refund.

Belk's innovative advertising often included lively and humorous newspaper ads, which he wrote himself. The slogan for his first store was "Cheap Goods Sell Themselves," and he referred to this and other early stores as "The Cheapest Store on Earth."

In 1891, William Henry persuaded his brother, Dr. John M. Belk, to leave the medical profession and become a partner in the Monroe store. They changed the company's name to Belk Brothers Company, and together they began expanding the business throughout the Carolinas and the Southeast. John continued managing the Monroe store until his death in 1928 at age sixty-two. William Henry remained active in the business until his death in 1952 at age eighty-nine.

The number of Belk stores grew to nine by 1910; 28 by 1920; 62 by 1930; 176 by 1940; and 280 by 1950.

Beginning in the 1960s, Belk began its migration from smaller downtown locations to modern, greatly expanded anchor facilities in regional malls. This enabled Belk to become the dominant fashion department store in most of its markets throughout the Southeast, offering a wide selection of top national brands of fashion apparel, shoes and accessories for men, women and children, cosmetics, home furnishings, housewares, gift and guild,

jewelry and other merchandise. Belk is also known for its private brand merchandise, which provides exclusive fashion, quality and value to its customers.

John M. Belk, son of the founder, is chairman of the board and chief executive officer of Belk, Inc. He served as Charlotte's mayor from 1969–1977, and is one of the community's most respected business leaders. Thomas M. Belk Jr., H.W. McKay Belk and John R. Belk, nephews of John Belk and sons of the late Thomas M. Belk, longtime president of Belk stores, serve as presidents of the company.

In May 1998, the former 112 separate Belk corporations were merged into a single company—Belk, Inc. Its four operating divisions are based in Charlotte, North Carolina; Raleigh, North Carolina; Greenville, South Carolina; and Jacksonville, Florida.

The company's mission is to be the leader in its markets in selling merchandise that meets customers' needs for fashion, quality, value and selection; to offer superior customer service; and to make a reasonable profit.

Reflecting the beliefs of its founders, Belk wants customers to feel confident of receiving honest and fair treatment, getting full value for every dollar and being satisfied in every respect, so that they will shop with Belk stores again.

Belk recognizes its responsibility to the people who make the company's growth and success possible. Belk remains committed today, as it has been throughout the company's long history, to maintaining relationships of integrity, honesty, and fairness with customers, associates, vendors, other business partners, stockholders, and the citizens of every community it serves.

Belk has a strong tradition of community service and philanthropy. Belk associates volunteer time, talents and leadership to innumerable civic and charitable organizations and community improvement efforts. Belk stores, along with the Belk Foundation, make generous contributions each year to schools, hospitals, churches and other human service organizations devoted to improving the quality of life in their communities.

✧

Above: John M. Belk, son of Belk founder William Henry Belk and former Charlotte mayor, is chairman of the board and chief executive officer of Belk, Inc.

Bottom, left: Belk Stores Services, Inc. began in 1927 as a buying office for Belk stores. In 1988, the year of the company's hundredth anniversary, it moved from its East Fifth Street location to a new 562,000-square-foot building on West Tyvola Road.

Bottom, right: The company's flagship store at Charlotte's SouthPark Mall opened in 1970.

WTVI

Since 1965, WTVI has provided quality public television for a 13-county area of North and South Carolina that now includes more than 326,000 households. From its beginnings as an instructional unit of The Charlotte-Mecklenburg Board of Education, WTVI has evolved into a sophisticated public television station offering a diverse mix of programs and services, everything from Big Bird to Ken Burns documentaries on The Civil War and Jazz.

WTVI's first broadcast, on August 27, 1965, was a children's show called *What's New* and a 60-minute program of folk songs starring Pete Seeger and Joan Baez. Other early programs included live broadcasts of The Charlotte-Mecklenburg School Board meet-ings, the popular PBS program *Upstairs, Downstairs* and *Someone Has to Listen*, an examination of racial conflicts in the public schools. The first broadcast of *Sesame Street* came in November 1969.

Also in 1969, WTVI received its first Public Broadcasting grant to produce a five-part series, *The Walls Come Tumbling Down*, based on *American Negro Folklore*, a book by a humanities professor at Livingstone College.

WTVI's growth was accelerated in 1982 when The Charlotte-Mecklenburg Public Broadcasting Authority assumed WTVI's license and the station began to assume a broader, more community-oriented role.

Improvements came quickly once WTVI became a locally owned public station. In 1985, the station began broadcasting with a new transmitter, made possible by a $705,500 federal grant. An even more powerful trans-mitter went into service in 1987, the result of a $3.1 million Mecklenburg County bond issue. Then, in 1989, ground was broken for a new building on Commonwealth Avenue. Another County bond issue provided $7.75 million for upgraded transmitting facilities and to upfit the new building.

Strong local financial support also enabled WTVI to keep pace with rapid technological improvements in the television industry. Satellite transmissions and local color production came along in the late '70s and stereo sound was added in 1985. The studios were expanded and renovated in 1990 and a new 1,200-foot tower and transmitter were dedicated in 1992.

WTVI's mission is to provide quality, educational, informative and entertaining programs and communication services, reflecting the values and cultures of its regional public television audience. One of the best examples of how WTVI fulfills this mission is the Ready to Learn service.

The Ready to Learn service combines PBS's award-winning children's television programming with a variety of community outreach efforts to help build children's learning skills. WTVI's Ready to Learn service currently serves 6,300 at-risk children in 175 sites located throughout the station's 13-county viewing area.

Ready to Learn provides free community workshops, books, curriculum materials and resources for area parents, teachers and day-care providers. The workshops are designed to train adults to teach children the basic skills that will help them enter school ready to learn and succeed throughout life.

Other landmark local programs originated by WTVI include *Carolina Business Review*, a weekly report of local and regional business news; *Spotlight*, a local performing arts series featuring well-known Charlotte pianist and composer Loonis McGlohon; and *Southern Piedmont Report*, a review of state legislative activity affecting the area.

Other notable locally-produced programs include *Healthwise*, a call-in show featuring doctors who discuss the latest in health trends; *Final Edition*, a weekly summary of local news;

For Pet's Sake, where local veterinarians answer questions from viewers regarding pet care; and *Charlotte Tonight*, a new weekly public affairs show with a focus on current news makers.

WTVI operates with an annual budget of more than $4 million and nearly 57% of this amount comes from the private sector, including memberships and program underwriting. Mecklenburg County provides 29% of the budget and the remainder comes from the Corporation for Public Broadcasting and a Ready to Learn grant.

As it moves into its fourth decade of distinguished service to the region, WTVI is gearing up for the next big revolution in broadcast technology—digital and high definition transmission. WTVI is out front locally as commercial and public television stations begin to comply with a federal mandate that all stations must convert to digital technology by 2003. Mecklenburg County commissioners have approved a $10 million investment for the digital makeover, which will provide a vastly improved image on the screen as well as much greater production capability. Ultimately, the new technology will increase WTVI's capacity to four channels. With this in mind, plans are underway for a 24-hour children's service, PBS University, as well as collaborations with major area non-profit organizations.

As this vision becomes a reality, WTVI will continue to adhere to its guiding principle: that the station's work inspire, inform, educate, entertain, or help unify the community.

✧

Above: As part of its comunity outreach, WTVI has strongly supported programs to improve Charlotte neighborhoods. Hal Bouton, left, president and CEO of WTVI, presents a check from WTVI to leaders of one local community program.

Below: WTVI's renovated and expanded studios on Commonwealth Avenue were dedicated in 1990.

SPEIZMAN INDUSTRIES

The fascinating story of Speizman Industries begins with David Speizman, who immigrated to the United States from Poland in 1905. David, then twenty-one years old, had been a weaver in Poland and was able to find a job working for his wife's uncle, who owned a silk-weaving mill in Patterson, New Jersey.

David later became foreman of the weave room and was able to save enough money to bring his wife and infant son, Morris, to the U.S. A few years later, David moved his family to a small town near Hamilton, Ontario, where he became a peddler and, later the owner of a small store.

The family then moved to Pennsylvania, where David worked in a weaving mill and began buying and selling used textile machinery and yarn. Morris Speizman worked in the same weaving room at night to earn enough money to attend college. After graduating from Philadelphia Textile School in 1928, Morris sold novelty-sewing threads in New York City for several years.

In 1936, Morris and his wife, Sylvia, decided to move south and start a new business. When they reached Charlotte, so the story goes, Sylvia said she was tired and maybe they should stop for the night. They looked around, liked what they saw, and never left. Later that same year, Morris Speizman Company, Inc., now known as Speizman Industries, was founded.

Morris sold a variety of used machinery, including dye machines, commercial laundry equipment and sock and stocking machines in North and South America. But he found he had his most success selling sock machines to the many hosiery mills in North Carolina.

A major event for the company occurred in the early 1950s when Hanes Hosiery Mills found themselves without any of the new seamless stocking machines, which were being used by their competitors. Hanes had stayed with "fully-fashioned" machines, which produced ladies' stockings with a seam. When they realized their marketing mistake, they called Morris Speizman and had him quietly purchase all the seamless stocking knitting machines he could find in the United States.

Morris bought over three thousand machines in a six-week period and sold them for a commission to Hanes. This enabled Hanes Hosiery to virtually corner the market on the production of seamless stockings for a one-year period.

Also during the '50s, Morris was able to buy and liquidate a hosiery factory in Galax, Virginia, which gave him the seed capital to become a force in the used hosiery machine business.

In 1958, Morris Speizman's oldest son, Larry, graduated from North Carolina State University and joined the company. Larry moved to New York and concentrated on selling sweater and circular fabric knitting machines. Morris Speizman's youngest son, Bob, graduated from the Wharton School at the University of Pennsylvania in 1962. The following year, Bob moved back to Charlotte to join the family business, concentrating his efforts on selling pantyhose and sock machines. In 1967, Morris Speizman retired from day-to-day business, turning operating control over to his sons.

Morris Speizman was an outstanding leader in Charlotte's civic and religious activities. His many accomplishments include president and honorary life president of Temple Israel; president, World Council of Synagogues; president, Mint Museum of Art; and chairman of

the board, Mercy Hospital. He was on the boards of the Charlotte Chamber of Commerce, the National Council of Christians and Jews, the Charlotte Mecklenburg Red Cross, and many others. He was awarded a Doctor of Humane Letters by Sacred Heart College in 1980.

The late '60s and early '70s, saw the company's outerwear division grow more rapidly than the hosiery division. Unfortunately, between 1972 and 1976, sixty-eight percent of all those who had purchased double knit machines from the company went bankrupt. Speizman Industries had to repurchase $18 million of the machines, whose market value had dropped from $50,000 to $50 per unit. Sales plummeted to about $12 million in 1977 but through the diligence of management and its loyal employees, Speizman Industries overcame the setback and repaid all debt.

During this period, Larry retired as president and Bob took control of the company. During the late '70s and '80s, Speizman Industries went back to what it knew best—the sock and hosiery business. The company began production of its Amy cushion-sole sock knitter, named after Bob's daughter, and sold more than five thousand of the machines throughout the world. The company also began selling double cylinder sock knitters manufactured by the Lonati Company of Italy. This part of the company grew and, in 1989, Speizman Industries decided to concentrate all its efforts on the distribution of sock and hosiery equipment manufactured by the Lonati Group.

The past few years have been years of rapid growth for Speizman Industries, acquiring Wink Davis Corporation, a distributor of commercial laundry equipment, and TMC Automation, a manufacturer of sock packaging machines.

During the '90s, Bob's sons, Bryan and Mark, joined the company and work in the sock and seamless garment part of the business. In addition, Bob's son, Barry, now works with the yarn machine division and son-in-law, Don Mullen, is in charge of the Wink Davis division. There now have been four generations of the Speizman family selling textile equipment in the United States and Canada.

"Our company tries to distinguish itself by adding more value to the products we sell than any of our competitors," says Bob Speizman. "We also try to align ourselves with the best suppliers who have technical superiority in their field."

"Most of all, we have always taken pride in honest, ethical business dealings We are aggressive and we want to get every deal, but only if we can close the deal in an honest and ethical manner."

Above: The Hosiery Machine Assembly Department at Speizman Industries in 1977.

Below: Speizman Industries moved into this 220,000 square foot warehouse and office building near Tyvola Road in 1999.

PERRY'S FINE, ANTIQUE & ESTATE JEWELRY

"It never ceases to amaze me what people have in their safety deposit boxes or jewelry cases," says Ernest Perry. For more than twenty years, Perry and his wife Priscilla have come across thousands of curious treasures which they pass on to the public at Perry's Fine, Antique & Estate Jewelry in SouthPark.

Intriguing stories often accompany the acquisition of the estate jewelry. One such story is the "Tale of the Potato Brooch." The story's beginning takes place in the late 1940s, when a woman was killed in a tragic plane crash. Her family searched for her cherished diamond brooch after her death but couldn't find it. Eventually, everyone quit looking and forgot about it.

✧

Ernest and Priscilla Perry

Weeks later, while she was cleaning her mother's house, the daughter came across a bag of potatoes sprouting in the pantry. As she carried the bag to the trash, she felt something hard at the bottom of the bag. Further investigation revealed that it was the diamond brooch. The mother had hidden it in the potatoes for safekeeping. The daughter almost threw it out!

Eventually, the brooch was sold and the tale was passed along with it.

Perry's at SouthPark has noticed through the years that the stories which accompany some of the antique and estate jewelry interest the buyers almost as much as the pieces themselves.

Ernest Perry went into business for himself in 1977 after having worked for a national chain for twelve years. He and Priscilla traveled across North Carolina, buying and trading estate jewelry. In time, Ernest and Priscilla accumulated fifty coffee cans full of unusual and unique jewelry which were too interesting to relegate to the scrap gold heap, despite the fact that the price of gold was unusually high at the time. Instead, they opened a jewelry store, convinced there was a market for such unusual treasures. Their hunch paid off; the public's interest in unusual antique and estate jewelry far exceeded their expectations.

Perry's at SouthPark greeted the new millennium and its twentieth year in business with a major store renovation and an expansion to twenty-six hundred square feet. In keeping with its tradition of mixing old with new, Perry's kept its magnificent century-old wooden showcases.

The massive oak and mahogany cases (two of which measure over twelve feet in length) are themselves curiosities. Manufactured by Wade Manufacturing Company of Charlotte in the early 1900s, a few of the cases are actually signed by the craftsmen who built them.

The cases debuted in the old Van Sleen Jewelry Store in Gastonia, reportedly delivered there by mule train. When Van Sleen's was sold, Ernest Perry recognized their value and bought them to use in his own store. The cases require precision balancing in order for their special pressure-sprung latches to work properly, but the extra effort is more than offset by the cases' aesthetic and historical value.

Estate jewelry is previously-owned jewelry, according to Ernest Perry, and antique jewelry is usually at least one hundred years old, although the term often describes any jewelry which was made before World War II. Perry's at SouthPark's impressive collection of fine, estate and antique jewelry includes necklaces, brooches of diamonds and precious gems, scatter pins (which were popular in the 1950s), and all kinds and sizes of watches, many of which are collectible.

Perry says the oldest piece of jewelry to find its way to his store was a diamond, pearl, and emerald necklace that had belonged to the daughter of a Russian czar. Industrialist

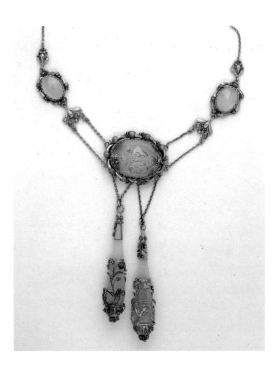

Top, left: A dainty platinum diamond pendant watch with a bow design brooch encrusted with old mine and rose cut diamonds and one natural pearl, c. 1900-1910. The watch features a pavé set puffed-style back.

Top, right: An exquisite fourteen-karat yellow gold negligée style necklace, featuring faceted cabochon and pendeloque shaped milky chalcedonys, c. 1820s-1830s

Below: This unique pierced leaf filigree design platinum pendant features a bezel set half-carat diamond enhanced by forty-three old European cut diamonds from the Art Deco period, c. 1920s.

Armand Hammer gave it to his banker, who, in turn, gave it to his wife, who later moved to Charlotte. The unusual piece sold for $15,000.

Although Perry's at SouthPark regularly sells items in the $50,000 to $100,000 price range, there are many pieces of interesting antique costume jewelry in their cases which carry price tags as low as $25.

Most jewelry brought to Perry's for appraisal and sale comes from private individuals and executors of estates. Perry and his trained staff offer free opinions regarding an item's potential market value. The jewelry store also offers thorough written appraisals, the cost of which depends on the complexity of the jewelry.

Although he no longer conducts estate auctions, Ernest still enjoys banging the gavel to help raise millions of dollars each year for local charities. His engaging personality and outstanding skill at the auction block have made him one of the area's most popular charity auctioneers. He helped plan the first auction for Charlotte Rescue Mission six years ago and has volunteered as auctioneer each year since. The Charlotte Rescue Mission auction raised $25,000 the first year and, in subsequent years, it has raised as much as $75,000.

Ernest is also involved with the Charlotte Symphony Guild's American Society of Interior Designers Showhouse, the International House, and North Carolina Chapter of the Leukemia Society, Dore Academy, and the Charlotte Philharmonic, among others.

One of the many stories that friends of the Perrys like to tell involves an auction for the Speedway Children's Charities. Two racing enthusiasts engaged in a hot bid for an autographed racing jacket donated by NASCAR legend Richard Petty. The jacket went to the high bidder for $24,000, but that wasn't the end of it. Ernest asked Richard Petty if he had another jacket for a second bidder. Petty brought a second jacket from his car, signed it, and presented it to the second highest bidder, thus fetching another $24,000 for the Speedway Children's Charity.

The Perry's appreciation for antique and estate jewelry has led them to a very successful business, but more importantly to them, it has provided a way for Ernest and Priscilla Perry to make significant contributions to the Charlotte community.

PEPSI-COLA BOTTLING COMPANY OF CHARLOTTE, INC.

❖

Above: Pepsi Limousine, c. 1940.

Below: Henry B. Fowler, Dale's grandfather and founder of Pepsi Cola Bottling Company of Charlotte, Inc., with a photograph of the first Pepsi truck.

When Dale Halton assumed management of Pepsi-Cola Bottling Company of Charlotte, she became the third generation of her family to own and operate the business, which was started in 1905 by her grandparents, Henry and Sadie Fowler. The first bottler to incorporate using the Pepsi-Cola name, the Fowlers thus became Pepsi's first franchise bottler. The company continues today as the oldest Pepsi bottler in the world.

The Fowlers and their two daughters, Margaret and Elizabeth, initially operated the business from their living room, with the women filling bottles at night and Henry peddling the drinks during the day. They then moved the operation into a barn next to a Charlotte blacksmith shop. They washed bottles by hand, filled them using foot pedal machinery, and delivered them in two horse-drawn wagons. Charlotte's iceman became the company's first salesman, delivering the product to a restaurant and two fruit stores among other stops to serve the city's fifteen thousand residents. Even though Henry Fowler had never learned to drive, he bought the company's first soft drink delivery truck in 1908, when roads were still in limited use.

A fluctuation in sugar prices forced the Pepsi-Cola corporation's owners to declare bankruptcy in 1923 and sell the parent company. Although many others abandoned the apparently sinking corporate ship, Henry continued to bottle and sell Pepsi during the

Depression. Determined and tenacious, he once lectured a route salesman on the evils of gambling, and then went to a gambling house near town and won back a route truck the salesman had lost shooting craps.

In the 1930s the company was moved to its present location on South Boulevard. Henry remained in charge of the Charlotte Pepsi franchise until his death in 1971 at age ninety-three. His long-term efforts and dedication to Pepsi-Cola later earned him a place in the Beverage Hall of Fame. The Fowlers also earned the title "Mr. And Mrs. Pepsi-Cola" in the industry and throughout the region. At his death, control of the company passed to his daughter, Margaret Fowler, who died in 1977.

In 1980, Halton, the Fowlers' only grandchild became president and CEO. She and her management team took charge and spurred the company to higher levels of success. Careful control of finances produced the cash flow needed to overhaul production machinery and purchase new delivery vehicles. To accommodate new growth, the facilities were rebuilt at the same location in 1985, adding a new office and a forty-two-thousand-square-foot warehouse. Greatly improved plant efficiencies and customer service were emphasized. Better employee benefits and policies improved morale, restored discipline and cut turnover. In 1987 the company built a warehouse distribution center in Midland, and about 1989

constructed a similar facility in Cherryville. Bulk delivery was moved in 1999 to an off-site warehouse in Charlotte. Greater concentration on profitability in all market segments, such as food stores, convenience stores, vending, schools and food service, reaped huge results. Market share increased from 25 percent to 34 percent and raw case volume increased by 240 percent, from 2.5 million to 8.5 million cases.

This overall increase in sales is a result of penetrating all segments of the market— schools, special events, little leagues, offices, swimming pools, golf courses and other recreational facilities, apartments, third party sales, drug stores, mass merchandisers, convenience stores, and large and small grocery stores. This growth has been accomplished without adding one square foot to the Pepsi territory. In the last twenty years, the company has never had a year that did not show Pepsi Brands sales increase. During this time the company has emerged to take its place as a prominent and well-respected member of the Charlotte business community.

Its leadership comes from a stable, but aggressive and competitive staff. The shortest tenure of service is thirteen years, and the longest is forty-nine years. The company's territory covers an area with a population of over 1.3 million, with delivery and service to more than eight thousand customers handled by 165 vehicles. Charlotte Pepsi, which employs approximately four hundred people, operates two production lines at its bottling plant and has four warehouses. Facilities also include a freestanding vehicle-repair facility and a large vending- and fountain-repair shop located away from the company's main plant and corporate offices in Charlotte.

Community involvement is a hallmark of the company. Staff members participate by serving on boards supporting the Arts, education and the business community. The company has also taken the rather unique approach of contributing ten percent of its pre-tax income to the Arts, including theater, ballet, and symphony, as well as youth and education projects and other charities. Among the many recipients of its generosity are the University of North Carolina at Charlotte and other colleges in the area; Boy Scouts and Girl Scouts; children's and women's health; drug rehabilitation; and medical facilities.

"Our company has been built on Service, Service and More Service," Halton says. "By giving outstanding service, keeping our prices competitive and our quality high, our market share has grown. We intend to continue our penetration of the market by giving excellent service and taking an uncompromising attitude toward meeting the needs of our customers."

D. L. PHILLIPS COMPANY

Each year, crowds numbered in the hundreds of thousands find their way to the Charlotte Merchandise Mart, an Independence Boulevard landmark. The crowds are attracted by such blockbuster events as the Southern Ideal Home Show and the Southern Women's Show. They collect holiday hints at the annual Christmas Show and indulge their hobbies at baseball card and model railroad shows. In addition, the Merchandise Mart is home to dozens of private trade shows.

The Merchandise Mart was the brainchild of D. L. Phillips, an enterprising businessman who was a leader in Charlotte's rapid development following World War II. But the Merchandise Mart was only one of his many accomplishments. Phillips built houses, apartments, shopping centers, skyscrapers, and hotels.

The company is now operated by the family's third generation, but its roots go back to 1938 when Phillips, who had been the

county's auctioneer, started building modest homes around Charlotte and Mecklenburg County. His specialty was affordable homes in neighborhoods such as Chantilly and Revolution Park.

When World War II came along, Phillips was called on to build homes for the military in Jacksonville, North Carolina. Later he would build housing units at the Cherry Point Marine Air Station, Hunter Air Force Base in Savannah, Georgia, Myrtle Beach Air Force Base and Charleston Air Force Base.

Phillips returned to Charlotte after the war and directed his company through a period of explosive growth.

In 1954 Phillips sold twenty-three acres along Independence Boulevard to the City of Charlotte for construction of the new coliseum and auditorium. The location at the edge of the city limits was considered remote at the time, but construction of the Charlotte Coliseum (now Independence Arena) and Ovens Auditorium stimulated tremendous commercial development along the busy boulevard.

Recognizing the need for a hotel near the new coliseum, Phillips built the Coliseum Inn, a 176-room hotel that is still owned by the company and operated as a Ramada Inn. As growth continued to spread out along Independence from the coliseum, the company built the Chantilly Shopping Center, which spanned both sides of the boulevard, along with two service stations and other businesses.

Success of the Chantilly Shopping Center encouraged the company to build the Hutchinson Shopping Center on North Graham Street and Freedom Village on Freedom Drive.

Responding to the growing city's need for apartments, the company branched out into multi-family development with such projects as Morningside Apartments and Briar Creek Apartments, now known as the Doral Apartments.

The company also expanded beyond Charlotte and Mecklenburg County, building the thirty-two-story Wachovia Center in Winston-Salem and developing commercial property in Durham and High Point.

The first phase of the Merchandise Mart, a 280,000-square foot structure that serves as the core of the current facility, was constructed on eighteen and a half acres next door to the coliseum in 1961. Initially, the Merchandise Mart appealed primarily to the apparel industry, with the first floor designed for exhibitions and trade shows. The project also provided thirty-five hundred parking spaces for the Mart and coliseum overflow.

The Merchandise Mart was expanded with a two-hundred-thousand-square foot, five-story addition in 1970. Two additions, totaling 135,000-square feet, were added in 1990. At the same time, the lobby was expanded and the older portions of the facility were updated. The Merchandise Mart now provides more than 225,000 square feet of exhibition space and the office tower is home to a variety of businesses, many of them involved in the apparel industry.

D. L. Phillips, the dynamo whose energy and imagination had propelled the company from its humble beginnings, died on Christmas Eve, 1973. His death left a major void, but other family members assumed leadership positions and the company continued to flourish.

Tom P. Phillips, D. L.'s son-in-law, succeeded D. L. as president. He retired in July 2000, after forty-five years with the company and was succeeded by his son, Andy Phillips. D. L.'s three daughters—Elizabeth P. Phillips, Iris P. Ostwalt and Peggy P. Crowder—remain principle stockholders in the company.

In addition to operating the Merchandise Mart, D. L. Phillips Company is involved in real estate management for apartments, warehouses and office buildings in Charlotte, Gastonia, Charleston, West Virginia, and

Jacksonville, North Carolina. But the company continues to be best known for the Merchandise Mart.

"This is one of the few merchandise marts in the country still owned by a private company, most are now owned by municipalities," explains Tom Phillips. "We fill a niche the City of Charlotte can't fill."

Tom Phillips believes the company's success can be summed up with one word—service. "This holds true for any business," he says. "If you give people value for the dollar and service, they will want to continue doing business with you. In our type business, you must make your customers feel appreciated and make them want to come back."

✧

Above: The Charlotte Merchandise Mart has been a landmark on Independence Boulevard for nearly half a century.

Below: The original Charlotte Merchandise Mart building (top right of the picture) was constructed in 1961. Freedom Hall (on the left) was added in 1970 and Liberty Hall (in the foreground) was built in 1990.

SHOWMARS

✦

Below: George Couchell and his family in front of the original Johnny's Grill on Monroe Road in 1953. Left to right: brother Pete, mother Anna, father John, sister Emily, and George. In front is sister Vivian.

Bottom: Young George Couchell and his wife, Helen, in the early '70s.

A growing, vibrant city can be identified by its success stories. The City of Charlotte is all about success stories and one of the biggest restaurant success stories is Showmars Restaurants. Owned by George Couchell, the local chain started in 1982 but its genesis began many years earlier.

The son of Greek immigrants, Couchell managed to obtain a Duke University education, become a Naval officer, and enjoy a successful career as a salesman for an international manufacturer–all before deciding that what he really wanted to do was run his own restaurant.

You might say that Couchell had the restaurant business in his blood. His parents immigrated to Charlotte from the Greek village of Karyae, where his father, John, operated a restaurant and served as mayor.

After settling in Charlotte, John Couchell opened Johnny's Grill, a forerunner of Gus' Sir Beef on Monroe Road. George was twelve years old at the time and he, his brother and two sisters worked at the restaurant alongside their father and mother. George was the carhop, shuttling curb-service orders from the kitchen to the cars parked at the drive-in.

Because they were such good students, the school principal excused them from a rule prohibiting students to leave the school grounds during the day. He understood they were needed to help run the family restaurant.

After attending Oakhurst School and graduating from East Mecklenburg High School, Couchell went on to major in economics at Duke.

Although successful in his sales career, Couchell decided to open his first restaurant, Mr. C's Southern Country Chicken, in 1967. The venture was financed with a $5,000 bank loan, co-signed by his brother. Couchell's wife, Helen, was instrumental in getting the venture going, putting in long hours at the restaurant and providing constant inspiration. Mr. C's, which served fried chicken, fish and pizza, proved so successful that two more locations were opened within the next six months.

Although the Mr. C's restaurants proved popular as well as profitable, health-conscious customers began to turn away from fried foods and, by the early '80s, Couchell felt it was time to try a new approach. He revamped the menu at his University City Boulevard location, adding several items still popular today, and gave the restaurant a complete makeover, including a new name–Showmars. Although the exotic name sounds vaguely Middle-Eastern, it was actually the name of the bookkeeper at Couchell's restaurant in Concord.

"What we tried to do with the Showmars' concept was fill the void between fast-food and full-service restaurants," Couchell explains. "We wanted to offer broader selection and better quality than fast-food while providing faster service and better value than full-service."

The Showmars menu includes a much greater range of choices than the typical fast-food outlet. Favorites include pita burgers, tenderloin tip dinners and flounder filet. The orders are placed at the counter and, at most locations, delivered to the diner's table.

The concept caught on quickly and Showmars restaurants could soon be found in most food courts in the Charlotte area. The first freestanding Showmars was opened on Independence Boulevard, near Matthews, in 1994.

There are now 17 Showmars locations with about 400 employees in Charlotte/Mecklenburg, Monroe and Rock Hill, and the expansion continues. A warehouse and commissary delivers fresh menu ingredients each day.

Couchell's general partner in twelve of the restaurants is Konstantantie Zitsos. In addition, each restaurant has a managing partner who has a piece of the action. "This way our managers are able to act as entrepreneurs," says Couchell. "Because they share in the success of the restaurants, they are determined to see them succeed."

Seeing the potential of Showmars, Couchell's son, John, decided to forego a medical career and joined the family business two years ago.

Couchell is modest about his success, insisting that it simply reflects the "wonderful opportunities America offers to hard-working, dedicated and honest people who want to succeed and contribute to the community.

"The success of Showmars, like any other business, is the result of determination and desire," he says. "You must have the zeal of a crusader and the involvement of competent managers and partners who are also dedicated and committed."

Although Couchell talks about slowing down and making more time for visits back home to Greece, friends say he loves the restaurant business too much not to stay fully involved.

In a recent magazine interview, former Charlotte Mayor Richard Vinroot described Couchell as "incredibly hard working and more. As a young man he was bright, honest and energetic. He's all those things grown up."

Vinroot should know. When they were both in high school, Couchell managed Vinroot's campaign for student body president.

✧

Above, George Couchell has found success with Showmars Restaurants by filling a void between fast-food and full-service restaurants.

Below: Managing partners surprised George Couchell with a sixtieth birthday party in 1999. At the far left is his brother, Pete. Looking over his right shoulder is his son, John.

WILTON CONNOR PACKAGING

You hear the phrase a lot from Wilton Connor Packaging employees: "We're not an ordinary company!" It's a slogan they've heard often from Wilton Connor himself. "We're not an ordinary company" neatly summarizes the company's approach to business and, in many ways, explains its success.

Innovative, out-of-the-box thinking and a sincere commitment to the welfare of its employees has helped Wilton Connor Packaging become one of the largest one-source display and packaging companies in the nation.

The firm provides value-added, turnkey packaging solutions for such well-known brands as Energizer batteries, Black & Decker power tools, Procter & Gamble consumer products and dozens of others.

Among the products and services supplied by Wilton Connor Packaging are point-of-purchase corrugated displays, structural and graphic design, contract packaging, inventory management and transportation logistics. Anytime you visit Wal-Mart, Home Depot or Food Lion you'll see a Wilton Connor product.

Wilton Connor and his wife, Catherine, leased seventeen thousand square feet of office and warehouse space and went into business as a contract packager in 1989. The fledgling company had eleven employees and one big customer, Energizer.

The demands of operating a capital-intensive business were staggering and the young company struggled for several years. "We nearly went bankrupt three times," Connor admits. To meet payroll and purchase inventory, he and Catherine cashed their IRAs, refinanced their home, and juggled thirty-six personal credit cards.

Connor credits Catherine, a CPA who operated her own accounting firm, with keeping the young company afloat. "She has always been very good with money and handled those troubled times very well," says Connor.

A partner in an accounting firm, Guy Forcucci, helped the young firm with its business plan during this difficult period and decided to invest his own money in the venture. "I could see the company had a good idea, but there was a shortfall of operating capital," he explains. "It's difficult to get bank loans for start-ups, so I decided to make an investment in the company."

Forcucci became the company's chief financial officer in 1991 and helped convince banks to loan the company much needed capital.

"Our strategy from the beginning was to be a 'one-source' operation," says Forcucci. "We wanted customers to be able to come to one location where they would obtain conceptual ideas, design capability, sales assistance, packaging and shipping. We've always tried to be pro-active and anticipate how we can help customers grow their markets."

Wilton Connor Packaging's unorthodox approach to solving packaging problems soon attracted additional customers and the

company began to grow. By 1996 sales had reached $26 million. In 2000 sales exceeded $70 million. The company now has about 600 full-time employees, although that figure doubles during seasonal periods.

The company recently moved into its new world headquarters in Westlake Business Park, off Westinghouse Boulevard. The offices occupy a 70,000-square-foot section of the firm's 330,000-square-foot Building VII, which also houses a seven-color printing press that is the largest of its type in the world. The company now operates out of seven warehouse and production buildings and additional buildings are planned.

In addition, Wilton Connor Packaging recently opened an office in Bentonville, Arkansas, to better serve Wal-Mart, one of its larger customers. Offices have also been opened in Hong Kong and Taipei, Taiwan, to assist customers doing business in those countries.

Connor's out-of-the-box approach to business extends to the way the company relates to its employees and the firm's human resources practices have attracted national attention. Employee perks include a household maintenance service with only the cost of materials charged to the employee, an on-site laundry, an employee van pool, a child

care subsidy, and an Angel Fund to help with financial emergencies.

Since many of the employees are immigrants, Wilton Connor Packaging offers one-on-one language skills training. To encourage better employee communications, Spanish speaking employees learn English, while those who speak English learn Spanish. The company has even hired an educational director to help children of employees perform better in school.

"A lot of companies use terms like empowerment and cooperation, but we really try to live that," comments Forcucci. "We hire and train people with talent and experience and we let them do their job. They take real ownership in it. Our employees know from our track record that the company is going to do well and that they will be rewarded for their efforts."

Inc. Magazine included Wilton Connor Packaging among its "Employees of the Year" and the company was selected for the book "Companies that Care," which lists the most family-friendly companies in America.

These unusual benefits result in a highly motivated workforce with very little turnover. There's also a long list of people who want to work for the company.

"Our business is built on providing solutions to complex packaging problems," Connor explains. "We recognized that there was a gap between what the customer is willing to pay for and what the suppliers provided and we filled that gap. In fact, one of our early customers called me 'the solution man.' People are interested in solutions."

✦

Opposite, top: Wilton Connor (left) and Dennis Smith inspect the first product run produced in 1994 by the company's five-color press.

Opposite, bottom: Signing the 1996 contract between Wilton Connor Packaging and Energizer were (left to right) David Bain, manager of contract packaging for Energizer, Guy Forcucci, and Wilton Connor.

Above: Gina Lundy addressing the opening of the plant.

Below: All the employees turned out to celebrate when Wilton Connor Packaging earned the Star Supplier Award from Energizer.

COCA-COLA
BOTTLING CO.
CONSOLIDATED

The second-largest Coca-Cola bottler in the United States and one of the world's highest per capita consumption bottlers, Coca-Cola Bottling Co. Consolidated (CCBCC) has a consumer base of more than sixteen million people.

In 1902 J. B. Harrison, great grandfather of Frank Harrison III, present chairman of the board and chief executive officer of CCBCC, established operations in Greensboro. In doing so, he became one of the first Coca-Cola bottlers in the world. In the early 1900s, Coca-Cola was purely a fountain drink sold at soda counters in drug stores. That same year, two other entrepreneurs also began marketing bottled Coca-Cola in North Carolina. J. Luther Snyder set up operations in Charlotte, while J. P. Gibbons opened a bottling plant in Hamlet. From that nucleus, CCBCC has grown to encompass franchise territory across the Southeast.

In Greensboro, J. B. Harrison found thirsty residents clamoring for his product, and hired C. S. Harper, Jr., to work in the plant. In 1903 he opened a plant in Raleigh. In 1906 Harper, with twenty-five percent of the stock that was then valued at $600, set up operations in Winston-Salem. Having covered the Triad and Triangle areas of the state, J. B. Harrison was quickly spreading the gospel of Coca-Cola.

Meanwhile, Luther Snyder rented a small facility in Charlotte and hired two helpers and a salesman. Although bottles promised for his operation failed to arrive on schedule, he began advertising Coca-Cola in a horse and wagon he rode. Having no bottled Coca-Cola actually available didn't stand in his way; he took orders for the future. Banners on his wagon urged people to "Drink Coca-Cola in Bottles" and proclaimed the news that Coca-Cola was "Now Served in Bottles at a Moment's Notice." Today, Snyder Production Center in Charlotte, one of the highest volume multipackage soft drink plants in the world, bears the family name.

Gibbons operated from a back-room shop in Hamlet, taking Coca-Cola to the streets in a horse-drawn wagon. At night, he washed his few bottles by hand and filled them for delivery the next day. As in Charlotte, the saloon business was strong competition, but Gibbons occasionally landed a case of Coca-Cola in a saloon for the saloonkeepers to drink. As the product became increasingly popular and more readily available, a few cases were shipped to other communities.

As sales increased, more facilities were needed. From 1905 to 1913, Charlotte Coca-

Cola Bottling Company plants opened in Salisbury, Gastonia, Concord, Shelby, Lexington, Albemarle, Statesville, Monroe and Lincolnton, North Carolina. Horse-and-wagon delivery vehicles gave way to trucks.

Despite a sugar shortage during World War I and a severe economic depression in the early 1930s, the company managed to remain strong. Consolidation of outlying plants during this time period led to today's CCBCC. Still able to meet the demand for Coca-Cola following a second sugar shortage during World War II, Coca-Cola plunged into the 1950s boom that found fierce competition in the soft drink industry. This led to package-size testing and evaluation, as well as the introduction of canned soft drinks. To distribute products, new sales techniques were blended with traditional route sales and advance calls to customers. The success of soft drink vending machines in selling Coca-Cola spawned partnerships with food vending services.

In 1972, the company's name was changed to Coca-Cola Bottling Company of the Mid-Carolinas, and the company offered its stock to the public for the first time. In 1973 Frank Harrison Jr., grandson of founder J. B. Harrison, directed the acquisitions of Greensboro, Winston-Salem, Burlington, and Raleigh, North Carolina, and Danville, Virginia. The company name was changed again, to Coca-Cola Bottling Co. Consolidated, to reflect its growth beyond the Carolinas.

In J. B. Harrison's day, the company had only one product. Coca-Cola is still the flagship, though today it's known as Coca-Cola classic (and also comes in a caffeine-free variety). But, the corporate family of products has grown to include diet Coke (and a caffeine-free version), Sprite, diet Sprite, POWERaDE, Mello Yello, Fruitopia, Fresca, Minute Maid flavored soft drinks, a wide variety of Minute Maid juices, and Dasani.

Well-planned development has added still more bottling plants in recent years. CCBCC now distributes Coca-Cola products in Alabama, Florida, Georgia, Mississippi, North Carolina, South Carolina, Tennessee, Virginia, and West Virginia. The Harrison family grew the company from modest beginnings to a company that today employs about 5,500

people, produces over 4.1 billion eight-ounce servings per year and operates some of the world's most advanced bottling equipment.

CCBCC's great success can be attributed to the dedication, integrity and energy of its employees. Throughout the company's history, the superior quality of its products, the high caliber of its employees and the leadership of the Harrison family have remained constant.

❖

Above: Inside North Carolina's first Coca-Cola bottling plant on South Church Street in Charlotte, 1902.

Below: Music and bottled Coca-Cola provided fun for soldiers and their wives at a "Spotlight of Bands" event in the early 1940s at the Morris Field Army Air Force Base in Charlotte.

LIONS JEWELERS

"When I opened Lions, I wanted a beautiful store that showcased unique jewelry," explains Mardi Tyson-Williams, owner of Lions Jewelers. "I wanted to create an environment that wasn't intimidating to the consumer. I think I've accomplished that."

Indeed she has. Walk into either location of Lions Jewelers and prepare to be dazzled. At every turn, the eye is drawn to flawless creations as unique as the people destined to wear them. Clients are greeted and immediately made to feel comfortable by a professionally trained staff ready to provide knowledgeable answers to any question and to serve in any way imaginable.

Mardi, a successful businessperson with a life-long love of jewelry, founded Lions Jewelers in 1987. She turned her passion into reality while attending a trade show in San Francisco and happened to walk into a booth that offered one-of-a-kind designer jewelry. She left with twenty-two pieces and a plan to open her own jewelry store.

"I'll be the first to say that my employees are the key to my success," offers Tyson-Williams. In fact, she and her staff have built a solid reputation within the community as the first choice among discerning shoppers. Clients enjoy the relaxed atmosphere and the fact that they have access to the owner—an owner whose enthusiasm for both her customers and her business is evident from the start. With two master goldsmiths, award-winning designers

and a gemologist on premises, Lions Jewelers is ready to satisfy even the most discriminating shopper's every wish.

Lions Jewelers specializes in only first quality pieces, all chosen by Mardi herself. The store is filled with jewelry designs by David Yurman, Roberto Coin, and Doris Panos, as well as fine Swiss timepieces, including Rolex. You'll also find gemstones of every type, opulent gold, striking sterling silver and, of course, diamonds of the finest quality.

Lions Jewelers is one of the few jewelers in the country chosen to attend the couture

Above: Mardi Tyson Williams, owner of Lions Jewelers.

Right: Lions Jewelers beautiful new location in Jetton Village at Lake Norman.

shows, while other buying trips include excursions to Italy and Antwerp to select and purchase diamonds. Clients look to Lions Jewelers to provide exquisitely designed pieces they won't see anywhere else—and they are never disappointed. Mardi literally travels the world in search of exciting new pieces to introduce to the Charlotte market.

"We establish special relationships with each of our customers," explains Mardi. "We get to know the pieces they need in their jewelry wardrobe and help them build their collections to something of beauty and value. We're always looking for special pieces for our customers."

Jewelry isn't the only facet of Lions Jewelers' exclusive commitment to their customers. The store's flagship location in Charlotte's SouthPark neighborhood is elegantly appointed and designed for comfort. The open, airy Lake Norman store at Jetton Village includes such amenities as children's room and media room where spouses or guests of clients may relax in complete comfort. The media room also accommodates groups for meetings and special luncheons.

Whether shopping for themselves or for a special gift, customers find an unparalleled selection of items for men and women alike. From Versace china and Waterford crystal to Limoges' and Fabergé, Lions Jewelers manages to combine the best of beauty, art and function.

"Strength and beauty, like the lion on our logo, is what the store stands for," says Mardi. "We back up every item we sell, unconditionally. This shows we are committed to excellence in every aspect of our business."

Lions Jewelers is very involved in the Charlotte community and actively supports a number of organizations, including The Family Center, American Heart Association, A Child's Place, International Brain Injury Association, Habitat for Humanity and local church and school benefits. The store also supports a SouthPark Little League baseball team each season.

Lions Jewelers offers incomparable beauty in design, unmatched knowledge of the industry and impeccable service, all of which adds up to a flawless buying experience. Those who seek the finest are encouraged to visit Lions Jewelers at Sharon Corners in SouthPark or Jetton Village at Lake Norman for truly unique creations from around the world.

✧

Above: Among the beautiful jewelry at Lions Jewelers are this sapphire and diamond bangles and beads by Doris Panos Designs.

Left: America's preeminent jewelry designer, David Yurman, introduced the new Quatrefoil Collection in eighteen-karat gold, carved black onyx, and pavé diamonds. The collection is available exclusively at Lions Jewelers.

BARNHARDT MANUFACTURING

✧

Above: Barnhardt Manufacturing Company, Charlotte, North Carolina.

Below: High-quality NCFI foam cushions are prepared for shipment to one of Barnhardt's Hickory furniture customers.

For Barnhardt Manufacturing, "a tradition of innovation" is not just an empty slogan—it's the way the company has been doing business since 1900.

Because of that approach, Barnhardt has bucked numerous trends over the years to stand-alone in a unique position among the Charlotte business community.

At a time when businesses change locations and ownership on a regular basis, Barnhardt Manufacturing has stayed at the same place on Hawthorne Lane since July 1900, when the firm was formally incorporated. The same family—now in its fourth generation—still owns the company.

While textile companies are leaving the state and the country, Barnhardt remains here—and is one of the few textile companies in the City of Charlotte. At a time when many manufacturers are abandoning cities' urban cores, Barnhardt has stayed in the inner city, providing good wages and benefits to local residents.

Barnhardt is also one of Charlotte's oldest companies. Throughout its history, its core business has stayed the same—cleaning and bleaching raw cotton for use in the dental and medical professions, pharmaceutical industry, health and beauty, feminine hygiene and industrial filtration.

The company's recent expansion of its cotton-bleaching operation makes them one of the largest cotton bleachers in the world. The Charlotte plant now encompasses approximately three hundred thousand square feet; an existing facility next door is fifty-five thousand square feet. Parts of the plant date back to 1900, when Thomas M. Barnhardt opened his company in a one-room facility.

Barnhardt topped $100 million in sales in 1999, when it was ranked the fifty-second largest privately-held company in North Carolina by *Business: North Carolina*.

There are seven product lines operating in five locations in Charlotte, Mount Airy, Hickory and High Point, North Carolina, and Dalton, Georgia, with a total of some 550 employees:

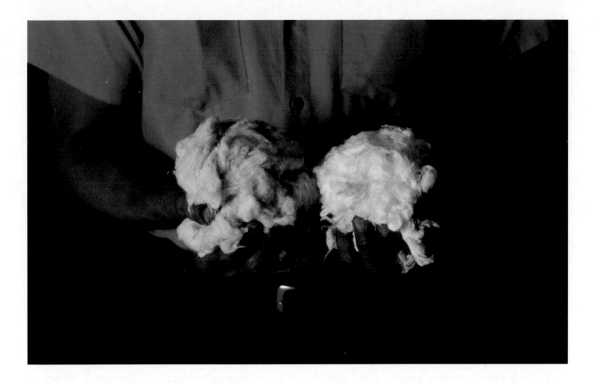

- Barnhardt Manufacturing: Supplier of quality bleached cotton and industrial cotton products;
- Richmond Dental: Supplier of single-use products to dentists around the world;
- Carolina Absorbent Cotton: Manufacturer of cotton, rayon and polyester pharmaceutical coils;
- Intrinsics: Supplier of single-use products to the salon, nail, and spa industries;
- North Carolina Foam Industries (NCFI): Manufacturer of flexible foam, carpet cushioning and chemical foam systems;
- Barnhardt Cushion: Manufacturer of fine cushioning products for the furniture industry;
- Dalton Foam: Manufacturer of re-bond carpet cushioning.

That's a long way from the company's original line of business producing cotton batting from cotton mill wastes for use as cushioning in horse collars, furniture, buggy seats, quilts and comforters. But over the years, the Barnhardts have shown willingness and an ability to successfully expand into new lines of related business while remaining focused on doing what they know best.

Observes John Smith, manager of the Barnhardt Cushion plant in Hickory, who has been with the firm since 1973, "The Company has had a lot of foresight. As the materials used in cushioning changed—like to polyester and foam—the Barnhardts changed the materials they worked in. But at the same time, they found new uses for the material they know best—cotton."

By taking this approach and being open to change and innovation, Barnhardt Manufacturing has become a diversified, successful and enduring company, able to weather the storms of economic downturns, changing markets and technological advances.

❖

Above: Robert shows the contrast in color between unbleached and bleached cotton.

Below: The Barnhardt family (from left to right): Lewis B. Barnhardt, Robert S. Barnhardt, Thomas L. Barnhardt, Lee Barnhardt Hatling, and Thomas M. Barnhardt III.

SONITROL SECURITY SERVICES, INC.

✧

Sonitrol Security Services located in Charlotte, North Carolina.

In 1984, five years after nineteen-year-old Bill Price started his own alarm company in Baltimore with a $1,000 investment borrowed from his father, he sold the company to the local Sonitrol dealer for $135,000 and moved to Charlotte as a partner of an existing Sonitrol franchise.

During the next four years—during which the franchise was headed by three different presidents—the Sonitrol franchise's sales and customer base grew tremendously, but the company was sliding ever closer to bankruptcy. By 1989 it was generating $1.4 million in sales—up from $300,000—and the customer base had grown from 165 to 900. But the burden of $4 million in debt overwhelmed those figures.

Finally the board of directors looked at the then twenty-nine-year-old Price and agreed, "Let the kid have a shot at it. He can't screw it up any worse than the other guys."

The decision was a gamble but despite his youth, Price had a promising track record. He had begun work as a sales representative for Flashguard Security in Baltimore, in 1977, providing consultation to businesses and homes throughout the Baltimore region. Beginning with a borrowed $1,000 from his father, he went into business for himself as president of Carroll Alarm, Inc., in Stevenson, Maryland.

He nurtured that business from nothing to revenues of over $395,000 in 1983, when he sold it to Sonitrol of Baltimore and moved his new wife, Carrington, to Charlotte.

The Sonitrol board's gamble on Price has paid big dividends. Working with stockholders to restructure the company's debt, the new fledgling manager followed his instincts, reducing expenditures, halting the steady increase in the company's debt, and explaining the financial situation with his employees.

"A vast majority of the employees from that meeting are still with the company today," he says proudly. "A number were scared–thought they wouldn't have a job left, but people generally respond favorably if you tell them the honest facts." Working together, management and employees turned the company around. With revenues in excess of $5.6 million and forty-eight full-time employees, the company is nearly debt free.

"We secure over 3,000 customers in both Carolinas—including 2,200 commercial/industrial clients and 800 homeowners," Price says. "We are in the electronic loss prevention security business, providing consultation through design, professional installation, local monitoring and on-going service to our customer base. Sonitrol has recently added Special Police, patrol services and on-scene runner response to his customer's alarm activity."

The company moved to its own seventy-five-hundred-square-foot state-of-the-art, fully computerized central monitoring station in 1995 and today is the only central station of its kind in North and South Carolina—UL listed, Factory Mutual and Insurance approved.

Previously started by the Sonitrol Southeast distributor in 1974, a group of investors, including Price, purchased Sonitrol of Gastonia in 1984, and acquired Sonitrol of Charlotte, merging the two companies in 1985. At that time the company had ten employees and combined revenues of $600,000.

A forty-percent annual sales growth and the whopping increase in debt occurred during the next five years. The board gave Price a clear directive when he became general manager in 1989—either save the company or put it up for a "fire sale." He chose the former.

Covering primarily the Charlotte seven-county region, the company also provides service in other parts of North and South Carolina. The company now services all of North Carolina with branches in Charlotte, Greensboro, Raleigh, and fifteen South Carolina counties, including Rock Hill, and branches in Greenville and Spartanburg.

"Every one of our employees is essential to our success," Price says without hesitation. "Our priorities are outlined on our company's mission statement: 'Every employee of Sonitrol should treat the customer as you would want to be treated–fairly, truthfully and above all, as a partner in their loss prevention needs.'"

He emphasizes, however, that employee relations are also vital, and says it is important that employees have fun at their jobs, explaining, "Every now and then we play upbeat music throughout the building or do a broadcast page to everyone with pagers, just to tell them to have a great day."

Price also knows how to enjoy life outside his business, listing first among his life's passions "my lovely and tolerant wife and two wonderful children." A thoroughbred horseracing enthusiast, he and his wife are the founders of the non-profit annual venue, the

Queen's Cup Steeplechase. But even his avocations include interests related to business including watching his employees grow within the organization and reach for new heights.

His business achievements have brought numerous rewards, including in the past few years his selection as Sonitrol "Dealer of the Year" for the Southeast Region in 1992 and 1994; "Outstanding Sonitrol Dealer of the Year" for 1995; and Charlotte Chamber of Commerce "Entrepreneur of the Year" in 1996.

Above: The Sonitrol UL listed monitoring station.
COURTESY OF MITCHELL KEARNEY.

Below: William J. Price.

BRADFORD BROTHERS, INC.

Few people are aware of it, but four major oil and gas pipelines, including the two main pipelines from Texas and Louisiana, sneak across Mecklenburg County on their way to the northeast. The lines are buried only three feet beneath the surface, but only the huge storage tank facility at Paw Creek indicates their existence.

The responsibility for constructing these pipelines, and keeping them safe through constant monitoring and maintenance, belongs to Bradford Brothers, Inc. of Huntersville.

Odd as it may seem, this family-run company began as a well-known dairy farm. Bradford family members are direct descendants of Hezekiah Alexander, one of the earliest settlers of Mecklenburg County, and the family has been prominent in the area for generations. By the 1930s, the family's Hiwassie Dairy Farm, operated by Cecil D. Bradford, Sr., known as "Dewitt," was well established, furnishing milk and dairy products to hundreds of grocery stores and individual customers in the Huntersville area. In those days, milk was delivered in glass bottles, the kind where the cream rose to the top; and the distinctive Hiwassie bottle was a familiar item in northern Mecklenburg households. William O. "Bill" Bradford started the bottling plant for Hiwassee Dairy Farm and both he and Cecil helped with the farm.

Following World War II, Cecil D. Bradford, Jr., Dewitt's son, purchased a dozer to dig some watering ponds for the dairy cows. Word of the laborsaving earth-moving machine spread and neighbors were soon asking Bradford to scoop out some ponds for them.

In 1957, Bill, Sr., sold the bottling plant, and, with his brother, Cecil, established Bradford Brothers. The grading business grew, and before long, the brothers were using the dozer to dig out streets, lay water and sewer lines and grade lots for the post-war subdivisions that developed around Huntersville and other northern Mecklenburg towns.

By the late '50s, Bradford Brothers was doing some small projects for Plantation Pipe Line Company, which was laying underground petroleum pipelines from the oil fields in Texas and Louisiana to Washington, D.C. This led to a major contract in 1960 to do earth work for Colonial Pipeline storage facilities at Spartanburg, South Carolina, Charlotte, and Mitchell Junction in central Virginia.

Once the earthwork was completed, Colonial contracted with Bradford Brothers to handle the maintenance on the line and the company started shifting its emphasis to pipelines exclusively. The company was formally incorporated in 1966.

Today, Bradford Brothers, Inc. provides construction, consulting, design and testing to the petroleum and natural gas industries and is the only petroleum pipeline contractor in North Carolina, South Carolina and Virginia.

Major company projects include the relocation of Colonial Pipeline's thirty-six-inch main line near Simpsonville, South Carolina; expansion of Plantation Pipe Line Company's storage terminal at Greensboro, North Carolina; construction of Colonial Pipeline's new two-mile long line to the Naval Supply Center in Yorktown, Virginia; and upgrading of petroleum facilities for the Exxon terminals in Roanoke, Virginia, and Newington, Virginia.

In 1997 Bradford Brothers completed a major program to inspect and repair 180 miles of Colonial Pipeline's original main line from the Saluda River in South Carolina to Greensboro, North Carolina. The project developed from a 1996 incident in which the thirty-six-inch mainline ruptured, spilling diesel fuel into a river in Greenville County, South Carolina. For thirty weeks, Bradford Brothers' employees helped locate problems and make repairs to the line, utilizing so-called "smart tools" that use an elastic wave to detect anomalies. In all, 575 locations in South Carolina and 875 locations in North Carolina were evacuated during the $6.1 million safety program.

Bradford Brothers has about 150 full-time employees and its territory ranges from Texas to Maryland. Although the company headquarters are still located in Huntersville, the firm also has offices in Richmond, Virginia, and Collins, Mississippi.

Bradford Brothers is still very much a family-run company. Cecil D. "Dee" Bradford, III, serves as president; Smith Bradford is vice president and runs the Richmond office; Ross Bradford is vice president; Bill Bradford is secretary/treasurer; Beverly Woods is controller/office manager; and Scott Bradford is a foreman. Bill, Jr., Ross, and Scott are sons of Bill Bradford, Sr. and Cecil III, Smith, and Beverly are the children of Cecil, Jr. The founders retired in 1988 and the four current officers have operated the company since then.

Drawing on its rich family heritage, Bradford Brothers has established a reputation for excellence in both the quality of its work and its response to customers needs. This approach has made the company a recognized leader in its unique industry.

✦

Following the rupture of a thirty-six-inch pipeline in South Carolina, Bradford Brothers was called in to recover the product, install a temporary section, and relocate two thousand feet of pipe.

PCA
INTERNATIONAL

✧

Above: PCA International's corporate headquarters.

Below: A photographer in session.

Walk the halls of the Customer Support Center of PCA International, Inc. in Matthews. On either wall at eye-level is a row of special photographic portraits. The framed images are of loved ones of PCA employees in individual and group poses. A sleeping newborn. A playful pair of twins. Three generations of Johnstons. And so on. The portraits serve as a daily reminder of what PCA does best and more often than any other company in North America: create memories. More than one hundred million memories each year.

What began modestly as a traveling portrait studio promotion in one S. S. Kresge store is now a network of more than 2,500 retail photographic studio locations, serving all fifty states, Canada, Mexico, and Puerto Rico. While compelling, that's only part of the ever-developing PCA story.

Since its founding in 1967 as Photo Corporation of America, the company has steadily and systematically refined the art and science of portrait photography. A camera designed by founder Bud Davis was instrumental in launching the industry. The "Framatic" single-lens reflex camera enabled photographers to shoot up to five hundred exposures between rolls of film. This introduced an operational efficiency that has since become a PCA hallmark.

Through the years, PCA has developed proprietary systems and processes that have become standard for the industry. Today, the company holds patents on technical innovations that range from protective camera housing to photo-processing techniques. Year in and year out, PCA made incremental improvements to the portrait studio concept: optimizing retail space, perfecting the promotional message, improving delivery, maximizing the print configuration, and more.

Then, during the 1990s, PCA began an association with fast-growing Wal-Mart, initially at stores in Canada. In 1997 the relationship grew when PCA acquired American Studios, a major Wal-Mart provider. As the relationship proved mutually beneficial, it led to an exclusive arrangement. Today, PCA operates in more than twenty-five hundred

Wal-Mart locations in the United States and Canada, Mexico and Puerto Rico.

The company's automated film laboratory prints more than 100 million portraits annually for more than five million customers. It's a daunting task, but PCA's Charlotte and Matthews lab facilities are fine-tuned operations that swell to one thousand employees during peak holiday seasons.

Even then, each order is quality-checked at least five times before a customer receives a portrait package. Film images are monitored by computerized systems. Color is assessed and optimized even before prints are produced. Lab technicians then inspect each processed print for quality and, if necessary, retouch them. At every step, it's a customer-centered service.

PCA was first in the industry to leverage digital technology by introducing instant portrait preview in the 1990s, and its impact was immediate. The new service gave customers an instant preview of their portraits and the opportunity to customize their collection of portraits on the spot, thus eliminating any surprises at delivery. Production processes were streamlined as a result, and quality assurance improved. It was another success in a longstanding corporate effort to create more value for the customer.

PCA has since pioneered a new retail concept, GoPortraits Digital Destination, which provides complete technical support and high quality printing services for digital photography. Located at the Carolina Place Mall in Mecklenburg County, the prototype store offers a state-of-the-art studio, photography equipment rental for professional photographers, a complete array of products, and digital processing services including the first E-box in North America, an advanced printing system from Agfa. Traditional film can also be processed and digitized.

The new venture in digital imaging is fully endorsed by Barry Feld, PCA's president, CEO and board chairman. It is one of several strategic initiatives that will redefine and reinvigorate the company beyond its core business of retail studio photography in the years ahead. Going forward, PCA will increase its efforts to serve the photographic needs of schools, churches, military posts, private clubs and organizations. A greater Internet presence looms on the horizon to provide online services and improved communication for all markets served.

Into the new century, PCA will continue to make changes and evolve as a company. Like millions of customers PCA serves each year and the family-oriented employees who walk the halls each day, PCA won't discard its favorite memories. Just reframe them.

✧

Above: A PCA Portrait Lab.

Below: GoPortraits Digital Destination Studio.

PREFERRED PARKING SERVICE, INC.

If you attend a Panthers game, enjoy an event at the Blumenthal Performing Arts Center, or work in the uptown area, chances are you'll park in a lot operated by Preferred Parking Service, Inc.

Preferred Parking Service provides commuters with more than 10,000 parking spaces in 45 lots and seven garages, most of them located in the uptown area.

The founder of Preferred Parking, B. J. Stacks, started his own company with a lot at Third and Church Street in 1961. Stacks had to sell his car to pay the first month's rent for that first lot but the business grew and he eventually branched out to Atlanta and Augusta, Georgia. In recent years, the company has concentrated its efforts in Charlotte.

Stacks' son, Roger, joined the family business in 1984 and, five years later, purchased the company from his parents, who are now retired.

Roger Stacks says "the goal of Preferred Parking is straightforward: to invest in uptown and the community while providing service-based parking and transportation services from a teamwork approach." In addition to managing parking lots and garages, Preferred Parking provides extensive consulting, design, and maintenance services that include construction, shuttle and valet services.

"The most critical features of a successful parking facility are safety, convenience, exceptional value, and usability," says Stacks. "For the customer, parking should be event-less, not a negative. Parking should be a seamless experience from the facility owner to the parking user."

Among the locations operated by Preferred Parking are the First Presbyterian Church lot at Trade and Poplar Streets, the Belk property at Trade and Brevard Streets, and the parking garage at the Carillon Building. Preferred Parking also manages parking garages for the Wachovia Center, BellSouth, the Charlotte/Mecklenburg Government Center, the CPCC campus, 600 North Tryon and many others.

The company has forty-eight full-time employees, plus a number of part-time workers for special events.

In addition to providing attractive and convenient parking, Stacks is also committed to historic preservation in the uptown area. Preferred Parking recently moved its headquarters from the historic Latta Arcade to a building at 221 South Tryon Street, which was built in 1897.

Not too many years ago, most of Charlotte's population lived in the area that now encompasses the center city. But, development of streetcar suburbs in the early twentieth century and construction of new suburban neighborhoods following World War II led to a gradual decline of downtown residential property.

In the last few years, however, thousands have rediscovered the advantages of living in the center city, leading to the restoration of Victorian-era Fourth Ward and construction of hundreds of new residential units. This center city renaissance has also given new life to the Frederick Apartments, one of the best examples of the city's 1920s prosperity.

The history of the Frederick mirrors the story of Charlotte over the past seventy-five years. The population increased seventy-eight percent in Charlotte during the booming decade between 1920 and 1930 and builders scurried to keep pace with the rapid growth. Record levels of new residential construction were recorded, including a significant new trend—construction of apartment houses.

Although apartment living was popular in large metropolitan areas such as New York and Chicago, single-family homes remained the norm in Charlotte and most of the South until the '20s. Then, apartment construction exploded. In the ten years from 1920 to 1930, the number of apartment buildings in Charlotte nearly quadrupled.

William Frederick Casey, a manufacturer's representative, built the Frederick Apartments in 1927 at 409 North Church Street in Fourth Ward (the street number is now 515). The red brick building, constructed by J. A. Jones Construction Company, featured an arched center entry and tiled roof that hinted at an Italian Renaissance Revival design influence. The polychrome facade with its three-dimensional clay tile detailing is unmatched in 1920s-era architecture in Charlotte.

The first newspaper ads for the Frederick appeared in September 1927, and boasted of "exclusive modern fireproof apartments with all modern conveniences." Specifically mentioned were "an electrical dishwasher, electric cooling and ventilation system, refrigerator, and many other devices."

The building had thirty-six units and the largest, a two-floor unit with two baths, was occupied by the owner and his wife. Other original tenants included two dentists, one physician, several salesmen, two insurance agents, and the local agent of the newly formed Federal Bureau of Investigation, or FBI. All lived within walking distance of their offices.

During the late 1930s, the Frederick Apartments was home to the acclaimed author Wilbur J. Cash, best known for his seminal social history *The Mind of the South*. It was here that Cash completed the manuscript for his classic study of Southern sociology.

Roger Stacks, the current owner, asked RE Services, Inc., a specialist in historic preservation, to retain as many of the building's original features as possible. In doing so, the Frederick is upgraded with the most modern conveniences available, and the Frederick retains the appearance, style, and ambiance that made it so popular in its early years. The Frederick is now home to a new generation of Charlotteans who are rediscovering the excitement of urban living.

❖

Above: The Frederick Apartments, built in 1927, helped popularize apartment living in Charlotte.

Below: The restoration of The Frederick Apartments retained many of the building's original architectural features.

UNIQUE SOUTHERN ESTATES

With a mission of preserving the tradition of Southern hospitality, Unique Southern Estates operates The Morehead Inn and The VanLandingham Estate Inn and Conference Center, two beautiful historic properties in Charlotte, North Carolina.

The elegant Morehead Inn is located in the heart of historic Dilworth, just minutes from uptown Charlotte in one of the city's most picturesque neighborhoods. This gracious Southern estate is endowed with quiet elegance and fine antiques. Built in 1917 for Charlotte businessman Charles Coddington and his wife Marjorie, it was designed and created by British-born architect William Peeps as a house for entertaining. It features five spacious public areas, intimate fireplaces, a magnificent staircase, secluded outdoor courtyard, luxurious private rooms and a lovely four-bedroom carriage house. It has earned a first-class reputation as one of the finest inns in the South, with numerous awards for renovation, cuisine and service. An ideal setting for a beautiful wedding or corporate reception, it employs a staff of thirty-two, including in-house event coordinators.

The VanLandingham Estate Inn and Conference Center, which was placed on the National Register of Historic Places in 1977, features over four acres of magnificent gardens for the use of guests. This distinctive California bungalow-style estate is located just three miles from the heart of uptown Charlotte. Easily accommodating a few to several hundred people, it provides an ideal backdrop for business or club meetings, seminars, corporate retreats, weddings, receptions, bridal luncheons and entertaining. A "social architect" is available to help with each occasion. Fine foods and catering are available, with menus to suit every taste and a wide range of budgets. Improvements to the bathrooms, plumbing, heating/air conditioning systems and gas log hearths have been carefully wrought to provide comfort without detracting from the estate's historic character. Outstanding antique furnishings and the use of stone in the structure of the house, in hearths and on the surrounding grounds enhance the quiet, "mountain" atmosphere. Built in 1913, the estate is the legacy of southern cotton brokers Ralph and Susie Harwood VanLandingham. It was designed by noted architect C. C. Hook.

Unique Southern Estates, founded in 1995 with Billy Maddalon as managing partner, acquired the properties. The company is active in the community. The Morehead Inn is particularly involved in aiding the Alexander Children's Center, and The VanLandingham Estate Inn and Conference Center has chosen the Metrolina AIDS project as its charitable cause.

✧

Above: The Morehead Inn.

Below: VanLandingham Estate Inn & Conference Center.

E. P. Nisbet Company and Nisbet Oil Company, which have been providing twenty-four-hour heating and air conditioning services for "as long as anybody can remember" is still headquartered in the historic Cherry neighborhood near downtown Charlotte.

E. P. Nisbet founded the company, which also provides wholesale petroleum products, in 1927. His interest in new mechanical devices led him to purchase a Williams Oil-O-Matic oil burner franchise, then an ultra-modern innovation in home heating. At his customers' request Nisbet bought a small oil truck and began home deliveries of heating oil. The business grew as Nisbet's company "looked after" his customers' heating needs.

In the 1950s, the E. P. Nisbet Company began installing Carrier air conditioners in homes. Leadership by Jim Kuykendall and F. H. "Bub" Orr contributed greatly to the company's growth and reputation in the heating and air business.

After a competitor offered to buy his business in 1955, Nisbet asked his son-in-law, Jim White, a Charlotte native who was then working "up north" with giant DuPont, if he would come to work at the Nisbet firm. White accepted and the business stayed in the family.

Jim began building the heating oil business, and operated the company after Nisbet's death in 1960. Seeing an opportunity in the wholesale gasoline business, he founded Nisbet Oil Company in 1962, and began supplying country stores and "filling stations" in then rural areas of Mecklenburg County, such as Mathews, Mint Hill, Pineville, and Shuffletown. As the business grew he began purchasing corner lots and building stations. In 1966 Jim teamed up with Wendell Boggs and bought Rhodes and Beal Oil Company, a small firm in Lincolnton,

North Carolina, selling petroleum products in Lincoln and Catawba Counties.

In addition to Nisbet's founder, the business has been led by Presidents Mary McLure Nisbet, 1933-86; James J. White III, 1986-2000 (now chairman); and James J. White IV, 2000-present. William F. Purvis, vice-president, 1964-86; Joseph W. Grier, Jr., Esq.; William S. Johns, Jr., CFO since 1981, have also greatly contributed to Nisbet's success. The management considers employees the company's greatest asset.

Nisbet, which grew from about $750,000 in sales in the 1950s to over $50 million in 2000, operates in ten counties around the Charlotte region. The company exists to provide customers with service and value, and strives to conduct its business with integrity and fairness. Active in the community, it underwrites programming on WTVI, Charlotte's PBS affiliate, and contributes to such groups as the Arts and Science Council, Crisis Assistance Ministry and Katawba Valley Land Trust.

✧

Above: The staff of E. P. Nisbet Company, c. 1955. Front row (from left to right): Jim White, Norman Williams, Charlie Wagoner, Jimmy Brown, Buff Deese, Bobby Williams, Van Tully, Garnet Jones, and J. W. Sellers. Back row (from left to right): Lester Hargett, Jim Kuykendall, Bub Orr, Ernie Helms, Calvin Brown, Harvey Ingram, John Taylor, James Medlin, Bill Thomas, David Long, Benny Peoples, and E. P. Nisbet.

Below: One of Nisbet's modern convenience stores, 1999.

HORNET'S NEST ELECTRICAL SUPPLY CO., INC.

❖

President Rick Gooding.

As one of the few remaining locally owned and operated companies of its type in the Charlotte area, Hornet's Nest Electrical Supply Co., Inc., has history of over 30 years' service. Opened in 1969 by Randall R. Gooding Sr., with Ross F. Bergamino, the company started small, with Gooding and Bergamino working alone in a 5,000 square foot location in Charlotte. Thanks in large part to their dedication and hard work, Hornet's Nest has grown and prospered.

A knowledgeable staff–a majority of whom have been with the business for over 10 years–provides assistance to customers on the company's inventory, which includes all the items used to provide electricity for any residential or commercial application. A few months into the business, Gooding and Bergamino hired Gary R. Helms and Tommy O. Smith. Gooding's son, Randall R. "Rick" Gooding Jr., began working there as a high school student in 1980.

Now operating at two locations–801 McNinch Street, Charlotte, and 1445 Stallings Road, Stallings, North Carolina. Hornet's Nest is led by Rick as president and owner, with Helms as executive vice president of the company and Smith as warehouse manager and sales supervisor at Charlotte. Other long-time key personnel include T. Ray Vickery, vice president in charge of the operations at Stallings, and Lisa L. Poole, office operations manager for both locations.

Trained and knowledgeable employees are the customers' first contact at both company locations. The first employee the customer talks to is usually able to provide solutions to his or her problems. In addition to selling quality products at competitive prices, Hornet's Nest employees help educate customers through classes, vendor counter days and direct mail, keeping them informed about industry changes and product development and improvement.

Servicing approximately 600 customers—more than 300 of them active every month—the company has grown consistently, even during times of recession. It is expanding service to other areas through an on-line catalog at www.ehornetsnest.com. Through this catalog, which contains over 500,000 items and is maintained through membership in "Wholesale America," customers can order many products other than electrical, ranging from hardware to plumbing to lawn mowers.

As it has been throughout its history, Hornet's Nest remains an active part of the Charlotte/Stallings community. Among its many charitable activities and projects are charter sponsorship of Hospice House of Monroe, North Carolina, sponsorship of local children's sports teams, and contributions to local high school yearbooks and sports programs. The company also sponsors Customer Appreciation Days, a golf tournament and other events.

Establishing long-term relationships with clients has proved to be a formula for success at Doggett Advertising. In a volatile profession where the average client relationship is about three years, Doggett Advertising's client retention average is more than ten years.

"What makes us unique is the tenure of our accounts," explains George Doggett. "We have lots of long-term relationships and some clients have been with us since the firm was established." Doggett Advertising, which represents local, national, and international clients, specializes in the logo apparel industry, automobiles, and real estate

Doggett, who has been in advertising for twenty-five years, founded the full-service advertising, marketing, and design firm in 1988 after serving as a partner with another ad agency.

Doggett Advertising began with a three-person staff with offices in Fourth Ward. The firm has grown to fifteen employees, including George's son, Jeff, who has been with the company ten years. "It's a young, energetic staff and we do a lot of exciting projects," says Jeff.

"It's also a very professional staff," adds George. "We've been able to recruit talented people from some of the top agencies in the country and we pride ourselves on our marketing and great creative work."

The agency's creative and marketing efforts have made it a consistent winner of major awards and honors from the advertising and printing industries.

George Doggett has a second career as a developer and has built and renovated several buildings in Charlotte's Fourth Ward and Dilworth neighborhoods. His interest in historic preservation resulted in the renovation of an East Boulevard home that now serves as the agency's offices.

It took ten months to renovate the 1920s-era home and convert it to a four-thousand-square-foot commercial structure. From the street the two-story brick house with its wide front porch still retains the look of a substantial Dilworth home. Inside, however, the converted home is a modern office facility filled with the latest technological marvels.

"We liked the pedestrian feel of the neighborhood and were able to preserve the charm of an old home while achieving a very creative environment," says Jeff Doggett.

The Doggett Advertising logo, a Greyhound, was adapted from the Doggett family crest and reflects the agencies approach to business. "The Greyhound conveys a lot of business principles we strive to apply in our daily interactions with clients," says George Doggett. "The Greyhound is quick, intelligent, friendly, and motivated to win—the same qualities prized in every Doggett employee."

The Greyhound also represents Doggett's ten guiding principles of client retention:
1. Surround yourself with the same breed.
2. Don't chase everything you see.
3. Get up to speed fast.
4. Stay lean.
5. Stay hungry.
6. Know when to change direction.
7. Don't bite the hand that feeds you.
8. Don't get distracted.
9. Go the full distance.
10. Run to win.

DOGGETT ADVERTISING

✧

Above: Jeff and George Doggett.

Below: Doggett Advertising's offices on East Boulevard.

CHARLOTTE MACHINE COMPANY

✧

Above: Charlotte Machine Company employees posed for this photo in 1941. Company founder Egbert Gribble is third from the left on the back row.

Below: Charlotte Machine Company has been located at 1618 Camden Road since 1926. The company sign is on the original building.

When it was established in 1914, much of Charlotte Machine Company's business consisted of producing parts for textile machines. Today the company's production includes parts for highly sophisticated industrial robots. This ability to adapt to changes in the economy has kept Charlotte Machine Company a strong and vital firm for nearly a century.

The owners of Charlotte Machine Company have endured through the boom and decline of the textile industry and seen the rise, decline and restoration of Charlotte's South End commercial district.

Mecklenburg County native Egbert Gribble in a small building on South Boulevard established Charlotte Machine Company. A machinist by trade, Gribble saw a need for a machine company that could supply component parts for the textile industry that dominated the area's economy at the time. As automobiles grew in popularity, the company added crankshaft regrinding and other automotive services to its line.

The company prospered and, in 1926, Gribble moved his machine shop to 1618 Camden Road. A couple of additions were constructed through the years but the original building is still occupied by the company today.

Since its inception, four generations of the Gribble family have been involved in Charlotte Machine Company. Egbert's two sons, Rex and Bill, joined the company following World War II. In the late '60s, Rex's son, Skip, came on board. Today, Rex, now semi-retired, Skip, Skip's wife, Nancy, and their son, Brian, all work for the firm. Bill Gribble was killed in a tragic plane crash in 1977.

Equipment for producing parts has become much more intricate over the years, but Charlotte Machine Company remains a small, family-operated business. Many employees worked for the company thirty five to forty years before retiring and several current employees can boast of twenty-five to thirty years service.

The business environment has changed completely since Charlotte Machine Company was established but the company has been able to react quickly to changing times. For example, as textiles declined in the 1950s, the firm produced parts for the Nike missile, which was being developed by Douglas Aircraft Company in a facility on Statesville Road. Today, Charlotte Machine Company produces custom machined parts for defense, medical, telecommunications and other industries throughout the world.

"We've been fortunate to have such a loyal work force," says Skip Gribble. "As a small firm, we are able to adjust quickly and adapt to changes in the marketplace.

"Our company is built on integrity, building good relationships with our customers, and doing good work," he adds. "Now that the fourth generation has joined the firm, we hope to be around for years to come."

If you grew up in Charlotte during the '30s, '40s, or '50s, Yates Louis Honey, "Y. L." to his friends, was an important part of your life. You might not have known his name, but you loved his food.

For three decades, Honey owned, or was involved with, many of the areas most popular eateries, including the popular Minute Grill at Morehead and Tryon Streets. Honey, along with his brother, Steve, and brother-in-law, Salem Suber, also operated several other Charlotte-area institutions—The Green Gables, located on Providence Road where the Manor Theater now stands, and the famed Townhouse, at the corner of Providence and Queens Roads.

Y. L. Honey established his first business, a small ice cream shop in Thomasville, North Carolina, in 1932, shortly after graduating from high school. A few years later, Honey moved to Charlotte, married Rose Suber, and entered both the restaurant and ice cream manufacturing business. His Blue Bird Ice Cream Company at the corner of Mint and Morehead Streets sold Honeydew Ice Cream, a flavorful treat still remembered fondly by old-time Charlotteans.

Honey's first Charlotte restaurant, Goody Goody BBQ, was located at the corner of Tryon and Morehead Streets and was the first of several restaurants Honey would operate on the site. His Minute Grill at that location introduced the concept of "curb service" to the area and became a Charlotte institution. Honey always considered the busy corner one of most important intersections in the city and the company he founded still owns the four-acre site today.

During the 1960s and '70s, Honey, who was both a dreamer and a doer, began to delve into other businesses, including hotels, convenience stores and commercial real estate investments. He built and operated two successful hotels and invested in one of the area's earliest convenience store chains. In addition, he built an assortment of other commercial real estate projects, including office buildings, retail stores and gas stations. But he always maintained his love for restaurants and the man who pioneered curb service restaurants was always willing to try a new concept.

Honey began to slow a bit in the 1980s and turned more control of the company over to others. His son, Yates Honey, Jr., became president in 1989. Y. L. Honey, Sr., passed away in 1997 at the age of eighty-six.

Today, Honey Enterprises is a privately owned firm specializing in two areas of business: real estate development/investment and hotels/restaurants.

Honey Properties, Incorporated, the real estate arm, invests in all kinds of real estate and owns and manages investments along the I-85 corridor from Greenville, South Carolina to Greensboro, North Carolina.

Honey's Incorporated, the hotel and restaurant operation, owns and operates Holiday Inns in Greenville, South Carolina and Gastonia, North Carolina and the one remaining Honeys Restaurant in Durham, North Carolina.

HONEY ENTERPRISES

❖

Above: Y. L. Honey in 1955.

Below. The Minute Grill, pictured in the early 1940s, introduced "curb service" to the area and became a Charlotte institution at the corner of South Tryon and Morehead Streets.

MEINEKE DISCOUNT MUFFLER SHOPS

❖

Below: This Meineke location in Pineville is typical of the company's modern service facilities.

Bottom: Each year, several hundred Meineke franchises attend classes at the company shop and training center on Independence Boulevard in Charlotte.

Sam Meineke had a background in the auto parts business and Harold Nedell had a franchising background when they decided to combine talents and establish a company that would supply one of the most basic automotive needs—the muffler—at discount prices. It proved to be the right idea at the right time.

A major milestone came in 1976 when Sam Meineke convinced a manufacturer to produce the first universal muffler, the UMAC, which changed the exhaust industry by reducing the number of mufflers required for inventory.

Since Sam and Harold opened the first Meineke Discount Muffler Shop in Houston, Texas, in 1972, the firm has grown to become an international franchiser of approximately nine hundred shops specializing in a full range of quality under-car services. In addition to exhaust systems, Meineke now offers brake service, front-end alignment, shocks and struts and a host of other services.

In 1983, Meineke was purchased by Parts, Inc., a wholly owned subsidiary of a British firm, GKN plc. After an exhaustive, nationwide search, management decided to move the company headquarters to Charlotte. A few of the twenty-one Meineke families who moved from Houston to Charlotte in 1986 are still with the company.

Today, Meineke employs approximately 115 employees at the corporate office in the First Citizens Bank Plaza on South Tryon Street and at the company-owned shop and training facility on East Independence Boulevard. Each year, several hundred Meineke franchisees attend classes at the state-of-the-art training facility to upgrade their skills and learn new management techniques.

As the result of an aggressive company growth strategy, Meineke now has locations in forty-eight states, largely locally owned and operated. These shops employ approximately forty-five hundred people. In addition, there are Meineke locations in Canada, the Dominican Republic, Guatemala, Puerto Rico, and its most recent shop openings in Mexico. Meineke's company goal is to have 2,009 shops throughout the world by the year 2009.

Meineke Discount Muffler Shops nationwide service an estimated 2.5 million vehicles each year.

Meineke recently became a subsidiary of Brambles Industries, PLC, a UK industrial services company with operations worldwide.

Since moving its headquarters to Charlotte, Meineke and its employees have become deeply involved in community activities. The company and its franchisees support Children's Miracle Network, a non-profit organization dedicated to raising funds on behalf of 170 children's hospitals across the U.S. and Canada. These hospitals serve more than 14 million children annually.

Meineke hosts an annual Golf Tournament for Champions that benefits local Children's Miracle Network hospitals including The Children's Hospital at Carolinas Medical Center, The Charlotte Institute for Rehabilitation, University Hospital, Mercy Hospital South, and Behavioral Health Centers.

Meineke is also a sponsor of the Charlotte Touchdown Club and the Bronco Nagurski Award Banquet.

When Wingate Inns made its debut at the spring 1995 AH&MA conference, industry analysts expressed expected surprise. Surprise that an all-new-construction mid-market hotel chain was being introduced for the first time in a decade, yet an expected move by industry giant Cendant Corporation (formerly HFS Incorporated), a company known for seizing opportunities.

"Not only was the occasion right for introducing a mid-market hotel chain designed for business travelers, we launched a product that is virtually timeless," said Wingate Inns' President and CEO John Paul Nichols. "We listened to what developers and consumers wanted, built a hotel chain around their requests and ensured that the technology we install will grow with the technology that comes out in the future."

Meeting with hotel developers and business travelers Cendant determined that the mid-market limited-service segment was the right niche, and then set out to offer business travelers a hotel product unlike any existing mid-priced chain.

Through extensive market research, Cendant learned that today's business travelers use modem-equipped laptop computers and fax machines that require state-of-the-art telecommunications; and that 60 percent of business travelers spend two to five hours a day working in their rooms. A survey showed that 69 percent of frequent business travelers carry their laptop computers on trips.

Wingate Inns then developed hotel specifications that include an in-room work area with a larger desk, office-like lighting, desktop dataport and two-line desk phone with voice mail, conference call and speakerphone capabilities. In addition, each Wingate Inn hotel offers automated check-in and check-out, an expanded complimentary continental breakfast, unlimited access to a free twenty-four-hour business center with fax, printer and copying equipment, and free local calls and long-distance access.

Adding free high-speed Internet access in every guest room further distinguished the Wingate Inn brand as the only hotel chain with this much-desired amenity.

"What we've done is turn guest rooms into satellite offices, and we're not charging travelers extra for the office-like capability and services," Nichols said.

Business travelers also like to relax on the road, with comfortable chairs, larger televisions with remote controls and a place to exercise, if they have the time. Wingate Inns satisfies all of these needs, as well as others, including in-room iron and ironing boards, a central commission pay program for travel agents and designated toll-free hotline.

The Wingate Inn-Coliseum, just off I-77 on Tyvola Road, offers 122 guest rooms, including seven suites, two meeting rooms plus the boardroom, an outdoor pool, and, of course, all other Wingate Inn signature amenities, including the complimentary twenty-four-hour business center, fitness center and spa.

WINGATE INNS

Since 1972, *The Leader* has been Charlotte's alternative voice for news, politics, cultural events, society news and commentary. Founded by media veterans Stan and Sis Kaplan, who still own the weekly newspaper today, *The Leader* has earned a reputation for in-depth, investigative reporting and award-winning writing. From political coverage to human interest stories to music and theater, Charlotteans can count on *The Leader* for insightful coverage of important issues facing Charlotte and Mecklenburg County.

And now, John Kilgo is back. *The Leader's* cover columnist and first publisher has returned to provide his unique brand of commentary. Kilgo headlines a group of columnists who provide readers with thought-provoking commentary every week.

The Leader has expanded its horizons to the north Mecklenburg area. A sister publication, the *North Meck Leader*, provides detailed coverage of news, features and more in the growing north Mecklenburg towns of Huntersville, Cornelius, and Davidson, as well as the University of North Carolina Charlotte area.

The Kaplans established themselves as leaders in the Charlotte media when they launched radio stations WROQ (FM 95.1) and Big WAYS (AM 610) in 1965. Then in 1972, Kilgo, the station's news director, helped the Kaplans launch their first newspaper endeavor, the predecessor of today's *Leader* newspaper.

The Leader's editor Andy Warfield maintains a focus on local news, including the pressing issues of growth and the challenges facing local public education and local government in a rapidly growing metropolitan area. Over the years, *The Leader* has received dozens of awards from the North Carolina Press Association, the National Association of Advertising Publishers and the Association of Free Community Newspapers for its writing, photography, advertising design, typography, and general excellence, among others.

The Leader and the *North Meck Leader* reach 140,000 readers throughout Charlotte and Mecklenburg County. Supported entirely by advertisers, *The Leader* is free, but its value to the community is priceless.

RADIATOR SPECIALTY COMPANY/ THE BLUMENTHAL FOUNDATION

Radiator Specialty Company manufactures and sells a wide variety of automotive aftermarket and household use products that solve problems most of us face daily. Founded by I. D. "Dick" Blumenthal in 1924, the company is headquartered in Charlotte, and has manufacturing and research/development facilities in Indian Trail, North Carolina and Mississauga, Ontario, Canada.

The stellar reputation of the company and its products is a matter of family pride. It started when Dick was stranded in Charlotte with a leaky radiator and was referred to George Ray, a tinsmith who had developed a powder that sealed the leak without removing the radiator. Blumenthal was so impressed that he began marketing the product and eventually established Radiator Specialty. Now earning over $100 million annually, the company has diversified and grown from a twelve-by-fourteen-foot office to over seven hundred thousand square feet of space.

Growing from one product—Solder Seal® Powder Radiator Repair—to over 2,000 products in 10 different market divisions in 78 countries, the company remains dedicated to producing and selling only the highest-quality products. Blumenthal family members have led Radiator Specialty from its beginning. Dick and his brother, Herman, worked together for forty years and upon Dick's death in 1978 Herman became CEO. Today, Herman is chairman emeritus and his son Alan, is chairman of the board. Son Samuel, a clinical psychologist, is a management consultant for the company.

A major Blumenthal legacy is Wildacres Retreat, in Little Switzerland, North Carolina. A fourteen-hundred-acre scenic mountain property purchased by Dick in the 1930s and dedicated to the betterment of human and interfaith relations. Wildacres has operated since 1972 as a public foundation hosting non-profit groups with planned educational programs. Herman's son, Philip, is director of Wildacres and the Blumenthal Foundation.

Through the Wildacres Leadership Initiative, twenty-five young emerging leaders from throughout North Carolina commit two years to an extensive leadership program grounded in the humanities. Both Ann Clark, 1994 "Principal of the Year" and now lead principal at Governor's Village, a four-school campus of the Charlotte-Mecklenburg Schools, and Leslie Takahashi-Morris, now executive director of the Initiative, were in the Initiative's first class. Its fourth class will begin in October 2001.

In addition to Wildacres, the Blumenthal family has given generously to hundreds of charities over the past four decades. Among these are the Blumenthal Performing Arts Center, Blumenthal Cancer Center, Shalom Park, Temple Beth El, and many colleges and universities. Hugh McColl Jr., chairman of the board for Bank of America, has described Herman Blumenthal, as "the most important philanthropist in Charlotte, and perhaps in the region."

✧

Above: Radiator Specialty produces a wide array of products, and recently opened at Indian Trail its third cone production facility which manufacturers 320 cones per hour.

Below: Radiator Specialty Company has grown from a single product (Solder Seal® Power Radiator Repair) to a modern diversified company that manufactures and sells over 2000 products in 10 different market divisions in 78 countries.

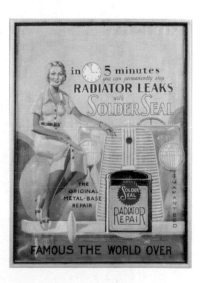

BUILDING A GREATER CHARLOTTE

Charlotte-Mecklenburg County's construction,

engineering, and real estate development

firms shape tomorrow's skyline

✦

*The 1908 Realty Building at Trade and
Tryon Streets was the first steel-frame
skyscraper in the Carolinas.*

E. C. GRIFFITH
COMPANY

In 1912, an ambitious young entrepreneur, E. C. Griffith, Sr., left a secure job with American Bank & Trust Company to launch his own land development business. Now operated by the third generation of the Griffith family, the E. C. Griffith Company has become one of the largest and most respected developers in the area.

A bold and aggressive businessman, E. C. Griffith, Sr., known as "Griff," financed his many projects by borrowing money from any source he could find, including his barber. According to which version of the story you choose to believe, the barber loaned Griff $2,000 on a four percent note or $4,000 on a two percent note. The story is told both ways. But there's no doubt it involved what was a large sum of money for its day.

Griff invested his borrowed money well and the company became highly successful during the 1920s, as Griff bought up farms and developed industrial parks and residential subdivisions in all sections of the growing city.

Among Griff's early developments was the exclusive Eastover Subdivision off Providence Road, which remains one of Charlotte's premier neighborhoods.

Like many other businesses, the young development firm, successful but highly leveraged, was nearly brought to its knees by the great economic depression that gripped the nation in the 1930s. At one point, the depression nearly cost Griff every property he had managed to acquire, but the banks showed a rare bit of compassion.

One banker, contemplating repossession, was quoted as asking his Board, "If Griff can't make it with these properties, what are we going to do with them?" The bankers gave Griff more time to pay off his loans and the company survived. The hardships of the depression and the threat of nearly losing all he had worked so hard to build, had a profound effect on E.C. Griffith, Sr. After struggling to pay off his loans and keep the business afloat, Griff taught his sons not to take risks and to seldom borrow money, the opposite of his original philosophy.

One story from the Great Depression tells how E. C. Griffith, Sr. built his dream house at the corner of Eastover Road and Cherokee Road for $60,000. Because of the terrible economic conditions, he was forced to sell it for $30,000—$15,000 in cash and $15,000 on a note.

Griff married Frances Rudy and they had five children, three boys and two girls: E.C. Jr., known as "Sonny," David, Francie, Jimbo and Sally. By the time Griff died in 1973 and the second generation took control of the company, the watchword was caution. Griff had set a clear direction; pay down debt and don't take chances. As a result the company was virtually free of debt and any development was done with cash.

The third generation, headed by James R. Griffith, Jr., and his brother, Preston, is now running the business. Their philosophy is somewhere between their grandfather's entrepreneurial risk taking and the second generation's Great Depression risk-aversion approach, with the second generation overseeing and approving all their projects. The current philosophy is best described as prudent, but progressive. The family is well aware of surveys that show only about 11% of family businesses successfully survive to the third generation because of punitive estate tax laws, the so-called "death tax."

James R. "Jim" Griffith, Jr. worked with Coldwell Banker Commercial Real Estate Services, Inc. before joining the family firm in 1988. Preston, formerly with Charter Properties, Inc., followed in 1990. They both have received their CCIM designation, referred to by some as a PhD in real estate.

Using the Total Quality Management business philosophy, Jim and Preston managed to restructure the company in a way that satisfied the interests of the second generation while providing new opportunities for the third, and, hopefully, future generations of Griffiths. The business plan that insured this orderly procession earned the company the prestigious North Carolina Family Business Forum award, presented by Duke University's Fuqua School of Business in 1997.

According to a recent inventory, E. C. Griffith Company and its associated entities total nearly one thousand acres of development, including apartment complexes, shopping centers, medical offices, industrial parks, office buildings and residential neighborhoods.

Recent successful investments include the Woodlawn Crossing retail center anchored by Harpers Restaurant; Tyvola Executive Park, a 45,000 square-foot office park; Four Points by Sheraton, an 11-story, 195-room hotel on McDowell Street; Museum Medical Plaza, a 10,000 square foot medical facility built for Presbyterian Hospital; a 1.2 acre uptown ground lease, known as Seventh Street Station, to Bank of America; Eastover Ridge Apartments, a two-phase luxury apartment complex on Randolph Road totaling 424 units; and Eastover Lakes, a 360 acre mixed use project.

❖

Above: E. C. Griffith Company was very involved in the commercial and residential development along West Morehead Street following World War I. This 1927 aerial photo shows the Wesley Heights Subdivision (lower left) and several of the commercial ventures developed by the company along Morehead.

Below: During the 1920s, E. C. Griffith, Sr. developed Eastover, which remains one of Charlotte's premier neighborhoods. This 1926 photo shows an Eastover construction site looking west toward Providence Road. E. C. Griffith, Sr. is pictured at the left.

BUILDING A GREATER CHARLOTTE

✧

Above: This 1930s photo shows Hempstead Place in Eastover, looking toward Fenton Place. Today the small oak saplings in the photo have grown to create a cathedral-like canopy over the street.

Below: E.C. Griffith, Sr. built his dream home in Eastover for $60,000. Because of economic conditions during the Great Depression, he was forced to sell the house for $30,000—$15,000 in cash and the remainder on a note.

Although conflict often exists between developers and environmentalists, the third generation members of the Griffith family consider themselves "concerned environmentalists." Their philosophy is to renew and replace the ecosystems that have been disrupted and even create new environmental wetlands where possible.

The company recently agreed to deed thirty acres of the wooded wetlands on the edge of Eastover to the Catawba Lands Conservancy. A stewardship fund has been established to maintain the property which has been described as "one of the last remaining urban forests and an attractive wetlands habitat."

The company also demonstrated its environmental awareness while developing Eastover Ridge Apartments. The apartments were oriented so that the balconies face a small creek that some believed to flow only when it rained. The City, however, wanted to "rip-rap" the entire creek, which would have eliminated a sandy streambed as well as the vegetation on the stream banks. Jim Griffith vigorously protested this policy because he had observed a variety of small fish in the pools of the slow-flowing system. "We worked hard to convince the bureaucrats, including one who said there was no wildlife in the creek because it was polluted with sewage runoff," Griffith explained.

At Griffith's insistence, the creek now has small weirs or dams to increase the depth and volume of water for aquatic and wild life. The stream is now home to mallards, great blue herons, kingfishers, muskrats, catfish, large mouth bass, and streambanks of ornamental plants and vegetation full of insects to support the food chain for the life that thrives around the stream.

E.C. Griffith Company is also deeply involved in a variety of civic activities. Generations of Charlotte families played on the ball fields along Randolph Road, which were "loaned" to the Myers Park/Trinity Little League for forty-two years. These were believed to be the oldest continuous-play Little League fields in the nation.

Preston Griffith has been deeply involved in the St. Frances Jobs Program, originated by Christ Episcopal Church to reach out to at-risk young adults, most of whom are school drops outs, and to give them a second chance. Preston became chairman of the Board of St. Frances and the program has grown to become BRIDGE (Building Responsible Individuals through Discipline, Guidance and Education) and provides mentors, education services and training for many at-risk youngsters.

The company is also a strong supporter of such organizations as United Way, American Cancer Society Research, Special Olympics, Down Syndrome Association, Cystic Fibrosis, Good Fellows, Goodwill, Salvation Army, Catawba Valley Land Trust and many others.

E. C. Griffith, Sr. was a founding member of the Mint Museum of Art, Inc. and donated the museum's thirty-acre site on Randolph Road around 1933. The company was also the marketing agent for the Stephens Company, which developed Myers Park. A June 1921 site plan for Myers Park, printed on linen, shows that lots at that time ranged from $500 to $4,000 for the most prestigious lots.

With 20/20 hindsight, those wonderful stories from earlier generations, which appear now to reflect such genius, were probably very risky at the time. For instance, the site for Westminster Presbyterian Church at Colville Road and Randolph Road was a land trade. E. C. Griffith Company received 360 acres, with three lakes, in the country. The land is located on what is now W.T. Harris Boulevard and Davis Lake/Statesville Road. Another storybook deal was the trade of a single lot in Eastover for ninety acres around the Quail Hollow Country Club.

A lot of luck is involved in the land speculation business and the growth and success of Charlotte is due to the efforts of many fine people and companies, which the E.C. Griffith family company will always appreciate.

Members of the E. C. Griffith family are descendants of Reverend David Griffith who served in General George Washington's Revolutionary Army. Reverend Griffith was a member of the Society of Cincinnati of 1787. An impressive document signed by George Washington has an engraved illustration on sheepskin, which depicts an eagle in a starburst symbolizing the birth of a new nation and, in the lower left corner, a vanquished King of England surrounded by storm clouds and lighting bolts which helped to keep British ships and reinforcements away. During the Great Depression, financier J. P. Morgan offered to purchase the document for $20,000. The offer was turned down.

With a solid family business structure in place and eighty-eight years of experience, E. C. Griffith Company is poised to remain one of the area's most progressive, and successful, development firms.

✧

Above: E. C. Griffith Company constructed small weirs to protect fish and wildlife at the Eastover Ridge Apartments. The project is typical of the firm's concern for the environment.

Below: Among the many successful and visible investments by the E.C. Griffith Company is the Four Points by Sheraton, an 11-story, 195-room hotel on McDowell Street.

THE DOWD COMPANY

Since it was founded in 1972, The Dowd Company has earned a reputation for building distinguished homes of exceptional quality.

Company founder Ken Dowd, whose background includes a degree in business and economics and experience as a mortgage banker, is a licensed contractor in both North and South Carolina.

The Dowd Company is proud to have been part of Charlotte's growth over the past three decades. Homes by The Dowd Company are currently being built in the neighborhoods of Highgate, Kensington at Ballantyne, Providence Springs and Seven Eagles. Homes and plans by The Dowd Company have been featured in *Good Housekeeping's Country Living*; *House and Gardens' Plans Guide*; and *Home* magazine.

The Dowd Company's continued success is due in great part to the relationships it has built and maintained over the years. Many of the company's subcontractors and craftsmen have been with the company since it's beginning and now several represent the second generation of their family in the construction industry.

"Our company goal has been to develop communities and build homes that reflect value and excellent workmanship," says Ken Dowd. "Our home buyers are confident in the quality of our product and our careful planning and attention to details." Backed by sound business practices, experience and imagination, The Dowd Company is looking forward to many more years of successful home building in the vibrant Charlotte community.

❖

Above: Ken Dowd, president of The Dowd Company.

Below: Seven Eagles, built by The Dowd Company.

HARRINGTON & ASSOCIATES

Charlotte's phenomenal growth during the past quarter century has created a demand for homebuilders of outstanding ability and a deep understanding of the local real estate market. One of the most successful and respected of these builders is Harrington & Associates.

Gene Harrington, who founded the firm in 1977, compliments his construction knowledge with efficient organizational skills, an extensive understanding of financing, and sound business principles. Harrington is also a licensed contractor in North Carolina (unlimited) and South Carolina, a senior residential appraiser (retired) and a licensed real estate broker.

Harrington served as president of the Charlotte Home Builders Association in 1982 and, in that same year, was honored by his peers as Charlotte's "Builder of the Year."

The reputation of Harrington & Associates has been built by innovative designs, financial stability and craftsmanship. This reputation is reinforced by job-site safety and cleanliness, a "walk through" inspection that promotes customer satisfaction, and unequalled service before, and after, the sale. In addition, all Harrington & Associates portfolio plans are reviewed and sealed by a structural engineer.

Harrington & Associates recognizes the importance of its management team in maintaining its reputation for quality and integrity. For this reason, senior staff members of Harrington & Associates are also licensed contractors and all staff members attend educational classes on a regular basis.

Homes by Harrington & Associates are located in many of Charlotte's finest neighborhoods, including Bellemeade, Berkeley, Crofton, Kensington at Ballantyne, Old St. Andrews at Piper Glen, Oxford Hunt, Providence Springs, Winterbrooke, Montibello, Quail Hollow, Hampton Leas, and Highgate.

Homes by Harrington & Associates are characterized by the excellent craftsmanship that discriminating homebuyers deserve, attractive designs that compliment a family's lifestyle, and, above all, standards that reflect the Harrington reputation.

❖

Above: Gene Harrington, President of Harrington & Associates

Below: One of the stately homes built in HighGate by Harrington & Associates.

HARRINGTON/ DOWD REALTY COMPANY

✧

The entrance to HighGate, a Harrington/Dowd development in Weddington.

Ken Dowd of The Dowd Company and Gene Harrington of Harrington & Associates formed Harrington/Dowd to develop exclusive neighborhoods and serve the marketing requirements of Charlotte's most recognized homebuilders.

Since planning its first neighborhood in 1981, Harrington/Dowd has continued to create neighborhoods that have a distinctive character. Harrington/Dowd has emphasized this uniqueness by inviting a select group of custom builders to create a variety of new home designs. All builders and their designs are required to meet the strict standards established by Harrington/Dowd through deed restrictions and by architectural control.

Harrington/Dowd is committed to continuing the tradition of marketing and developing exclusive neighborhoods. Street lamps, sidewalks, cul-de-sacs, and the preservation of natural terrain characterize these neighborhoods.

Every member of the Harrington/Dowd on-site staff is an experienced professional, helping buyers make informed comparisons of value and assisting them in choosing the right property and design, which best suits their personal needs and lifestyles.

The fine neighborhoods created by Harrington/Dowd include Bellemeade, Berkeley, Crofton, Kensington at Ballantyne, Old St. Andrews at Piper Glen, Oxford Hunt, Providence Springs, Winterbrooke and HighGate.

Christopher Phelps established his residential design firm twelve years ago in a small upstairs office in an old commercial building in Concord.

The timing could not have been better. The tremendous growth of the Charlotte area was creating a demand for unique, upscale homes and Phelps' residential designs provided the style and elegance buyers were seeking.

Working with nearly thirty of Charlotte's premier homebuilders, Christopher Phelps' hallmark is innovative design ranging from European/contemporary and Georgian, to low-country style homes. His European reproductions—French country and chateau, English Tudor, Italian Renaissance—reflect England, France and Italy's ageless charm and grace.

A native of upstate New York, Phelps earned a degree in architectural technology from the State University of New York. After working a few years for a family-owned commercial architectural firm he decided to exchange the snow and cold for the sunny Carolinas and moved to Charlotte, where he landed a job designing stores for the Belk department store chain. His first love, however, was designing innovative homes and, in 1989, he decided to establish his own residential design firm. In the company's early days, Phelps was also a homebuilder, an experience that provided useful insights into the practicalities of building a custom home.

Phelps' background as a successful builder of upscale homes and his design expertise enable him to look at building a home from the owner's perspective as well as the builder's viewpoint, considering all aspects of the process from style and budget to the actual lot and building materials.

Builders who work with Phelps say he can intuitively sense what a family needs and wants in a home, based on his discussions with them. A photographic memory enables Phelps' vision to become reality through a comprehensive, hand-drawn sketch, and a dying art form since the advent of technology. A staff of skilled designers and draftspersons put the finishing touches on the design with detailed drawings for the builders.

Award-winning homes designed by Christopher Phelps and Associates are located in some of Charlotte's most prestigious country club communities, including The Peninsula, The Point, and Ballantyne. The firm has also designed new, historically correct custom homes for established neighborhoods such as Eastover, Myers Park and Dilworth.

Christopher Phelps and Associates grew quickly from a one-person operation to eight employees by 1995. At that time Phelps decided to move the firm to Charlotte, where it has grown to 14 employees.

Due to its continued growth, the company is moving its offices to a new arts and crafts style building in South End. The Phelps-designed building reflects the architecture of the neighboring buildings and blends well into the historic Dilworth neighborhood.

✧

Above: Christopher Phelps homes are designed for the art of living.
COURTESY OF PAT SHANKLIN.

Below: Innovative designs by Christopher Phelps range from European/contemporary and Georgian to low-county style homes.
COURTESY OF PAT SHANKLIN.

CROSLAND

Recognized as one of the Southeast's leading real estate companies, Crosland traces its roots to the 1930s when John Crosland, Sr. began building houses in Charlotte's growing neighborhoods.

By 1937 he had founded the John Crosland Company, moving into new areas with his popular single-family homes. Shortly thereafter, he expanded into retail development, adding small shopping centers to the Crosland communities.

The John Crosland Company thrived during World War II by building homes for defense industry workers in Eastern North Carolina. Its homebuilding reputation was solidified as it developed neighborhoods to serve many families during the post-war housing boom. Often doing business on a handshake, Crosland built his company on sound business principles and was known for his personal integrity.

Crosland's only child, John, Jr., joined the business in 1955 after serving in the U.S. Army during the Korean conflict. Hardworking, thorough, and committed to his father's values, the son developed his father's solid business into a burgeoning enterprise. He was named president in 1965.

Assembling a management team known for its talent and experience, John, Jr., built upon the company's foundation in homebuilding to expand into multi-family residential development, commercial and residential land development, and more sophisticated retail projects. Having sold its mid-Atlantic homebuilding operations to Centex Homes in 1988, Crosland recently re-entered the homebuilding business. Today known as Crosland, the company's portfolio has grown to a market value exceeding $600 million.

Whether developing its own projects or working on behalf of investors, the company's commitment to quality is evident wherever it does business. Crosland has earned a reputation for exemplary customer service and for maximizing value at every stage of a real estate project's lifecycle—acquisition, land planning, design, financing, construction, marketing, management, and disposition.

Crosland uses innovative planning and design to make the communities where it does business better places to live, work and shop, and the company retains most of the assets it develops.

In 1999, after conducting an international search to identify his successor, John Crosland, Jr., named Todd W. Mansfield the company's CEO. Crosland acceded to the position of chairman of the board of directors. As former executive vice president and general manager of the Disney Development Company for eleven years, Mansfield had supervised the development of more than $3 billion in commercial and residential properties worldwide.

Today, Mansfield and Crosland lead a company distinguished by excellence. Sharing their commitment to integrity and customer satisfaction, the company's 230 employees work through six product areas—Office and Industrial, Apartments, Retail, Land Development, Contracting, and Homes. Often collaborating, these specialists integrate residential, office, retail and commercial uses into distinctive destination communities.

Throughout the years, Crosland has helped shape the Charlotte region into one of the country's most desirable places to live. Dotting the area's landscape are such signature projects as:

- Whitehall in southwest Charlotte, a 680-acre development that features a technology park, corporate office park, retail district, residences, two hotel sites, and appealing greenspaces with several lakes.
- StoneCrest at Piper Glen offers 467,000 square feet of retail, entertainment, dining, and service space, and includes an innovative Children's Village that clusters a variety of stores catering to children.
- Sharon Corners in SouthPark was the first specialty center of its kind in Charlotte and was recognized in 1995 by the International Council of Shopping Centers with the International Design and Development Award.
- Crestmont at Ballantyne is an elegant, custom-built apartment community that fulfills Crosland's vision to provide comfortable, convenient living.

The company also builds affordable housing with partners like The Affordable Housing Group and North Carolina Low Income Housing Corporation and has been active in the retirement and continuing care markets for seniors.

Each Crosland project supports the company's philosophy of "building community." Extending that commitment into community service, Crosland contributes both time and money to programs for families, youth and seniors, as well as those that address education, the environment, historic preservation and the arts.

Setting high standards for leadership, the company has been recognized with numerous awards for project excellence, including the National Association of Home Builders' Pillars of the Industry Award for Olmsted Park, a landmark apartment community near uptown Charlotte.

John, Jr. has been recognized as "Builder of the Year" by *Professional Builder* magazine, was named to the National Housing Hall of Fame by the National Association of Home Builders, was recipient of the U.S. Housing and Urban Development Commissioner's Award and served as founding chairman of Habitat for Humanity of Charlotte.

Over the past six decades, Crosland has developed, built or managed more than 15,000 multi-family residential units, over 13,500 single-family homes, 35 retail centers, 25 commercial buildings, 2,000 acres of commercial property, and 110 residential communities in the Carolinas, Tennessee, and Georgia. In addition to its Charlotte headquarters, Crosland has a Raleigh office, and also operates in Durham, Greensboro, Winston-Salem, Asheville, Columbia, Augusta and Nashville.

The vision for the years ahead includes mixed-use developments—creating destination communities with a mix of housing types, lifestyle amenities, retail options and commercial development that respond to customer preferences. One example of this type of "placemaking" is Birkdale Village. Developed in partnership with Pappas Properties, it brings several of the company's disciplines together to create an exciting commercial and residential venue.

The company has earned a reputation for quality development, unsurpassed customer service and for conducting business with uncompromising integrity. By continuing to focus upon building lasting relationships with customers, partners, and associates, Crosland is well positioned to fulfill its mission of becoming a leading diversified community builder throughout the Southeast.

✧

Above: Sharon Corners was the first specialty center of its kind in Charlotte. It was recognized in 1995 with the International Design and Development Award, presented by the International Council of Shopping Centers.

Below: With its variety of thirty-six shops, restaurants, galleries, salons, and innovative Children's Village, StoneCrest at Piper Glen is a favored destination for shoppers in South Charlotte.

John Crosland: A Tribute

Throughout its history, Charlotte has been blessed with outstanding leaders—men and women whose vision and determination built the city we enjoy today. One of the greatest of these giants was John Crosland, whose mark on Charlotte's home building industry may never be surpassed.

When Crosland died in 1977, his firm had built 6,500 homes over a 40-year period. At the same time, he earned a reputation as a fair-minded, serious businessman who tried to satisfy his customers, even if it meant fixing a serious problem in a house years after its completion and sale.

Crosland was born in 1898 in Richmond County, the son of the second largest cotton planter in North Carolina. But it became clear early that his interests were more in business than in farming.

After attending Davidson College and North Carolina State University, Crosland came to Charlotte. His first job after college was as cashier and teller at American Trust Company, a forerunner of today's Bank of America. In 1924, he went to work for a local lumber company and ten years later started his homebuilding career with a few houses on McDowell Street that sold for $1,800.

Crosland's first major project was Club Colony, off Selwyn Avenue near Myers Park Country Club. Other well-known Crosland neighborhoods include Morningside, Forest Park, Ashley Park, Plaza Hills, Hampshire Hills, Huntingtowne Farms, Beverly Woods, Stonehaven, Coventry Woods, Foxcroft East, Clanton Park, and Sardis Woods.

His son, John Crosland, Jr., joined the firm in 1956 and took over the company in 1973 when his father retired. The younger Crosland, who went on to enjoy his own successful career as a homebuilder and developer, remembers that his father put his greatest emphasis on fairness and honesty. "He really believed in doing the right thing and following through," he says.

His son also remembers his father's business philosophy: "He never wanted to be obligated to someone and be in the position where he could not meet his obligation." This philosophy reflected his father's struggles during the devastating economic depression of the 1930s.

Crosland was also respected as a man who lived up to his agreements, whether they were spelled out in a legal document or not. "Too many people try to use a contract to get out of something they agreed to do," recalled a long-time friend. "But, if he made a business promise to someone twenty years before, he would fulfill it to the *nth* degree. It didn't have to be in writing."

In a report to his employees a year before he died, Crosland expressed his business philosophy in his own words: "Honesty is not subject to criticism in any culture. Shades of dishonesty simply invite demoralizing and reprehensible judgments. A well-founded reputation for scrupulous dealing is itself a priceless company asset."

Above: John Crosland, Sr., 1898-1977.

Right: This brochure promoted John Crosland's first major project, Club Colony.

Retaining the beauty and charm of an older home requires the skills of an experienced home remodeler. For the past decade, owners of many of Charlotte's most distinguished homes have depended on Construction Management of Charlotte to preserve their investments.

Construction Management of Charlotte was founded in 1991 by Dave Scholl, who has more than thirty years experience in the construction business. The firm's specialty is renovating and updating older homes in classic neighborhoods such as Myers Park, Eastover and Dilworth.

CMC's project portfolio reveals a wide variety of remodeling projects, including additions, bathrooms, garages, and finishing basements and attics. Many of the projects have required major "house surgery" and load transfers to correct structural problems and bring the homes into compliance with modern building codes. Working closely with designer Jeanine DeVaney of Charlotte In-Vironments, Inc., Scholl and his crews have transformed outdated kitchens into masterpieces of craftsmanship as well as beautiful, workable living spaces.

"We have three priorities," says Scholl. "Quality, cost and time. They are all priorities, but they come in that order."

CMC provides clients with a unique contract that guards against unexpected expenses during renovation. "We prepare a detailed budget estimate, then we assign a fixed fee based on the budget," explains Scholl. "This way there is no incentive to cut corners or escalate the cost."

CONSTRUCTION MANAGEMENT OF CHARLOTTE, INC.

Scholl holds North Carolina and South Carolina general contracting licenses and is a member of the National Home Builders Association, Remodeler's Council, and the National Association of Remodelers Institute (NARI). He serves as a member of the NARI membership committee and is a member of Central Piedmont Community College's Construction Industry Advisory Board.

Scholl and his superintendent, Buz Knight, have earned their certified remodelers certificates and several of CMC's carpenters are certified lead carpenters.

Scholl is general manager of CMC and his wife, Faith, is president. Buz Knight, who has been with CMC for more than eight years, is the company's general superintendent. Ethelyn Scholl, Dave's sister-in-law, is the company's administrative assistant. CMC has thirteen employees and contracts with a number of highly regarded subcontractors.

Scholl started CMC with just himself and a helper. The company has grown from a first-year volume of $250,000 to an anticipated volume in excess of $2 million for 2001.

With the renewed emphasis on preserving the best of Charlotte's historic neighborhoods, Construction Management of Charlotte antici-pates continued growth and a bright future.

Above: Dave Scholl.

Below: Construction Management of Charlotte specializes in renovating and updating older homes, such as this kitchen remodeling in the historic Dilworth neighborhood.

COURTESY OF LESLIE WRIGHT DOW, WRIGHT COMMUNICATIONS.

SIMONINI BUILDERS, INC.

❖
Above: Simonini Builders' homes are located in the Charlotte area's finest neighborhoods.
PHOTO COURTESY OF ROBERT STARLING PHOTOGRAPHY, ORLANDO, FL.

Below: This cape cod inspired home by Simonini Builders is located at The Point on Lake Norman.
COURTESY OF SOUTHERN EXPOSURE PHOTOGRAPHY, CHARLOTTE, NC.

Bottom: This residence, located in The Peninsula on Lake Norman, received a National Sales & Marketing Silver Award, one of the many local, regional, and national distinctions earned by Simonini Builders.
COURTESY OF SOUTHERN EXPOSURE PHOTOGRAPHY, CHARLOTTE, NC.

Simonini Builders, whose custom-built homes have set the standard for quality and luxury in the Charlotte area, was formed in 1994. But the company's construction lineage goes back nearly a century.

It all started with Paul Simonini, who founded Industrial Cork Comapny in Chicago in 1905. As the story goes, Paul Simonini, the son of Italian immigrants, designed an indoor ice rink as part of his master's theses while working on an engineering degree. Shortly after starting his company, which installed rigid insulation systems, Paul called on the builders of Chicago Stadium, hoping to sell them cork insulation for the big project.

"Grandfather discovered they were including an indoor ice rink and the only plan they could find for such a project was the master's theses my grandfather had written several years before," recalls Alan Simonini, chief executive officer of Simonini Builders.

Paul got the job, the first major project for his young company, and Chicago Stadium with the ice rink designed by a college student became home to the Chicago Blackhawks hockey team and, later, Michael Jordan and the Chicago Bulls. The stadium was only recently demolished to make way for a new arena.

In the late '40s, Al Simonini, Paul's son and Alan's father, joined the growing family firm, which had become the distributor and installer for all types of rigid insulation. In 1971 Al decided to retire to Atlanta and sold his half of the business to his brother. Then, in 1973, Al moved to River Hills, a new community on Lake Wylie.

"Dad had retired when he was only about fifty, but he started joint-venturing a couple of houses in River Hills with a friend," Alan explains. Pretty soon he was back in the construction business.

Alan graduated from Arizona State University in 1975 and started working for some of the subcontractors building his father's homes in River Hills. He joined his father and brother, David, when Al decided to start building in Charlotte.

After trying to compete with other builders for a couple of years in the highly competitive market for popularly priced homes, Al and his two sons decided to return to the luxury home market, starting with several homes on Myers Park Drive. By the time The Peninsula at Lake Norman started developing in the early '90s, Simonini Builders' reputation was growing.

In 1991 Simonini Builders built the first million-dollar spec home in Charlotte for the Street of Dreams promotion at The Peninsula. But it was only the beginning. In 1998 Simonini Builders constructed the first $3 million spec home in The Peninsula.

David Simonini left to start his own business in 1994, and Alan Simonini decided to focus on the construction of fine quality, custom homes. At this time developer Ray Killian, Jr. became a 50-50 partner with Alan in Simonini Builders. Al is now permanently retired and living in Florida.

Killian, who graduated from St. Andrews College, serves as executive vice president and CFO of Simonini Builders. Killian has more than a quarter-century's experience in real estate and

development and has earned the prestigious Certified Commercial Investor Member (CCIM) designation, the highest recognition in the field of real estate and investment brokerage.

Other key executives of Simonini Builders are Phil Hughes, vice president/construction, and Bill Saint, vice president/operations and controller.

Soon after joining forces, Alan Simonini and Ray Killian, Jr. set new goals for the company that were little short of a management revolution. This undertaking was designed to (1) transform Simonini Builders from a family-run enterprise into a true business with strategic plans, goals and objectives, but to do so in a way that combines the best of both cultures; (2) create a team of employees and trade contractors that support each other, both in their professional development and personal growth; and (3) put before every team member—including the customer—a computer system that provides the information he or she needs to satisfy a client the first time, and every time.

These efforts were rewarded in 2000 when Simonini Builders became the first builder in the Carolinas to receive the National Housing Quality Gold Award from the National Association of Home Builders, the most prestigious honor in the home building industry. Simonini Builders is also the first custom builder in the nation to receive the Gold Award.

Simonini Builders has earned its reputation for excellence through dedication to quality, commitment to service, and an uncompromising desire to build the very finest home possible.

A recent customer feedback survey by the well-respected national consulting firm, Woodland & O'Brien, found that a stunning one hundred percent of Simonini Builders' customers would refer the firm to a friend or associate, and "satisfaction with home" rated an unparalleled ninety-seven percent.

Simonini Builders' homes are found in the Charlotte area's finest neighborhoods, including Myers Park, Eastover, The Peninsula, Challis Farm, Ballantyne, and Morrocroft. Simonini Builders homes are also found in River Hills and Riverpointe on Lake Wylie and Governor's Island, Alexander Island and The Pointe on Lake Norman.

The company has also earned a reputation for building in-fill homes, such as Myers Park City Homes, that enhance and revitalize the city's older and more desired neighborhoods. Myers Park City Homes were designed specifically to blend in with the Myers Park neighborhood and to reflect the neighborhood's traditional architecture.

Simonini Builders' success more than validates the efforts of its thirty-five team members to create a company that makes good on its mission: to deliver superior quality homes, outstanding customer service, and forge relationships with clients built upon trust. "We're building our company the way we build a house," says Killian, "a solid foundation to support a lot of activity within."

BUILDING A GREATER CHARLOTTE

SOUTHERN ENGINEERING

❖

President Charles Saleh.

Southern Engineering has built its reputation as one of the top steel fabrication companies in the Southeast, utilizing assets that include a ninety-year company history, a financial infusion by new owners, talented new management, experienced employees, and the loyalty and trust of suppliers and satisfied customers.

The company's two-hundred-thousand-square-foot facility, located on a thirteen-acre site on Charlotte's Wilkinson Boulevard, has undergone over $7 million in improvements since 1994.

The Berry family of Charlotte founded Southern in 1911 and operated the company for three generations. Known as "Little Pittsburgh," the company flourished as one of the premier steel fabricators in the region. Its steel built many of the major buildings in Charlotte for years, including the Charlotte Coliseum, Ovens Auditorium, and most of the power plants in the region.

By the time the recession of the early 1990s rolled around, Southern Engineering was in trouble. When Charles Saleh, company president, arrived at Southern Engineering in 1994 he faced a formidable task. He found the company in bankruptcy and reeling from the aftermath of a tornado. The handful of remaining workers was working with obsolete equipment. Under his leadership, Southern rehired laid-off employees and encouraged creative problem solving while overhauling inefficient and outdated practices.

Southern Engineering has been restored the hard way: "one employee, one supplier, and one customer at a time."

The company's management and employees are serious about achieving Southern's mission to be the premier steel fabricator in the region, providing superior quality and on-time delivery in every project. This objective is based on each employee's performing with the highest integrity, commitment, and loyalty to customers and the company.

Charlotte's central location is a key factor in Southern Engineering service to an increasing number of clients throughout the Southeast. The company's ties to Charlotte are strong, depending not only on the company's long history of operation there, but also on the desire of its officials and employees to continue playing a part in the region's success and growth. "We need to be known for our ethics and for making our community a better place to live," Saleh says, demonstrating his own dedication and that of the company through participation in many community, charitable, and professional organizations and programs.

During the past several years, Southern's operations have climbed steadily, thanks in large part to new investments in state-of-the-art technology for production and process automation. Computerized equipment assures increased efficiency, higher quality, and greater accuracy.

In a policy aimed at expanding Southern's geographical and job reach, the company provides contractor support on design/ build projects for cost-efficient construction and quick occupancy. Southern has been involved in all types of building projects including major industrial plants, offices, shopping facilities, commercial skyscrapers, warehouses, heavy installations and custom structural steel fabrications.

Among its customers are such firms as Duke Power, DuPont, Shimizu American Corporation, J. A. Jones, Beers Construction, and Whiting-Turner Contracting.

A look at Charlotte's skyline reveals scores of well-known buildings on which Southern has worked, including earlier work on Eastland Mall, Wachovia Center, Westinghouse Nuclear Turbine Plant, and the old Charlotte Coliseum.

When the coliseum was built in 1955, its structural steel dome, spanning 322 feet, was the world's largest. More recent work includes the Concord Mills Mall, Ballantyne Shopping Center, Davidson College, and many Charlotte-Mecklenburg schools.

Southern's operations remain on Wilkinson Boulevard and are located within easy access of two interstate highways.

The engineers, draftsmen, estimators, and technicians, some of whom have worked for Southern Engineering for more than forty years, are highly skilled and experienced. Its professional technical teams consistently receive the highest ratings from the American Institute of Steel Construction.

Officials at Southern Engineering are enthusiastic about the company's long history in Charlotte and look forward to being a part of its promising future.

"We want to continue to grow with Charlotte," Saleh emphasizes. "This city provides us a central location to serve our expanding client base across the fast-growing southeastern region, and we build our success by helping our customers in being successful."

DAVID SIMONINI CUSTOM HOMES

If you have driven through Myers Park, Eastover, South Charlotte or any prestigious community in Charlotte, you have most likely driven past one of David Simonini's custom homes and not even known it was there. David Simonini Custom Homes prides itself on its ability to blend its new creations into the existing charm of Charlotte's established neighborhoods.

This expertise comes from David Simonini building architecturally correct houses based on years of studying home styles and visiting cities around the world to determine what is truly authentic in each style of architecture.

After being involved in the family's home-building business for over twenty years, David Simonini sold his fifty-percent share in the business and started his own company in 1994. He left the family's business in order to create one-of-a-kind masterpieces. Under his father's tutelage, David learned that strong values and principles lead to continued success. He follows his father's advice of never sacrificing on quality, being fair and remaining true to your word.

David incorporates quality materials, innovative designs and fine architectural details with excellence in construction to bring each homeowner's vision to life. He combines old world-style architecture and traditional interior details with maximum comfort, convenience and gracious sociability, which results in "elegant works of art."

Rich woods, ambient lighting, arched windows and doors, and natural materials such as tumbled marble and limestone are signature elements of the interior designs, which blend interesting textures, subtle colors, and timeless charm. Features include such touches as hand-carved stone lintels, elegant handmade wood mantles, reclaimed European/French architectural artifacts, slate roofs, copper cupolas, custom wrought iron fixtures, hand-laid

flagstone porches, custom shutters and authentic European chimney pots. Admitting that he is a perfectionist, David carefully coordinates each facet of the creation for overall perfection—right down to the hinges and screws.

David has even brought his own vision to life, Courance, a seven-acre village of French Country-styled homes in south Charlotte. After touring France, Simonini finalized his idea of building an authentic European village complete with cobblestone streets, unique fountains and a pond with black swans. Centuries-old building materials and furnishings have been combined with modern techniques to create a village of fifteen homes located in the gracious neighborhood, Pellyn Wood. It is viewed as a perfect example of how old world authentic architecture can be brought to fruition through David's creative vision.

One man alone could not build these works of art. That is why David Simonini has surrounded himself with an experienced team of field, office and management personnel. All stand behind the same integrity and exacting standards that David has set forth. This belief is set forth in the initial meeting with a customer and is based on the promise of customer satisfaction, which is backed by David's personal guarantee and an unparalleled company warranty. Every member of the David Simonini Custom Homes group is committed to fulfilling the customers' wishes.

David Simonini not only wins accolades from his homeowners; he also receives them from his peers. In 1997 David was awarded the Gold Award for Best One-of-a-Kind Spec House Under 4,000 Square Feet in the Nation from *Professional Builder* magazine and the National Association of Home Builders (NAHB). In 1998, David's star continued to shine with awards for Outstanding Abilities to Achieve Excellence from Elite's *Who's Who, The Business Journal's* Charlotte edition awarded him the 40 Under 40 award and the Charlotte Chamber of Commerce selected him as its Entrepreneur of the Year. The company won the HBAC's Excellence in Home Building Award in 1999 and was recognized two consecutive years, in 1999 and 2000, by *Charlotte's Best* magazine as the Best Custom Home Builder Overall. The year 2000 ended with a bang for the company as it was selected by *Custom Home* magazine to be the winner of the coveted Pacesetter Award for Best Design.

David Simonini Custom Homes will continue to build one of a kind masterpieces for its clients while continuing to look for new opportunities to build enclaves of high-end custom homes in prestigious neighborhoods throughout Charlotte. Strong values and principles will always be the backbone of David Simonini Custom Homes' continued success.

✧

Above: David Simonini.

Top, left: David Simonini Custom Homes creates unique masterpieces for each and every homeowner. Attention to detail and architecturally correct houses are the hallmark of David Simonini.

Below: Antique heart of pine flooring, European kitchens, and state-of-the-art professional appliances are just a few of the many features that can be found in a custom home by David Simonini.

FIRST LANDMARK, U.S.A., INC.

First LandMark in conjunction with subsidiaries SYNCO, Inc. and Guardian Management Inc., acquires, develops, holds, manages, and selectively sells investment real estate. Generally limited partnerships are formed as syndicated ventures to acquire properties, primarily rental apartments, office buildings and land. Since 1971 the company or its SYNCO subsidiary have organized eighty-one investment real estate ventures involving properties in Atlanta, Charlotte, Gastonia, Greensboro, Greenville, Hickory, Nashville, Raleigh, Richmond, Rocky Mount, Southern Pines, Spartanburg, Wilmington and Winston-Salem. Aggregate purchase costs have substantially exceeded $250 million.

The restoration of historic residential and commercial properties and the construction of new townhouses in a blighted area of Charlotte's center city have been among the most satisfying of the company's many successful ventures. In 1978, when Bank of America announced intentions to fund revitalization of Charlotte's historic Fourth Ward, local developers were highly skeptical and unresponsive. As banker Hugh McColl recollects, "I remember how difficult it was to get any developer to have a conversation about it, much less get interested. Only one person was able to visualize what we had in mind, and that was Reitzel Snider. He and his company entered into a joint venture with us and took the plunge into building very fine and relatively expensive townhomes in the center of Fourth Ward. Most people thought we were crazy. The first project, which was Hackberry Place, led to the renovation of The Poplar and the development of Hackberry Court. These three projects, with the restored Victorian homes, formed the nucleus of Fourth Ward redevelopment. Because of the high quality, upper income people were attracted back to the center city, which was our goal in the first place."

Other projects undertaken by the company in the 1980s involved the restoration of two historic commercial edifices, The Court Arcade and The First National Bank of Charlotte. The Court Arcade, designed in 1926 by London-born architect William H. Peeps is one of Charlotte's most notable buildings from both architectural and historical perspectives. Its arched stone façade and expansive skylight arcade are characteristic of the neo-classical style which was popular following World War I. Located in the courts and municipal offices area, the building was traditionally occupied by members of the Bar until a fire rendered it uninhabitable. After standing vacant for several years, the building was marked for demolition. Acquired, renovated and restored by a company partnership in 1980, today The Court Arcade is a proud element of Charlotte's governmental plaza area.

acquired in 1980 by a SYNCO partnership, the building was entirely vacant except for the ground floor. In 1982 the company completed an $11-million renovation that was acclaimed for successfully combining modern technology and historic preservation.

The Swiss American Realty Group was organized in 1989 at the initiative of First LandMark and Overterra AG of Zurich, Switzerland. This consortium is comprised of private companies and individual investors from Europe and the USA. The initial purpose was to provide realty investment banking services; however, the primary objective has evolved to a direct investment function. To date, six ventures

At its grand opening in 1927 more than twelve thousand guests admired the elegantly classical features of the First National Bank's new headquarters. For more than three decades this building at 112 South Tryon dominated the Charlotte skyline, having achieved distinction as the first twenty-story "sky scraper" between Philadelphia and Birmingham. Many of the city's most prestigious business and professional firms have had offices here; however, when

Opposite: One Tryon Center, originally First National Bank of Charlotte.

Top: The Poplar.

Middle: Hackberry Place and Hackberry Court.

Bottom: Court Arcade.

have been organized to acquire realty investment assets for a purchase cost of $21.1 million.

At year-end 2000 the company's twenty-nine currently operating partnerships owned realty investment properties valued at more than $135 million. The portfolio, consisting of properties located in the two Carolinas, included thirteen rental apartment properties containing 2,381 units, two commercial properties containing approximately 60,000 square feet, and seven land tracts consisting of approximately 265 acres. Net of first mortgage indebtedness, the portfolio's gross equity value was estimated at more than $75 million.

BUILDING A GREATER CHARLOTTE

MARSH PROPERTIES

With a proud history dating back three-quarters of a century, Marsh Properties has earned a stellar reputation for quality rental homes and commercial development. Founded by twenty-six-year-old Lex Marsh in 1926, the company now owns and manages seventeen hundred apartments, as well as neighborhood shopping centers and office buildings in the Charlotte area.

A Marshville, North Carolina native, nine-year-old Lex Marsh moved to Charlotte in 1909 with his family, who owned several tracts of farmland in Mecklenburg County, including the area now known as Sedgefield. After a stint in the military at the end of World War I, Marsh attended Wake Forest University Law School, earning his law degree at age twenty, and becoming North Carolina's youngest licensed attorney the following year.

Marsh began his real estate career selling Biltmore Drive lots priced at $2,500 before the 1929 stock market crash—and $250 afterward, when he could find a buyer. In the early 1940s he obtained approval as a FHA mortgage banker, bringing much-needed capital into the area. The housing crunch after World War II led him to build FHA-financed apartments, including many in Sedgefield and Camp Green. He also developed Charlotte's first suburban shopping center at Sedgefield, founded the multiple listing service for the Charlotte Board of Realtors, and organized and led Charlotte's Home Builders' and

Mortgage Bankers' associations. Marsh also founded the Charlotte Apartment Association.

In the early 1960s Marsh brought John Sikes Johnston and David L. Francis into the organization. During the next decade mortgage loan servicing grew from $10 million to over $100 million.

The firm's many developments have included Forest Pawtuckett and Windsor Park subdivisions. Marsh Properties is now one of the largest owner/manager of apartments in the Charlotte area, including Sedgefield, Salem Village, Strawberry Hill, Providence Park, and Queens at Granville luxury apartments.

In 1999 the Marsh Companies began development of land on Providence Road at the intersection of I-485, which Lex Marsh purchased over time beginning in 1956. Currently 164 apartments have been completed and over 320,000 square feet of office space have been built in this project known as Providence Park.

Currently, the Marsh Companies are headed by Lex Marsh's daughter, Gretchen Marsh Johnston; her son-in-law, Jamie McLawhorn; and George Warren. The present management team plans to continue making significant contributions to Charlotte's growth through quality real estate development and superior customer service.

SHOOK DESIGN GROUP, INC.

Across America, historic districts and downtowns are back in vogue. The shift to urbanism is a trend grounded in changes in the demographic and sociographic profile of today's society. Shook[SM] understands and capitalizes upon the positive and immediate reaction consumers have to a sense of history. Shook's designers replicate, emulate and draw inspiration from history and from pop-culture icons of the past and present.

Shook's strategic brand consultants, architects, and interior and graphic designers approach each project first from a marketing perspective, and then from a design perspective. Employing a cross-disciplinary process, Shook's work cues and triggers consumers in ways that enhance clients' return on investment.

For Camden Square, the firm's urban designers renovated a collection of crumbling warehouses, and created two new facades to replace the existing storefronts. For Southend Brewery, Shook's restaurant group developed a new concept that taps consumers' nostalgia for the Industrial Age. Located in a renovated warehouse, the new eatery quickly became the city's top grossing restaurant, proving that Charlotteans are hungry for a connection with the city's past.

Both projects are located near a formerly abandoned rail corridor that now serves the Charlotte Trolley. Shook has been widely recognized for creating a vision for the economic and aesthetic rehabilitation of the trolley corridor, as well as for being a brand author of Historic South End. Having worked on several of the district's top renovation projects, Shook recently organized a two-day planning charrette for an eight-block area within South End. The area, branded as Morehead Central, will become the gateway between downtown and South End, as well as home to a prominent trolley stop.

In a city longing for a sense of history, South End provides visitors a rewarding glimpse into the past.

✧

Above: Camden Square's new façade (top, left) and before Shook's renovation (top right) and Southend Brewery before (bottom, left) and after renovations (bottom, right).

RENOVATED CAMDEN SQUARE PHOTO COURTESY OF STEVE LITTLE. RENOVATED SOUTHEND BREWERY PHOTO COURTESY OF TIM BUCHMAN.

Below: Terry Shook (left) and Kevin Kelley (right).

MECA
PROPERTIES

✧

Above: President Anthony T. (Tony) Pressley.

Top, right: The Design Center of the Carolinas, housed in an old mill, is part of MECA's Camden Square Village, a mixed-use complex that includes studios and showrooms for the design industry.

Bottom, right: Infill residential development like Olmsted Park has helped revitalize Charlotte's South End.

Below: Executive Vice President Robert M. Pressley.

More than half-a-century ago, Robert H. "Bob" Pressley established a real estate company in Charlotte with the purchase of a single house and two vacant lots. From that simple beginning, the company has evolved into one of the most respected commercial-investment real estate firms in the area.

Bob's son, Anthony "Tony" Pressley, took the company helm in 1980, and was later joined by his brother, Robert M. Pressley. Today, Tony's two sons are key parts of the company, establishing a three-generation legacy.

MECA's services include development, brokerage and management of commercial and investment real estate, with projects including new construction and adaptive reuse of existing properties. A proponent of urban redevelopment, Pressley has focused the firm's services on Charlotte's central core. The firm is committed to creating models for recycling and revitalizing urban properties in a way that will have a positive impact on neighboring communities and that may be replicated in other parts of the country.

Pressley was the founding president of the South End Development Corporation (SEDC) and led the charge to reclaim the original "South End" of Charlotte's center city.

South End is one of Charlotte's original urban corridors, adjacent to Charlotte's oldest rail corridor (1852) and located between the historic Dilworth and Wilmore neighborhoods. In the 1890s, the area became a bustling industrial district. When Charlotte's industries headed for the suburbs after World War II, many of the industrial and manufacturing buildings in this urban corridor were abandoned.

Today, South End's restored historic buildings house distinctive shops, diverse restaurants, and a growing office and residential community. Reaching this goal wasn't easy. Working with SEDC, Pressley encouraged the City of Charlotte to apply for a grant through the Environmental Protection Agency's (EPA) Brownfields Economic Redevelopment Initiative. Charlotte received a $200,000 grant in 1996 for a model project in the South End/Wilmore area. Pressley also lobbied for the North Carolina Brownfields Reuse Act of 1997, which became law on October 1, 1997. Without these steps, rehabilitation of these industrial properties would not have been feasible.

MECA's projects in Charlotte's urban center have included Olmsted Park, Atherton Mill, Camden Row Live-Work Condominiums, and Camden Square Village, a mixed-use complex that includes studio and showroom space for the greater design industry. The Village is home to the Design Center of the Carolinas.

As a "home-grown" company, MECA is committed to preserving and respecting the community's past with an eye on its current and future needs. The firm's appreciation for the past provides a unique perspective as it develops new projects and rehabilitates vintage properties.

Whelchel Builders, Inc., is a builder who is not interested in following the footsteps of others. CEO Don Whelchel has successfully adapted the discipline acquired as a dedicated long-distance runner to his business philosophy, recognizing that performance is the key factor in both endeavors. The company's success in the construction industry is based on the same sense of commitment, competition, and response to challenge that sustains Don in his daily run.

The company has constructed buildings ranging from churches and schools to banks, medical and manufacturing facilities throughout the Southeast since 1983, earning a solid reputation for getting the job done, no matter what the task.

Whelchel Builders considers energy, momentum and a unified effort of the entire general contracting team—from project managers, estimators and field superintendents to subcontractors and inspectors—essential resources for successful performance.

The Whelchel team provides solutions that work, eliminating unnecessary steps and costs, carefully monitoring job progress, maintaining realistic schedules, and offering reliable construction alternatives. Through this approach, Whelchel consistently meets the specialized needs and expectations of its clients and ensures the highest quality construction standards.

Each project is unique, offering its own challenges and rewards, from working with a church building committee whose members have no previous construction experience to cooperating with a veteran architect to providing design/build services in-house. Areas requiring a high degree of technological expertise, such as medical facilities, are among Whelchel's many successes, as are secondary and university level institutional projects. Commercial projects may involve transforming difficult tracts of land into marketable resources, from retirement centers to shopping malls to superstores. Familiarity with each client's special concerns and decision-making processes enables the company to meet these varied challenges.

Unlike most builders, Whelchel's interior and exterior renovation and addition projects have comprised a significant portion of the company's work, involving successful renovation of over five million square feet, from high-rise office towers and medical complexes to church expansions and small retail shops.

Since opening its doors in 1983, Whelchel Builders has focused on building results-driven project teams reflecting strong leadership direction and extensive engineering and project management experience of CEO Don Whelchel. Throughout this development process, the company has recruited and maintained the best available technical, management and field expertise, resulting in successful completion of a diverse range of project types throughout the Southeast.

WHELCHEL BUILDERS, INC.

✧

Above: CEO Don Whelchel.

Below: Merchandise Mart.

PROVIDENT DEVELOPMENT GROUP, INC.

❖

Above: Tom Waters.

Below: The Enclave at Piper Glen is among the fine communities developed by Provident Development Group.

Tom Waters established Provident Development Group, Inc. in 1991 with a commitment to developing family-oriented communities offering refreshing and creative amenities through well-planned neighborhoods.

Provident Development Group, Inc. projects include several master-planned communities throughout Charlotte and surrounding areas. Thus far, The Crossings is the firm's largest master-planned community with more than 540 single-family homes and several townhome and apartment sites. Other projects include Huntington Forest in South Charlotte with a large swim club and more than 420 home sites; Wyndham Place in the University area with 192 home sites; Brookfield on Sunset Road with 72 home sites; and The Woodlands, with over 244 home sites. Carrington Ridge, located in Huntersville, will bring together single-family homes and townhomes in a unique neo-traditional style, pedestrian-friendly setting. Additionally, two developments on Lake Norman have spectacular lake front views.

Other developments include The Enclave at Piper Glen, which features twenty-three luxurious homes overlooking the Piper Glen Golf Course; Sardis Grove and Reverdy Glen, both located in Matthews, and Stonecroft, the 2001 HomeArama site, where Charlotte's top builders have come together to offer the finest in exclusive and elegant residential living.

Before moving to Charlotte, Waters spent more than thirteen years with Centex Homes in Texas and four years with Lennar Homes in

Florida. A native of Austin, Texas, Waters received a Bachelor of Business Administration degree from Southern Methodist University.

As a veteran homebuilder, Waters organized Provident Homes, Inc. in 1997 to provide custom homes in Charlotte's growing in-fill market. Residences by Provident Homes, Inc. reflect traditional neighborhood designs and can be found in many of Charlotte's finer communities such as Morrocroft, Providence Country Club, Piper Glen, Sardis Grove, Reverdy Glen, and Stonecroft. Provident's $1.7-million show home at Stonecroft won seven awards at the 2001 HomeArama, including "Best of Show," "Reader's Choice," and even the most prestigious "People's Choice" award.

In addition to his extensive land development and homebuilding businesses, Waters is actively involved in various organizations. He has served as president of the Home Builders Association of Charlotte, chairman of the Real Estate Building Industry Coalition (REBIC), and the Board of Directors of SPPACE, the homebuilder's political action committee. He is a graduate of Leadership Charlotte and served as a precinct delegate to two Republican Conventions.

Provident Homes, Inc. and Provident Development Group, Inc. have found harmony in many areas, as they continue to provide quality homes in environmentally sensitive communities by emphasizing good land design and superior amenities. Creating neighborhoods that are family oriented is the hallmark of Provident Development Group, Inc. and Provident Homes, Inc.

"We understand today's new home buyers and their active lifestyle," says Waters. "We realize that building a beautiful, functional home requires more than just providing the latest features or fads. Our care and concern for every aspect of a new home includes good working relationships based on attention to detail, trust, commitment, and accurate communication."

Tom and his wife Claudia, son James, and daughter Cammie love to call the Charlotte region home. Waters says his family was attracted to Charlotte by its natural beauty, dramatic growth, quality of life and positive attitude toward business. "My family and I plan to be permanent fixtures in Charlotte and give back what we can to this great city," he says.

INDEX

SPONSORS